The Battle for Jerusalem

John Hagee

Publishers Since 1798

THOMAS NELSON PUBLISHERS®
Nashville

Published in Nashville, Tennessee, by Thomas Nelson, Inc.

Library of Congress Cataloging-in-Publication Data

Hagee, John.
    The battle for Jerusalem / John Hagee.
      p. cm.
    Includes bibliographical references.
    ISBN 0-7852-6379-9
    1. Bible—Prophecies—Jerusalem. 2. Jerusalem in the Bible. 3. Jerusalem. I. Title.

BS649.J38 H33 2001
263'.042569442—dc21

2001018035

Printed in the United States of America

03 04 05 06 07 PHX 6 5 4 3 2

To my children:
The Fabulous Five
Tish, Chris, Tina, Matt, and Sandy

Contents

Introduction

I'm writing this in December 2000, and never has any season looked less like a season of peace on earth. Every day seems to bring another assault upon innocent civilians in the Middle East. The U.S. Department of State has warned American citizens to defer all travel to Israel, the West Bank, and Gaza. Beneath ill-fitting masks of diplomacy, murderous tempers are raging.

The last thing I need at this busy time of year is to be writing another book, but I felt compelled to write this one. Why? Because what happens in Jerusalem matters to you, whether you believe it or not.

Medieval mapmakers (quite rightfully, in my opinion) placed Jerusalem at the center of the world. They understood what Bible scholars have known for years—Jerusalem is the center of the universe, the focal point of things to come and things in the past. Scripture tells us that God is not finished with Jerusalem:

> Again the word of the LORD of hosts came, saying,
> "Thus says the LORD of hosts:
> 'I am zealous for Zion with great zeal;
> With great fervor I am zealous for her.'
> "Thus says the LORD:
> 'I will return to Zion,
> And dwell in the midst of Jerusalem.
> Jerusalem shall be called the City of Truth,
> The Mountain of the LORD of hosts,
> The Holy Mountain.'" (Zech. 8:1–3)

vii

My purpose in writing this book is simple: I want you to understand the age-old divisions that are still tearing the Holy Land apart. I want you to be able to distinguish between truth and propaganda in the media reports, and I want you to understand God's plan for His Holy City. These things are important because with every passing sunset we move one day closer to the day when Jesus will descend for His church and Jerusalem will take its place on the center stage of world events.

In Romans 9:33, Paul quoted the prophet Isaiah:

> As it is written:
> "Behold, I lay in Zion a stumbling stone and rock of offense,
> And whoever believes on Him will not be put to shame."

You and I know that the "stumbling stone" was Jesus Christ, the cornerstone of our Christian faith and of the world itself (Eph. 2:20). That stone was laid in Zion, also known as Mount Moriah, today called the Temple Mount.

Now the Temple Mount where Jesus walked is a "stumbling stone" to peace and a "rock of offense" that ignites passions unlike any other bit of real estate in the world. And in the years to come, Mount Zion will become the platform from which the Antichrist will reveal himself to the world.

Make no mistake, friend, the ancient city of Jerusalem and the Temple Mount in particular will never fade from the world's stage. And hearing these two names in the world press is like hearing the distant hoofbeats of the approaching horsemen of the Apocalypse.

We must understand those who are battling for the soul of Jerusalem—and we must pray for the peace of the Holy City.

One

The Heart of the Current Battle

Jerusalem today is a detonating device with no fail-safe, a loaded pistol at a poker dispute, a driverless coach careening toward a blind curve. No other item on the entire Middle East peace agenda forebodes such potential mayhem as the city's future status.

—*John L. Lyons, "Jerusalem: Besieged by the Sacred"*[1]

Jerusalem is the very soul which unites and fortifies the nation [of Israel] in its entirety.

—*Natan Sharansky, Israeli diplomat*[2]

An ancient text records a debate of Jewish sages about why Cain murdered his brother, Abel. By identifying what drove Cain to kill, the sages hoped to discover the root of human violence on earth.

According to one sage, a twin sister was born with Abel, so the two brothers fought over a woman. Another sage said the brothers agreed to divide everything in the world, so one promptly claimed the clothes on his brother's back and ordered him to disrobe, while the other claimed the ground beneath his brother's feet and ordered him to fly.

A third sage agreed the brothers must have decided to split the world. But then, he said, one claimed the land where the temple would be built, the other insisted the place was his, so Cain rose up and killed his brother.

1

The history of murder began, said the rabbi, in an argument over who would own Jerusalem. Specifically it began with an argument over the Temple Mount.[3]

The Timeline

In mid-July 2000, Israeli Prime Minister Ehud Barak and Palestinian leader Yasser Arafat came together at the presidential cabin in the Catoctin Mountain retreat at Camp David. American President Bill Clinton had invited them to the meeting, and before both men was a copy of a peace agreement that had been years in the making.

The Israelis had made remarkable concessions. They would relinquish nearly all of the West Bank occupied in the 1967 war, including the highly strategic Jordan Valley. They would set up joint patrols with Palestinian security forces. They would recognize the right of Palestinian refugees to return to the "State of Palestine" and accept a number of refugees into Israel.

In return, the Palestinians would "demilitarize" their land. They would allow the Israelis to maintain three reinforced battalions and other forces on the West Bank within military compounds. The Israelis would also operate three early-warning stations and three air-defense units on the West Bank until May 2007, or until peace agreements had been achieved between Israel and other Arab foes.[4]

Then President Clinton addressed a thorny question: What about Jerusalem?

Barak was willing to make concessions never before considered by an Israeli prime minister. Though he did not want to divide the city, he was willing to consider the idea of a neighborhood swap—exchanging Palestinian neighborhoods for Israeli ones.

When Clinton took the idea to Arafat, the Palestinian leader became enraged. Furthermore, he and his delegation became incensed over a casual suggestion Barak had made: in exchange for giving the Palestinians de facto control over the Temple Mount, the

Israelis could build a small synagogue on the northeast corner of the holy site.

Arafat, an international terrorist whose hands are stained with a river of blood from the veins of innocent women and children, a thug so repugnant that he was not permitted to enter the U.S. until recently, glared at Clinton and said, "These arguments are explosives and will set off massive fires in the region . . . Do you want me to throw the region into a new age of religious conflict?"[5]

Arafat's words proved prophetic—but only because he lit the fuse that ignited tensions into violence.

Tempers Grow Short in Autumn

In late September 2000, Ariel Sharon, the seventy-two-year-old retired Israeli general and military hero, planned to visit *Har Habayit* (the Hebrew term for the Temple Mount), the holiest site in Israel. Before arranging this trip on the day prior to Rosh Hashanah, Sharon spoke with the police and Israeli security services. They approved his visit. Shlomo Ben-Ami, the minister of foreign affairs, then talked with Jibril Rajub, the head of Palestinian security, who promised there would be "no problem" with Sharon's visit to the holy site, currently administered by Muslims.[6] Rajub also told Ben-Ami that as long as Sharon did not enter the mosques, there would be "no reason for concern."

But even before Sharon got into his vehicle that breezy day in late September, Islamic violence cast its threatening shadow over the proposed outing. Earlier in the month, Israeli security officials had noted a sharp increase in violent attacks by Palestinians against Israeli security forces and civilians in the area of Netzarim.[7]

Wednesday, September 27

On Wednesday, an Israeli soldier was killed and two others wounded by a roadside bomb detonated by remote control at the Netzarim Junction. According to Voice of Israel radio, Palestinian police did not assist their Israeli counterparts in pursuing the three attackers, but neither did they prevent Israeli security forces from pursuing.[8]

On this same day, youth activists from Fatah, the first guerrilla/terrorist movement, called upon supporters from Jerusalem and Yesha to come to Jerusalem to participate in a demonstration to block Sharon's procession from reaching the Temple Mount. The Fatah organization, one of the most disciplined and loyal groups aligned with Palestine Liberation Organization (PLO) Chairman Yasser Arafat, spent the day before Sharon's proposed visit distributing flyers that called upon the masses to protest the visit by Sharon and other Likud Knesset members.[9]

Thursday, September 28

Nerves tightened. On Thursday a Palestinian police officer participating in a joint security patrol on the West Bank suddenly shouted "Allahu Akbar!" (God is greater!) and opened fire at point-blank range on his Israeli partner, Yossi Tabaja, who died shortly after arriving at the hospital. Joint Israeli-Palestinian security patrols, which had been considered an important part of the peace process, were suspended as a result.[10]

Also on Thursday, as planned, Israeli Knesset member Ariel Sharon visited the Temple Mount with a six-member Likud Knesset delegation, including Moshe Arens, Reuven Rivlin, Naomi Blumenthal, Joshua Matza, Gideon Ezra, and Ayoub Kara. Because security forces were concerned about disruptions, one thousand police officers escorted the group as they walked to the entrance of the Temple Mount at the Mughrabi, or Western, Gate. At no time did Sharon or any members of the entourage enter the mosques.

At the time of Sharon's entry to the Temple Mount, approximately 150 Muslims were praying in the mosques, including members of the Palestinian Authority's Legislative Council and Arab

Knesset members. At first the Arab Knesset members walked along-side the Likud delegation, talking and even joking with them. The images were captured by Israel Television's Channel 2. According to the Israeli daily *Ha'aretz*, however, as soon as the Arab Knesset members saw the television cameras, "they began hurling abuse at Sharon."[11]

The delegation stopped at the area called Solomon's Stables, where they were provided a briefing on the site. Demonstrators tried to approach but were pushed back by police. One Palestinian boy was slightly injured and given medical attention.

While Sharon and the others made their way back to the Western Gate, dozens of Palestinians began to run after them in an apparent attempt to break the police line. As they departed, a crowd of one thousand Palestinians threw stones at the police. Sharon's delegation left the site after only an hour's visit, and thirty policemen and four Palestinians were slightly wounded in the ensu-ing scuffle.[12]

The serious violence spread throughout the country twenty-four hours later, following the broadcast of inflammatory statements by official Palestinian radio and television stations. Four hours after Sharon's visit to the Temple Mount, at noon, the Voice of Palestine radio broadcast a statement by Yasser Arafat declaring the visit to be "a serious step against Muslim holy places." Arafat called upon the Arab and Islamic world to "move immediately to stop these aggressions and Israeli practices against holy Jerusalem."[13]

By four o'clock that afternoon, Palestinian Legislative Council speaker Ahmad Qurei had taken to the airwaves, asserting on Voice of Palestine radio that the visit "defiled" the mosques and was "a clear and flagrant expression of the Israeli schemes" against Muslim holy places. In the same broadcast, Palestinian Culture and Information Minister Yasser Abed Rabbo declared that Israelis from both ends of the political spectrum have a goal of "Judaizing" or controlling Jerusalem.[14]

Friday, September 29

During Friday prayers on the Temple Mount, A'akramah Sabri, the Palestinian Authority's officially appointed mufti of Jerusalem, called for a jihad, or holy war, "to eliminate the Jews from Palestine." At 1:00 P.M., immediately after the conclusion of prayers in the mosques on the Temple Mount, hundreds of Palestinians attempted to overpower Israeli border guards at the Mughrabi Gate leading to the Western Wall Plaza (the Wailing Wall), where Jewish worshipers were engaged in prayer prior to the Rosh Hashanah holiday. Many of them threw rocks from the platform of the mosque onto Jewish worshipers in the plaza below. When rioters broke through the gate that leads into the plaza, Israeli border guards entered the Temple Mount and opened fire with rubber bullets.

Israeli Police Inspector General Yehuda Wilk noted that Israeli police never enter the Temple Mount under normal circumstances while Muslims are praying: "For all the years that I have been an officer and also when I was the Jerusalem Police Chief, I never prevented any prayers at the Temple Mount. But there cannot be a situation whereby the Muslims pray on the Mount and then attack policemen and try to stone Jewish worshippers below."[15]

In the initial outbreak of violence, four Palestinians were killed and more than one hundred wounded in clashes with Israeli police. Over the ensuing weekend, fifty-eight Palestinians were arrested for throwing rocks and firebombs throughout Jerusalem. Sixty policemen were injured, including Jerusalem Police Commander Yair Yitzhaki, who suffered a concussion from being hit in the head by rocks. On Saturday, a Palestinian mob attacked Joseph's Tomb in Nablus, burning Jewish religious texts and destroying the building. An Israeli of American origin, Hillel Lieberman, was brutally murdered as he ran to the tomb in an effort to save the texts. The attack occurred just after Israeli troops withdrew from the site after the Palestinian Authority assured them that they would keep order in the area.[16]

In the Gaza Strip, Palestinian and Israeli security forces engaged in a furious gun battle for more than an hour at the entrance to a Jewish settlement. A Palestinian policeman was killed in the exchange, and a father and son were caught in the crossfire. They clung together, twelve-year-old Mohammed Aldura and his father, Jamal, and tried to shield themselves behind a wall. "The child, the child!" the father yelled, waving his arm in the smoke.

The incident, caught on television and broadcast on Israeli television Saturday night, revealed the instant when the boy screamed in panic, then slumped in his father's arms as he was fatally struck in the abdomen. The father, also wounded, trembled with convulsions, then rolled his eyes and lost consciousness. He was later hospitalized in Gaza and was expected to recover.[17]

His son was not so fortunate. But at a news conference in late November, Israeli General Yomtov Samia stated that an inquiry found that the boy had been hit by a volley of gunfire from a Palestinian position.[18]

Saturday's fighting was one of the bloodiest confrontations between Israelis and Palestinians in recent history. In a blunt official statement, Prime Minister Ehud Barak said Israel "is exercising maximum restraint but is determined to preserve public order and protect its citizens."[19]

Bassem Naim, a Palestinian activist in the West Bank, said, "The battle over Jerusalem has begun. With our blood and with our souls we fight for you, Jerusalem!"[20]

Aftermath

On October 7, the United Nations Security Council adopted a resolution stressing the importance of establishing a mechanism "for a speedy and objective inquiry" into the violence that claimed the lives of more than one hundred Palestinians over a three-week period. The United States, Israel's ally, abstained from that resolution but did not veto it, and U.S. Ambassador Richard Holbrooke said that if the Security Council agreed to debate the issue a second time, the United States would veto any resolution on the subject.[21]

The Israelis did not welcome the American action. The extremely one-sided resolution did nothing to quell Palestinian violence. I'm disappointed that our country did not veto the resolution. The action is nothing more than Arab propaganda designed to influence the world community against Israel, and it teaches one valuable lesson: violence pays. Stir up a little strife, charge another nation with bully tactics when it acts to stem your violence, and smile as the rest of the world chastises the stronger nation.

On October 12, two Israeli reserve soldiers were brutally murdered by an enraged Palestinian mob when the soldiers took a wrong turn and entered the West Bank city of Ramallah. There they were brutally lynched by a bloodthirsty mob. I have seen video of the incident—with my own eyes, I watched as one man's body was tossed out a window, then subjected to burning, stomping, beating, and dragging by an infuriated crowd of shouting Palestinians. I saw the blood-stained window, men lifting their arms in celebration, flags waving, and one flag in flames—the Stars and Stripes of the United States of America.

One of those murdered men was thirty-five-year-old Vadim Norzich, son of Anna and Issai, residents of Or Akiva. The Norzich family fled from Russia in the early 1990s and had been living in Israel since then.

Vadim had married his sweetheart, Irina, one week before his death. The wife pulled out wedding pictures to show a reporter, and there was Vadim—handsome and strong, wearing a white satin kipah beneath the canopy with his bride.[22]

On that same day, Arab terrorists attacked the *U.S.S. Cole* as the ship refueled at a port in Yemen. The explosion killed seventeen sailors and injured thirty-nine. Yemen, the poorest nation on the Arabian Peninsula, has cooperated with the U.S. in the past, but the country's leaders sympathize with the Palestinians and are angered by American support for Israel. To appease his people, Yemeni President Ali Abdullah Saleh asked that the injured *Cole* be removed as soon as possible.[23]

In November, U.S. Defense Secretary William Cohen warned that the Israeli-Palestinian conflict could spin out of control and spread to other countries in the region.[24]

A Media Barrage Incites Violence

Since the beginning of the Palestinian-initiated violence against the Israelis, the Palestinians have consistently broadcast extreme incitement, calling upon the Arab masses to harm Jews and Christians wherever they may be found. I have watched video of Arab children racing to assemble guns as a sort of game. I have heard Palestinian broadcasters, reporting against a background image of the mosque on the Temple Mount, proclaim, "The supreme Monitoring Committee of the National Arab and Islamic Forces calls upon the masses of our people to immediately assemble in the streets and public squares in order to express their rage and strong stand against the barbaric Israeli aggression, and their determination to continue the intifada [uprising]."

During the Friday sermon broadcast live on Arafat's official TV station, the cleric at a Gaza mosque made the following statements:

> The Jews are Jews, whether Labor or Likud, the Jews are Jews. They do not have any moderates or any advocates of peace. They are all liars. They are the ones who must be butchered and killed. As Allah the Almighty says, fight them . . . Have no mercy on the Jews, no matter where they are, in any country. Fight them, wherever you are. Wherever you meet them, kill them. Wherever you are, kill those Jews and those Americans who are like them, and those who stand with them. They are all in one trench, against the Arabs and Muslims.[25]

I watched a video of this sermon, saw the earnestness of the cleric, who wore white from head to toe, saw the agreement flashing on the faces of men who sat cross-legged on carpets in the mosque.

I have seen video footage of Arab children, probably not more than six or seven years old, who are trained to quickly assemble automatic weapons while blindfolded. I have heard these children boldly proclaim in treble, childish voices, "But if I starve, I will eat the flesh of my conqueror! Beware of my hunger and rage!"

On October 16, television cameras also caught a young Arab man who told the media, "We shall remind them that the Palestinian people and the Palestinian mothers bear their sons in order for them to become martyrs."

One of the most distressing realizations to come from the days of violence was that many of the protesters were not Palestinians proper, but Arab Israeli citizens. Thirteen Israeli Arabs were killed in the early days of violence when police fired on protesters who were blocking roads and throwing stones in towns stretching across northern Israel. Until the uprising of autumn 2000, the 20 percent of Israelis who are ethnically Arab had never demonstrated, thrown stones, or identified with the Palestinians of the territories in such a public way.[26]

In early November, three Israeli soldiers and six Palestinians died in gun battles throughout the West Bank and Gaza Strip. The Israelis said the struggle was no longer a civilian uprising. "This isn't an intifada," said an Israeli captain as he fired tracer bullets that cut red streaks through the dark sky during one battle north of Jerusalem. "This is a war."[27]

The Truth of the Matter

Yasser Arafat would like the world to believe that a bellicose and bullying Israel is to blame for the latest bloodshed, or that Ariel Sharon's approved and preplanned visit to the Temple Mount provoked the unrest. But Thomas Friedman put his finger on the matter in a *New York Times* editorial:

> The roots of this latest violent outburst can be traced directly back to President Clinton's press conference after the breakdown of the Camp David summit. At that time, Mr. Clinton pointedly, deliberately— and rightly—stated that Israeli Prime Minister Ehud Barak had offered unprecedented compromises at the summit—more than 90 percent of the West Bank for a Palestinian state, a partial resolution of the Palestinian refugee problem and Palestinian sovereignty over the Muslim and Christian quarters of the Old City of Jerusalem— and that Yasser Arafat had not responded in kind, or at all.[28]

Arafat and his cronies couldn't believe their ears. Barak's offer was like an unexpected gift, more than they had expected and certainly more than anyone else had ever offered. And there was Clinton, smiling and sure, telling them that Barak and the Israelis deserved an answer—a good one.

Friedman continues:

> Mr. Arafat had a dilemma: make some compromises, build on Mr. Barak's opening bid and try to get it closer to 100 percent—and regain the moral high ground that way—or provoke the Israelis into brutalizing Palestinians again, and regain the moral high ground that way. Mr. Arafat chose the latter.[29]

The concessions Barak made addressed every demand Arafat had previously made, but the PLO chairman flatly refused them in hopes of gaining more. It has been said that the Palestinians never miss an opportunity to miss an opportunity. Because Barak's concessions were so extraordinary and totally unexpected, he went home to face an openly hostile Israeli public and Knesset. His administration collapsed.

Here is the dilemma Arafat now faces: because he refused to negotiate, and because Barak has dwindling support in the Israeli government, there is little hope that Arafat will see such a generous offer again. The door of peace seems to have been slammed shut by the hand of Arafat himself.

The cycle continues. Israel offers an olive branch; the Palestinians swat it away with both hands while screaming for world pity and support. If this latest uprising is a war—and it certainly looks, sounds, and smells like war—then let's name it after the man who bears responsibility for it: Yasser Arafat.

The Heart of the Conflict

On my desk I have a stack of published news reports that claim the unrest was sparked by Ariel Sharon's visit to the Temple Mount. Listen to the voices of reporters who have again missed the big picture:

Israeli officials yesterday claimed that Palestinians, provoked by sermons at Friday prayers, had attacked Jewish worshippers at the Western Wall . . . But Hanan Ashrawi, a respected Palestinian leader, said later that this was untrue and that Israeli police had invaded the grounds of the Dome of the Rock. ("Bloodbath at the Dome of the Rock," *Independent,* 30 September 2000)

Violence continues for the fourth day today . . . the trouble began with a visit last week by Israeli opposition leader Ariel Sharon to Jerusalem's Temple Mount, the city's holiest and most contested site. Palestinians charge the visit triggered a religious war. ("Violence in Jerusalem Continues Between Palestinians and Israelis Over the Temple Mount," National Public Radio, 1 October 2000)

To thousands of Palestinian youths throughout the West Bank, Gaza Strip and Jerusalem, it was Sharon who drove them into the streets by leading a delegation of hard-line Israeli lawmakers on a one-hour tour of Jerusalem's Temple Mount, Judaism's most sacred place. ("Arab Uprising Spreads to Israel; Israeli Defends Visit to Contested Site," *Washington Post,* 2 October 2000)

Palestinian leaders said Wednesday as Sharon planned the visit that the hawkish opposition leader wanted to show Israeli sovereignty claim over the contested holy site by the tour. Meanwhile, Israeli Environment Minister Dalia Itzik also told Israel Radio that in her opinion, Sharon made this visit without good intentions, and only wanted to ignite hatred and violence between the two ethnic sides. ("Sharon's Visit to Temple Mount Causes Violence," *Xinhua* [China], 28 September 2000)

I believe that Ariel Sharon's visit—which had been approved by the Muslim authorities—was only an excuse, a convenient and public situation that would give Arafat an opportunity to storm and release the intifada and create terrorism and strife in the battle for Jerusalem.

But knowing as he did that the situation was touchy, why did General Sharon risk so much for a visit to a holy place? The general said his purpose was to reaffirm the Jewish claim to the site and to demonstrate his firm conviction that Jerusalem's Old City and the Temple Mount—captured in 1967 when Jordan attacked Israel—must remain under Israeli sovereignty and not be surrendered in a bid for peace.[30]

"You must understand," he told a reporter, "the Jewish people are having one tiny small country, and that is Israel. And in this tiny small country, Jews, thank God, are having the right and the power to defend themselves by themselves. And we are going to keep it. All our history is here. That's where we started as a nation. And no one will be able to prevent any Jew from going to the Temple Mount."[31]

The Temple Mount Today

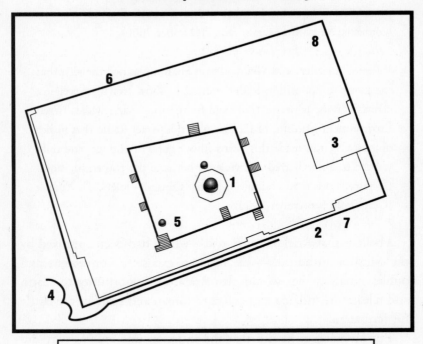

1	Dome of the Rock	5	Dome of the Spirits
2	Western Wall	6	Eastern Gate
3	Al-Aqsa Mosque	7	Mughrabi Gate
4	Entrance to the Western Wall Tunnel	8	Solomon's Stables

The Temple Mount, or *Har Habayit*, is the ancient site of the first and second temples. Nothing remains of either temple but the holiest shrine in all of Jewish civilization, the Western Wall. When the Romans burned and demolished the temple in A.D. 70, just as Jesus prophesied in Matthew 24:2, all that remained was a single outer wall. According to traditional Judaism, the temple cannot be rebuilt until the Messiah comes, and religious Jews regard the Western Wall, or *Ha'Kotel*, as their most sacred shrine. The wall is commonly known as the Wailing Wall, where the Jewish people come to mourn the destruction of their temple.

When the Jordanians captured the Old City of Jerusalem in 1948, Jews were forbidden to worship at the wall. So in June 1967, when the Israeli army retook the Old City, people watched in awe as television cameras revealed footage of Israeli soldiers praying and weeping at the Western Wall. General Moshe Dayan, who handed the Islamic mosques back to Muslim control a week after their capture, came to the wall and said Jews had "returned to their holiest of holy places, never to part from it again."[32]

The Israelis, on the other hand, have never forbidden the Muslims to visit their holy sites atop the Temple Mount. Immediately upon the reunification of Jerusalem in 1967, Israel passed the Protection of Holy Places Law, which guarantees the sanctity of all holy sites and makes it a punishable offense to desecrate or deny freedom of access to them. Under Israeli rule, Christians and Muslims have always administered their own holy places and institutions. The principle of free access to holy places for all religions was reaffirmed in the *Basic Law: Jerusalem, the Capital of Israel,* enacted by the Israeli Knesset in July 1980. Under these procedures, since 1967 Israel has authorized and allowed the Muslim holy sites on the Temple Mount to be administered by the Islamic religious authority, the Waqf.[33]

Yet the rhetoric of war has inflamed passions to the point where a man called Khalil, an administrator at a United Nations office in Nablus, told a reporter, "They [the Jews] took our land in 1948, they took our land in 1967, they stopped us from putting food on the table, and now they want to take away our religion. What is left for us but to fight?"[34]

This is pure Palestinian propaganda. Arafat is engaging in the politics of fear. A National Public Radio (NPR) report on the uprising quoted Arafat as he spoke about the Palestinian fighters: "A salute to the heroes and the faithful ones for your noble battle for dignity," he said, "the battle for holy Jerusalem and for Palestine." The NPR reporter went on to add that while political analysts disagree on whether Arafat planned the current spasm of violence, he clearly hopes to gain from it. Yiev Aluaha, a spokesman for Arafat's Fatah, says the days of violence "will only benefit the peace process."[35]

When asked if the Palestinians had used his visit to the Temple Mount as a pretext to start a planned outbreak, Sharon said,

> Yes. They had several motives. They wanted to get some more concessions from [Prime Minister] Barak. But almost nothing was left. Being inexperienced in negotiations, he thought that he would come to Camp David and put all the concessions on the table and that Arafat would embrace him, thank him, kiss him and love him, but Arafat is experienced. He immediately took everything and started to demand more . . .
>
> Maybe he [Arafat] wanted the last phase before establishing an independent state to be a battle. Our intelligence says [the uprising] was pre-planned and orchestrated by Arafat. He is using the Tanzim, a paramilitary force that reports directly to him. I believe there are thousands of them, equipped by the Palestinian Authority. Arafat signed an agreement that their weapons would be confiscated, but he never implemented it.[36]

As I write this in December 2000, the intifada continues. *Newsweek* magazine reports that a gray-haired mourner at a funeral deferentially asked Marwan Barghouti, a leader of the Tanzim, when the dying might end. "We are at the start of this intifada," Barghouti answered, dry-eyed and relaxed. "It has only been two months." As the violence continues in the weeks and months ahead, he said, "Israeli politicians will start to take us seriously."[37]

Twenty-six years ago, Yasser Arafat made his first appearance in the United States. He gave a dramatic speech at the United Nations, telling the General Assembly that he had come "bearing an olive branch and a freedom fighter's gun." He ended with a warning: "Do not let the olive branch fall from my hand."[38]

Arafat is far more willing to lower the olive branch than the weapon . . . and in the next chapter, you'll learn why.

Two

Why Jerusalem Matters

> Yet I [God] have chosen Jerusalem, that My name may be there . . . For now I have chosen and sanctified this house [the temple], that My name may be there forever; and My eyes and My heart will be there perpetually . . . In this house and in Jerusalem, which I have chosen out of all the tribes of Israel, I will put My name forever.
>
> —*2 Chronicles 6:6; 7:16; 33:7*

Jerusalem! No city on the face of the earth is like the Holy City. Other cities are known for their massive size, their climate and beauty, or their economic strength, but none can compare to the majestic city of Jerusalem. Why? Because Jerusalem is the city of God, the capital city of the nation God created by His spoken word (Gen. 12:1–3; 13:14–15), and with which He later made an eternally binding and unconditional blood covenant (Gen. 15:8–18).

Jerusalem is the city God has chosen as His habitation. King David, the man after God's own heart, wrote of the city of God with a holy passion, saying:

> Great is the LORD, and greatly to be praised
> In the city of our God,
> In His holy mountain.
> Beautiful in elevation,

The joy of the whole earth,
Is Mount Zion on the sides of the north,
The city of the great King . . .
As we have heard,
So we have seen
In the city of the LORD of hosts,
In the city of our God:
God will establish it forever.
Selah (Ps. 48:1–2, 8)

Jerusalem is a small city by many standards. With a population of approximately 620,000, it is certainly not the most populous city in the world. And yet it dominates headlines of newspapers and is known as the Holy City to Muslims, Christians, and Jews.

The Jewish claim to Jerusalem, however, is rooted in three thousand years of history. The words *Jerusalem* and *Zion* are mentioned more than eight hundred times in the Jewish Bible. And even during the Diaspora, when millions of Jews were scattered throughout the world, the Holy City remained foremost in the thoughts of the Jewish people. Everyday rituals such as saying grace over meals were filled with references to yearning for Jerusalem.

Not all the Jews were scattered. Despite all their national suffering, the Jewish presence in Jerusalem has remained constant and enduring. They have never abandoned the land. In fact, since 1840, the Jews have constituted the largest ethnic group in Jerusalem. They have held an uninterrupted majority in the city since 1860.

Though other nations have gained political sovereignty over the area, none but the Jews have ever made Jerusalem their capital city. It belongs to the Jews. Though all nations are welcomed there, and though many have trodden the city underfoot and massacred its citizens, the City of God is held for the Jewish people not by treaty, not by a peace process, but by *divine decree*.

Jerusalem, my friend, is not just another city. God chose Jerusalem as a place where His name would be worshiped forever. Jerusalem is a spiritual lighthouse to the entire world, sending its beacon of hope to a world staggering in despair. Jerusalem is the city that says by its very presence, *There is a God of might and majesty,* and as the mountains are about Jerusalem, so is the Lord God Almighty around His people. He is eternal, unmovable, and unshakable!

As Christians, we are proud to join together in supporting the continued sovereignty of the State of Israel over the holy city of Jerusalem. We support Israel's efforts to reach reconciliation with its Arab neighbors, but we strongly believe that neither Jerusalem nor any portion of it should be negotiable in any peace process. Jerusalem must remain undivided as the eternal capital of the Jewish people.

History of the Holy City

Jerusalem, whose very dust is adored in Scripture, was first settled by Canaanites in the twentieth century B.C. The earliest recorded reference to the city is found written on Egyptian clay bowls.[1] Though only a little larger than twelve acres in size, the city was naturally well defended and had at its base one of the most abundant springs in the area. By about one thousand years before Christ, Jerusalem was inhabited by Jebusites, a group of people related to the Hittites of the Old Testament.

The Bible tells us that David bought a threshing floor on Mount Moriah from a Jebusite and built an altar on the site (2 Sam. 24:16–25). Many scholars believe the area was a holy place, for threshing floors and altars naturally went together in pagan rituals of harvest and fertility gods. In any case, writes Gershom Gorenberg,

> If Jerusalem wasn't already holy, it's hard to understand why a city stood there. It's on the edge of a desert; the soil is rock; the sole

21

spring is grade C; the trade routes cross to the north. You wouldn't come here for gold, wheat, or spices. Only to stand at the gate of heaven.[2]

By the time David was anointed king of Israel in the last decade of the eleventh century B.C., the nation of Israel needed a strong central capital. David searched for a location among the tribes, and in 1004 B.C. he conquered a Jebusite city and felt led of God to make it his capital. Today we call it *Jerusalem*. The Palestinians call it *al-Quds*, and the Israelis, *Yerushalayim*.

David's passion for the Holy City is revealed in his writing:

> If I forget you, O Jerusalem,
> Let my right hand forget its skill!
> If I do not remember you,
> Let my tongue cling to the roof of my mouth—
> If I do not exalt Jerusalem
> Above my chief joy. (Ps. 137:5–6)

As you may recall, David was a musician as well as a warrior king. With his right hand he played the harp and sang the songs of Israel with such power that the demons of King Saul were silenced. David's message was simple—if he were to forget Jerusalem, his life would have no meaning. If Jerusalem was not the source of his deepest joy, he felt there was no need to exist. He saw Jerusalem as the Holy City, the place God and God's people called home.

In Jerusalem, David's son Solomon built his magnificent and ornate temple upon Mount Moriah, the place where David had erected his altar upon a threshing floor and Abraham had offered his son Isaac as a sacrifice until God sent an angel to spare the boy (Gen. 22:1–19; 2 Chron. 3:1). Jewish tradition also holds that Mount Moriah was the place where God collected dust to create Adam and where Cain killed Abel.[3] Incidentally, the Muslims believe that it was Ishmael, not Isaac, whom Abraham nearly killed upon Mount Moriah.

In Jerusalem, Jeremiah and Isaiah uttered thoughts that molded the spiritual foundations of half the human race.

In Jerusalem, the first temple was destroyed by the Babylonians when they captured Jerusalem in 587 B.C. Many of the Jews were led away into the Babylonian captivity, but they returned in 536 B.C. and began to build the temple again. The resulting structure, which was far less ornate than Solomon's temple, was known as Zerubbabel's temple.

In A.D. 70, Titus sent his troops into Jerusalem and slaughtered the Jews until their blood literally streamed down the streets. The Romans completely sacked the city and destroyed the second temple, which had been completed only six years before. The Romans continued the slaughter of the Jews of Jerusalem. In A.D. 135, Hadrian, a second-century Roman emperor, barred Jews from Jerusalem and had survivors of the massacre dispersed across the Roman Empire. Many fleeing Jews escaped to Mediterranean ports, only to be sold into slavery.

In A.D. 313, Constantine, the first Christian emperor of the Roman Empire, legalized Christianity and encouraged the construction of churches in the Holy City. At that time churches were built over locations that had to do with the life of Christ—the supposed sites of the birth of Jesus, His death, and His resurrection.

In A.D. 638, the Muslim forces of Omar, the second successor after Muhammad, captured Jerusalem from the Romans. Though Omar set about making the city a sanctuary for Muslims, he regarded Jesus and the Hebrew patriarchs as prophets, so their religious sites were preserved and protected.

The story is told that when Omar entered the city, he approached Sophronius, the city's Christian patriarch, to ask where the temple had stood. Sophronius, according to legend, in essence quoted Matthew 24:15: "Here is that appalling abomination, as prophesied by Daniel, standing on this holy site." Without a clear answer, Omar ordered the mount cleared of rubbish, then built a wooden mosque at the southern end of the mount.

Caliph Abd al-Malik ibn Marwan had the Dome of the Rock built between A.D. 685 and 691, and most people think of this magnificent gold-domed building when they think of the Temple Mount today.

In 1099, the crusaders, marching under the sign of the cross, stormed into Jerusalem to claim the city for Christ. Again the streets of the city ran with blood as the crusaders slaughtered more than forty thousand people and set fire to mosques and synagogues. In one particular situation, 969 Jewish men, women, and children were herded into a synagogue and set ablaze by crusaders. As the people screamed and burned alive, the crusading warriors stood outside and sang, "Christ, We Adore Thee."

Recent History

Jerusalem means "city of peace," but it has known more war, more bloodshed, more tears, and more terror than any city on earth. It has been conquered and reconquered thirty-eight times by Babylonians, Greeks, Romans, crusaders, and Ottomans, yet it stands today as a testimony to the faithfulness and intent of God.

In 1947, the United Nations voted to partition Palestine into two states, one Jewish and one Palestinian. The Jewish population, then about 600,000, was allotted large swaths of barren desert as a land reserve for the absorption of numerous Jewish refugees waiting to arrive. While the Palestinian population of 1.3 million was expected to grow through natural increase, the Jews were expected to take in Jews of all nationalities, particularly refugees from the Holocaust. So the land was almost equally divided between the two peoples, with more than 70 percent of the fertile land granted to the Palestinians.[4]

But when the British withdrew on May 15, 1948, five Arab armies immediately invaded in an effort to "push the Jews into the sea." They attacked Israel full force, trying to murder the Zionist state in its help-less infancy. By the time the fighting ended, tiny Israel survived intact (a miracle of God!), but Egypt occupied the Gaza Strip and Jordan held the West Bank. The Palestinians were left empty-handed.

Israel, Surrounded by Arab Countries

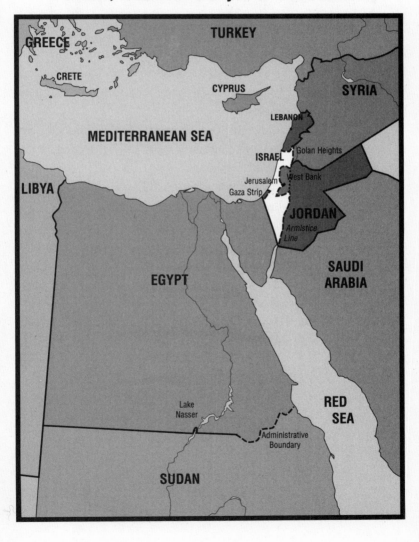

The Israelis didn't create the Palestinian refugee problem—the Arabs did. They forgot that when you start a war, you must be prepared to live with the consequences of losing that war.

From this war of 1948 was born the "Palestinian refugee problem" that the media have used to brainwash the Western world for the past fifty years. This "refugee problem" was created, sustained, and manipulated by Arab leaders against their own people to portray the Jews of Israel as heartless. It proved to be very effective.

In her book *From Time Immemorial,* historian Joan Peters charts in painstaking detail, with irrefutable documentation, that just before the war of 1948 began, Arab leaders told the Palestinians to leave their homes. "As soon as we drive the Jews into the sea," they promised, "you can return."[5]

To the Arabs' shock and surprise, they lost the war, and soon an estimated 600,000 Palestinian refugees were asking Jordan, Iran, Iraq, and Syria to let them immigrate.

But the Arab states would not welcome them, even though they had plenty of land and money. Despite sharing a common language, religion, and culture with the refugees, those states denied them permission to immigrate. Why? Because the refugees had become a lightning rod for the world media to attack Israel. "See how heartless the Jewish people are?" moaned the newspapers and reporters. "See how unreasonable Israel is? Look at the poor Arabs without homes!"

A. B. Yehoshua explains that the Palestinian refugees are not really refugees at all, but displaced persons:

The Jews who fled or were expelled by Arabs from the Old City of Jerusalem, the Etzion Bloc, Atarot, Kfar Darmon or Beit Ha'arava, into Israeli territory, were never refugees but only displaced persons, who were immediately allocated new homes in the Israeli homeland. However, the Palestinians did not call their uprooted people displaced persons. They were instead referred to as refugees, even though most remained in the Palestinian homeland and lived at most only 20 to 40 km away from their homes . . . There were also Palestinians who fled, or were expelled, from Palestine and went to Arab countries . . . where they did not receive local citizenship and their status remained that of refugees. But during the 19 years in which the Palestinian territory of the West Bank and the Gaza Strip were under Palestinian, Jordanian, and Egyptian control, all of these refugees could have at least returned to their homeland, becoming displaced persons rather than refugees, and building themselves new homes in their homeland.[6]

Yehoshua goes on to say that the blame for the refugees' unhappy existence lies directly upon themselves and the Arab countries. Nothing stood in the way of these people making new homes for

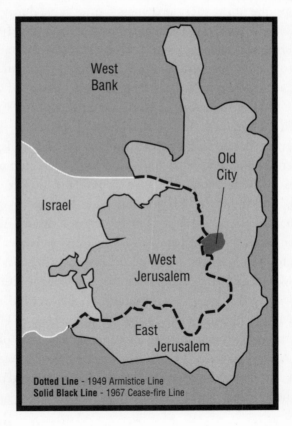

themselves in Arab countries, yet the truth is clear: they are more valuable politically as refugees than as prosperous, productive citizens in an Arab nation.

Few people know that the Israeli government and the United Nations put up $150 million to resettle any Arab families that wanted to return to their homes. But those who did return were shot by the Palestine Liberation Organization. That's the PLO, led by Yasser Arafat, the same man who refused to compromise and has walked away from the peace negotiations.

Since 1948, five brutal wars have been fought in Israel. A river of blood has been shed over control of Judea and Samaria (the West Bank), the Golan Heights, and the Holy City, Jerusalem.

Perhaps one of the most amazing victories came during the Six-Day War in 1967. Only the mighty hand of God could have preserved Jerusalem from its birth until the stunning moment when Jewish soldiers broke through the Jordanian front and prayed together at the Western Wall. After almost two thousand years, the ancient city of Jerusalem once again was restored to Jewish hands through a supernatural victory of the Israeli army.

This turn of events dramatically affected the State of Israel. Not long after the war, one rabbi told a meeting of Orthodox cabinet members that "the Holy One gave us the land through obvious miracles," and therefore, "He'll never take it from us."[7]

But not all the Israeli leaders were religious. Many more were pragmatic and realized that the Messiah had not yet come. The Jews still had to live alongside Arabs, and the Arabs still considered the Temple Mount a holy place. Almost immediately the Jewish religious authorities issued a statement warning Jews not to tread upon the Temple Mount. Because no one knew where the Holy of Holies had actually stood, Jews ran the risk of entering that holy place with unclean hands and feet. The time for entering the Temple Mount, they said, was still in the future—when the Messiah would come and rebuild the temple.

Within a week, the Israelis turned control of the Islamic religious sites back to the Muslims and made an effort to channel Jewish religious fervor from the mount to the Western Wall.

For generations, the Israelis have struggled to keep peace with their Arab neighbors, responding with violence only when threatened. Yet the Palestinians, armed with hot tempers, stones, and weapons, continue to wear away and call upon the sympathies of world opinion.

The Palestinian-Israeli peace process began with secret talks in the early 1990s and reached a historic peak with the signing of a peace pact at the White House in September 1993. Israeli Prime Minister Yitzhak Rabin stood in the White House Rose Garden with Yasser Arafat. President Bill Clinton stood between the two men, eager to announce that Rabin and Arafat had, the previous day, signed the West Bank accord. At that signing, Rabin declared that the land flowing with milk and honey should not become a land flowing with blood and tears. In a speech delivered only a few days before, Rabin had said,

> We, the soldiers who have returned from battles stained with blood; we who have seen our relatives and friends killed before our eyes; we who have attended their funerals and cannot look in the eyes of their parents; we who have come from a land where parents bury their children; we who have fought against you, the Palestinians—we say to you today, in a loud and a clear voice: enough of blood and tears. Enough.

That was a desperate and sincere cry from the soul of a warrior, but two years later, in Jerusalem, Rabin was assassinated. Blood and tears flowed again, and the leaders of the world stood at his graveside and mourned the man who had tried to bring peace to his country but failed.

Since that time, as the nation has continued to strive for peace, Israel has been handing over land to the Palestinian Authority—most of the Gaza Strip and about half of the West Bank. The Israelis have pulled out of important defense positions and trusted the Palestinians to keep their word about protecting religious sites and disarming those who would commit acts of terror. For their part, the Palestinians arrested several anti-Israel extremists of Hamas and the Islamic Jihad.

But a final peace had not been achieved, and in the summer of 2000, the entire process fell apart. The stumbling stone? Jerusalem and the Holy Mount.

The All-Important Temple Mount

> As the navel is set in the center of the human body,
> so is the land of Israel the navel of the world . . .
> situated in the center of the world,
> and Jerusalem in the center of the land of Israel,
> and the sanctuary in the center of Jerusalem,
> and the holy place in the center of the sanctuary,
> and the ark in the center of the holy place,
> and the foundation stone before the holy place,
> because from it the world was founded.[8]

This text, from ancient Jewish writings, gives a clear indication of just how revered is the Jewish Temple Mount. It is a place too holy to traverse. It was the site of Solomon's temple and, later, Herod's, the temple where Jesus worshiped. Most important—and this is the most explosive concept—it is the place where the Messiah will rule His kingdom from a third temple.

If words could cause tremors, that last statement would evoke a ten on the Richter scale. Gershom Gorenberg, a Jew living in Israel, explains why:

The dispute over who owns the Mount is one of the most intractable issues of real-world Middle Eastern politics. The conflict

30

is intense because of the Mount's place in history—but even more because of its place in the future. For a small but growing group of Jews on the Israeli religious right, every day since 1967 has been a missed opportunity to begin building the Third Temple. For a far larger number of conservative Christians elsewhere in the world—and particularly in the United States—building that Temple is an essential condition for the Second Coming. And for many Muslims, any attempt to destroy the shrines of Al-Aqsa is a sign that the Hour is at hand . . . The Temple Mount is potentially a detonator of full-scale war, and a few people trying to rush the End could set it off.[9]

Each of the faiths represented in Jerusalem has its own script for how the end of days will come. The Jewish people look to the Bible and read Scripture of how the Messiah will rule from the temple and from Jerusalem. The prophet Malachi wrote,

> "Behold, I send My messenger,
> And he will prepare the way before Me.
> And the Lord, whom you seek,
> Will suddenly come to His temple,
> Even the Messenger of the covenant,
> In whom you delight.
> Behold, He is coming,"
> Says the LORD of hosts. (3:1)

The Jewish Perspective

Because of the prophet's words, religious Jews are convinced that a third temple will be built. They differ, however, in their ideas about how the temple will come to the Temple Mount.

Many Jews believe the Messiah Himself will build the temple, and it is folly to try to force the issue. Another group believes the temple will descend from heaven, wrought by the hand of God.

Since the destruction of the second temple in A.D. 70, Jewish prayers have risen for the rebuilding of the temple. Orthodox Jews today pray the following words three times daily: "May it be thy will that the Temple be speedily rebuilt in our own time."[10]

The predominant school of thought holds that Israel's duty is to rebuild the temple as soon as possible. According to this line of thought, the nation has been sinning through omission since 1967, when God restored the Temple Mount to Jewish control. These people argue, quite convincingly, that no temple was ever built without human assistance, and many of them note that Israel's former two temples were built with the help of Gentiles.

Contemporary Gentiles are more than willing to help build the temple. Many Christians, both as individuals and as corporate entities, have aligned themselves with those who desire to see the temple rise upon the mount.

According to Temple Institute spokesman Rabbi Chaim Richman, detailed blueprints for the third temple have existed for years. The plans were drawn from the Bible, Josephus, and Middot. Under the auspices of Rabbi Shlomo Goren, the seventy-seat Supreme Court building that housed the Sanhedrin in biblical times has already been constructed. Goren states that its location next to the Temple Mount is correct for the coming temple, which will be thirty times larger than the previous temples, according to the prophet Ezekiel.[11]

Not only are the blueprints being prepared, but so are the personnel. According to rabbinic tradition, those of the priestly tribe of Levi, the *Kohanim*, were forbidden to alter their names as they were scattered during the Diaspora. Recently a more scientific test to verify those of priestly lineage has arrived. In studies of male Jews descended from Aaron, the brother of Moses, it was discovered that as a group they carry a unique aberration of the Y chromosome.[12] God has managed to preserve His priests!

But with the preservation of the priests arises another problem: in order to enter the Holy of Holies and sacrifice to the holy God of Israel, a priest had to be ritually cleansed by a mixture containing the ashes of a perfect red heifer. Because all Jews became unclean during the Diaspora, the only way to purify priests and establish a priesthood is through the ashes of a red heifer.

The Jewish sage Maimonides taught that there were nine red heifers between the beginning of the tabernacle and the end of the second temple. When the tenth arrived, said Maimonides, it would be prepared by the Messiah.[13]

In 1997, a red calf was born at Kfar Hassidim, a small religious kibbutz near Haifa. The calf, born of a black-and-white holstein, was hailed as a miracle. Tour buses began driving out to see her, rabbis came to consult about the significance of her birth, and the Muslims raised their radar. Editorials in Jerusalem papers called the calf a "ticking time bomb," and the *Boston Globe* ran a story with the headline "Portent in a Pasture."[14] An Islamic tract on the approaching apocalypse mentioned "the red cow" born in "what they call Israel." The author, Amin Jamal al-Din, went on to say incorrectly that when the calf "reaches its full development in the third year of its life, it will be sacrificed at the Temple of Solomon, and the person who will do this will be their king, their redeemer, the Antichrist."[15]

Al-Din was correct in his statement that the cow could not be declared a kosher red heifer until it had reached three years of age. After a few months the calf, called Melody, developed a few white hairs in its tail, thereby disqualifying itself for temple sacrifice. But the calf's unexpected arrival stirred the embers of temple passion, and American Clyde Lott, a preacher and Mississippi cattle rancher, has since joined forces with Israeli cattle breeders to create the perfectly red heifers that will be needed for temple sacrifice.

Lott says, "I've devoted my entire life to this; God has placed it on my heart." He sees himself as the spiritual heir of "the righteous Gentile from Ashkelon," who, according to the Jewish Midrash, provided the rabbis with the last known red heifer during the time of the second temple.[16]

At this writing, Clyde Lott is planning to take herds of cattle to Israel, ostensibly to aid with Israeli beef production, but undeniably to pave the way for the third temple.

The advent of a red heifer pointed toward another problem: the ashes of the red heifer will purify the people, but who among the Israelis was ritually pure and therefore qualified to handle the sacrifice of the red heifer? According to the laws of *Halacha*, anyone who has walked upon ground containing the bones of the dead or entered a building with dead people under its roof is ritually impure. Therefore, anyone who has walked in Israel (which is rife with cemeteries) or has been born or spent time in a hospital is unfit to handle the sacrifice of the red heifer.

To handle this thorny problem, a group of religious Jews has asked for volunteers—pregnant women whose children will be descended from Aaron, and therefore part of the priestly class. These women will live in special buildings, elevated above the ground, and when their children are born, these baby boys will be shielded from all forms of impurity as defined in Jewish law. At the age of thirteen, they will be old enough to serve as priests.[17]

In 1997, Reuven Prager, a Jew living in Israel, began minting silver half-shekels. When the temple stood, he says, every Jew was required to contribute a silver half-shekel annually to pay for sacrifices and temple maintenance. He took out a *Jerusalem Post* ad after minting his first coins, and in 1998 he sold five thousand, with 10 percent of them "coming back" to his temple fund. Three times a year he and two Brinks guards, both *Kohanim*, venture into the city to pick up lockboxes filled with sacred half-shekel coins dedicated to the third temple. When they finish their collection, they deliver the coins to a safe in the Chief Rabbinate building.[18]

In Israel today, you can find people who are convinced that the Jews must make the country ready to receive the temple and the Messiah. You can also find people who believe that God will do all the work.

What you'd be hard-pressed to find are people who think the Temple Mount is meaningless.

The Christian Perspective

Most Christians who study Bible prophecy also look for a third temple in which the Messiah will reign. We'll discuss this in more detail later, but we know that the Messiah will not reign in the temple until the millennial kingdom, when the earth will finally receive its King. Prior to this, however, a false messiah will stand in the temple and cause the entire world to worship him and take his mark. He is the Antichrist, and he will be revealed in the seven-year period known as the Tribulation.

For now, know this: the third temple will be rebuilt by human hands, and a false messiah will stand in it. He will probably oversee or orchestrate the project. But when his doom is sealed, the Lord Jesus Christ will reign from the Temple Mount, and His glory will fill the earth, just as the prophets foretold.

The Muslim Perspective

You may be surprised to learn that the Muslims also have an eschatology. They call the coming battle *the Hour*, and Islamic tradition quotes Muhammad as saying, "Behold! God sent me with a sword, just before the Hour, and placed my daily sustenance beneath the shadow of my spear, and humiliation and contempt upon those who oppose me."[19]

Like the early Christians who believed the Lord was coming soon, Muslims of the seventh century, when Islam was still in its infancy, rode out to conquer the world because they were convinced the end was near. Notice the difference, however: Christians sought to win the world through the gospel of love. The Muslims sought to win the world through domination and conquest.

Islam teaches that wars and immorality will increase in the latter days. It also holds that a false messiah, known as *al-masih al-dajjal,* will conquer the world. According to Islamic belief, he will be a Jew, leading an army of Jews from the East. Then Jesus will return to defeat the false messiah in a battle near Jerusalem. He will kill all pigs, break all crosses, and leave Islam as the world's true faith. The dead will rise, and every man and woman who ever lived will face judgment at the valley of Jehoshaphat next to the walls of Jerusalem.[20]

During the Gulf War, many Muslims believed the Hour was approaching. Palestinian newspapers published a purported tradition from the Prophet—probably produced, says Gershom Gorenberg, by Saddam Hussein's propagandists—that claimed the Hour would come when "yellow-haired people, Byzantines and Franks" gather with Egyptians "in the wasteland against a man named Sadim."[21] The yellow-haired Byzantines and Franks, of course, were the Americans.

In 1999, a book called *The Great Events Preceding the Appearance of the Mahdi* (the Muslim end-times leader) began selling briskly in the Islamic bookstores of Jerusalem. Other Muslim leaders began to calculate times for the appearance of the Mahdi,[22] but most Muslim leaders insist the time cannot be calculated. "Anyone who fixes the time of the appearance," say Muslim clerics, "is telling a falsehood."

But, like Christians, Muslims look for certain signs of the end of the age. Among them are the presence of "Byzantines invading Hijaz," the northwest portion of Saudi Arabia. Muslims believe that American presence in Saudi Arabia fulfills this prophecy. Another prophecy of Muslim end times is a Jewish presence in Palestine, which is, in their view, another sign of the approaching Hour.[23]

When the Mahdi appears, they believe, the sun will rise from the west. Also during the latter days, a man will arise who will appear to be an "outwardly pious person who will take care to remember God at all times. But in reality he will be the most wicked person on earth. He will deceive a large number of people and will rally them around himself. He will gain control over five regions."

Sound familiar? This outwardly religious deceiver sounds very much like the biblical description of the Antichrist who will arise during the time of tribulation to come.

"At the world's end," writes Gorenberg, "the believers of three faiths will watch the same drama, but with different programs in their hands. In one Jesus is Son of God; in another he is Muslim prophet . . . The infidels in one script are the true believers of another."[24] The Jewish perspective holds that Messiah, a mortal man, will come to usher in the golden age of peace.

Notice that Jerusalem is the setting for all three events. In fact, Muslims believe that at the end of time, the Kaaba—the most holy shrine in Mecca—will supernaturally come to Jerusalem and plant itself on the Temple Mount, of course.

Muslims call the Temple Mount *Al-Haram al-Sharif*, or the noble sanctuary. According to their tradition, it is not only the place where Muhammad arrived on a winged horse before ascending to heaven; it is also the site of the world's second mosque, built by Adam (of Adam and Eve) after he built the mosque in Mecca.[25]

Present-day Difficulties

Three major religions, each followed by millions of people, and each looking to one small piece of real estate for the future culmination of their faith. Is it any wonder that the rocks surrounding the Temple Mount are frequently bathed in blood?

In the fall of 1996, in order to help celebrate the three thousandth birthday of the city of Jerusalem, the Israelis allowed visitors through a 450-yard tunnel that ran parallel to the Western Wall. The tunnel was not a new excavation, but a route dating back to the time of the Maccabees in the third century B.C. The tunnel was also in use at the time of Herod the Great.

The Muslims reacted with great protests and hysterical caterwauling. The media picked up the story and all too often left the impression that the Israelis had been tunneling beneath holy Islamic sites. Nothing could be farther from the truth, but you'd never know it from the news reports.

Fighting broke out between Palestinians and Israelis, and before the week ended, more than seventy people lay dead. Israel was soundly denounced throughout the world.

The *Washington Post* reported that "it should come as no surprise that violent passions were aroused by Israel's tampering with the ground beneath the Dome of the Rock and Al-Aqsa Mosque." National Public Radio commentators stated that the Palestinians claimed "the project threatens the stability of the Al-Aqsa Mosque."[26]

In truth, the Muslims weren't as threatened by the centuries-old tunnel as they were by the fact that the Jews were visiting their own holy site. "In the tunnel," reports an Islamic Web page,

> they have an electronic screen explaining the main elements of the city according to a Biblical vision, suggesting that the city is a Jewish city, including all the buildings, the markets, and the "Temple." In that picture there is no record of any Islamic holy sites, and that includes the Al-Aqsa mosque, clearly reflecting the actual plans to destroy the Al-Aqsa mosque and to build the "Temple" in its place.[27]

As frantic as the Muslims were about the Jews and their Western Wall tunnel, no one has said a word about the recent Muslim digging beneath the Temple Mount. The Waqf, which administers the Temple Mount, requested and received a permit to open an emergency exit in the new mosque built in Solomon's Stables. They are building a third mosque on the Temple Mount. To build this structure, they dug a hole 60 meters long and 25 meters wide. For the first time since 1967, a fleet of bulldozers and trucks was put to work on the mount, carrying out six thousand tons of earth.

Alarmed by the haphazard digging, Israelis from the Antiquities Authority investigated and found articles from the first and second temple eras in the discarded earth, dumped unceremoniously in the channel of the Kidron River.[28]

When three Jews protested the illegal Waqf construction on the mount, 150 Arabs attacked, smashing the windshield of the Jewish protesters' car. But the Muslims' behavior is not surprising when you consider that they are trying to prove that Jews have no connection to the Temple Mount at all.

In another incident, a Jewish Quarter resident was arrested on the Temple Mount when she went up to walk in the areas permissible by Jewish law. When she sat on a bench and closed her eyes, the Waqf police accosted her and interrogated her. When she said she was a student at Hebrew University studying the second temple period, the Arab police responded by saying, "You really believe there was a Second Temple? You plan to destroy the dome [of the Rock] and build the Second Temple!"

The Waqf officials then turned her over to a detachment of the Israeli police stationed in the Old City, where she was held and questioned for four hours. During the questioning, an Israeli police officer told her she had been charged with the crime of "praying on the Temple Mount." Her sentence? She was forbidden to return to the Temple Mount, and she was required to report to the police every two days until she left the country or risk a 4,000 shekel fine.[29]

The Temple Will Rise Again from Mount Moriah

Many Jews see a vivid picture of the Temple Mount's future in Isaiah 2:1–5:

> The word that Isaiah the son of Amoz saw concerning Judah and Jerusalem.
> Now it shall come to pass in the latter days
> That the mountain of the LORD'S house

Shall be established on the top of the mountains,
And shall be exalted above the hills;
And all nations shall flow to it.
Many people shall come and say,
"Come, and let us go up to the mountain of the LORD,
To the house of the God of Jacob;
He will teach us His ways,
And we shall walk in His paths."
For out of Zion shall go forth the law,
And the word of the LORD from Jerusalem.
He shall judge between the nations,
And rebuke many people;
They shall beat their swords into plowshares,
And their spears into pruning hooks;
Nation shall not lift up sword against nation,
Neither shall they learn war anymore.
O house of Jacob, come and let us walk
In the light of the LORD.

Many modern Jews look forward to walking in the light of the Lord on His Temple Mount. On the Web, I found a site maintained by Gershon Salomon, a secular Jew who earnestly awaits the rebuilding of the temple. He writes,

In Israel we are now living in exciting, prophetic end-times. G-d is moving in the midst of the people of Israel to redeem the people and land of Israel and to rebuild His House on Mt. Moriah in Jerusalem. We believe that Mashiach ben David [the Messiah] is soon to come. At the same time these are very critical times that will be followed by troubles and difficult events. One important result of these times is that the preparations for the rebuilding of the Temple and the worship in it are continuing at full speed.[30]

Make no mistake, the temple will stand again upon the Temple Mount. And that fact begs a question: Must the Muslim mosques be destroyed before the temple can be built? Although no one knows for certain, there are several possibilities.

Where Did the Temple Stand Originally?

To rebuild the temple, the Jews must first determine exactly where the previous temples stood. Scripture indicates that the site for the temple was divinely appointed (Gen. 22:2; Ex. 15:17; 2 Sam. 24:18; 1 Chron. 21:18), so the builders cannot arbitrarily choose any site they please.

Each of the previous temples was built with the Holy of Holies enclosing a rock known as *Even ha-Shetiyah*, or Foundation Stone. Because it was on this stone that the ark of the covenant rested and the shekinah glory descended (1 Kings 8), departed (Ezek. 8:4; 11:23), and promised to return (Ezek. 43:1–7), no other place can be substituted.[31]

The problem lies in locating the Foundation Stone. The Temple Mount proper has existed through the centuries, but its surface has been changed and its archaeological depths have been largely unexplored due to tensions between the Israelis and the Muslims.

One theory puts the original temple at the southwestern corner of the Temple Mount platform, near the present Al-Aqsa Mosque. Tel Aviv architect Tuvia Sagiv cooperated with an Israeli firm that does aerial infrared survey work. In the resulting pictures, he saw thick subterranean lines beneath the Dome of the Rock and the mosque to the south. He believes that Hadrian's Roman temple to Jupiter once stood in this southern region, and it would be logical to assume that the Roman emperor built his temple over the ruins of the Jewish structure.[32]

Most Israeli archaeologists believe that the Dome of the Rock sits directly upon the ruins of Solomon's temple, and that the rock under the dome is, in fact, the Foundation Stone. Archaeologist

Where the Third Temple Could Be Built

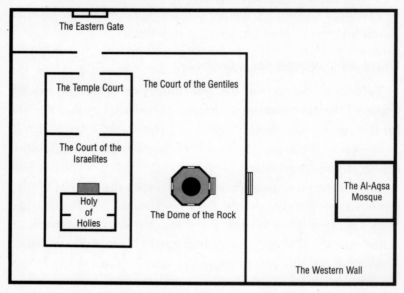

Leen Ritmeyer believes that the foundation, trenches, and walls of the Holy of Holies are discernible. His opinion is the most commonly held and the most dangerous. In order to rebuild the Jewish temple, the Dome of the Rock would have to be destroyed. No one can imagine that coming to pass without engaging in a bloody war with the Arab nations.

Another school of thought, however, places the original temple in the wide-open area to the north of the Muslim Dome of the Rock. According to several sources, including the Bible, the Mishnah Torah, Josephus, and the Talmud, the five temple gates lined up in a straight line opposite the Eastern, or Golden, Gate.

The Mishnah Torah, for instance, declares that the priest would sacrifice the red heifer (used to purify uncleanness so people could enter the temple) on the Mount of Olives directly opposite the

Eastern Gate. From this position, he could look above the Eastern Gate and through the five gates of the temple and see the veil surrounding the Holy of Holies. None of this would be possible unless the temple was located directly opposite the Eastern Gate and not situated in the center of the Temple Mount.[33]

Asher Kaufman, Ph.D., was the first to propose this theory. He mapped the first and second temples, with the rock under the current Dome of the Spirits marking the Holy of Holies. In time he heard from American preacher David Lewis, who cited Revelation 11: "Then I was given a reed like a measuring rod. And the angel stood, saying, 'Rise and measure the temple of God, the altar, and those who worship there. But leave out the court which is outside the temple, and do not measure it, for it has been given to the Gentiles. And they will tread the holy city underfoot for forty-two months'" (vv. 1–2).[34]

Do you see the possible picture? By some miracle, perhaps performed by the Antichrist himself, peace could be arranged so that the Jews could build their temple to the north of the current mosques. And the "Gentiles," or Arabs, would be treading it for the first three and a half years of the Tribulation period.

I cannot be dogmatic about this, but I believe this is a strong possibility and lines up with prophetic Scripture. It is entirely possible that the coming "man of peace," the false christ, will be able to work such a miracle of diplomacy. The nations will wonder at his genius, his diplomacy, and his ability to make peace.

Time will tell.

Three

The Birth of the Battle

> Ten measures of suffering were sent by God upon the world. Nine of them fell on Jerusalem.
>
> —Hebrew proverb[1]

> The dew which descends upon Jerusalem is a remedy for every sickness, because it is from the gardens of Paradise.
>
> —Excerpt from the Hadith, the sayings of the prophet Muhammad[2]

I don't know whether you ever fought with your siblings, but whenever my brothers and I got into a tussle, my mother would come into the room and want to get at the root of the problem. "Start at the beginning," she'd say, and we'd be forced to explain who did what to whom before the fists started flying.

Having the Jews and Arabs sit down for a let's-go-back-to-the-beginning talk isn't so simple—the roots of their strife go back for more generations than we can count. Their ancient rivalry began in the time of Abraham.

Abraham, Father to Arab and Jew

Abraham, son of Terah, lived until the age of seventy in his native country of Chaldea and in the city of Ur, a pagan place. There he was called of God to leave his home, and Abraham obeyed: "By faith Abraham obeyed when he was called to go out to the place which he would receive as an inheritance. And he went out, not knowing where he was going" (Heb. 11:8).

To honor Abraham for his faith and obedience, God dispatched an angel to tell him that he would be the father of a great nation: "And behold, the word of the LORD came to [Abraham], saying . . . 'One who will come from your own body shall be your heir.' Then He brought him outside and said, 'Look now toward heaven, and count the stars if you are able to number them.' And He said to him, 'So shall your descendants be'" (Gen. 15:4–5).

Abraham was more than a little surprised at this revelation because his wife, Sarah, was already postmenopausal and had never borne a child. Sarah, trying to help God out a bit, asked Abraham to visit the tent of her Egyptian maid, Hagar, and have a child with her—not an unusual practice in those days. Abraham said, in effect, "Sounds like God's will to me, Sarah. No problem!"

So Abraham slept with Hagar, and Ishmael was born. Later, just as God had foretold, Sarah conceived and gave birth to a miracle baby, Isaac, whose name means "son of laughter."

And there you have the root of the problem: the people of Israel, the Jews, are descended from Isaac; the Arabs are descended from Ishmael.

Isaac was the child of promise, a miracle sent by God. Ishmael was the child of Abraham's attempt to fulfill God's promise through his own efforts.

Notice what the angel of the Lord told Hagar about her son:

And He said, "Hagar, Sarai's maid, where have you come from, and where are you going?" She said, "I am fleeing from the presence of my mistress Sarai." The Angel of the LORD said to her, "Return to your mistress, and submit yourself under her hand." Then the Angel of the LORD said to her, "I will multiply your descendants

exceedingly, so that they shall not be counted f~~r~~
the Angel of the LORD said to her:

> "Behold, you are with child,
> And you shall bear a son.
> You shall call his name Ishmael,
> Because the LORD has heard your affliction.
> He shall be a wild man;
> His hand shall be against every man,
> And every man's hand against him.
> And he shall dwell in the presence of all his brethren."
> (Gen. 16:8–12)

The New Living Translation puts it this way: "This son of yours will be a wild one—free and untamed as a wild donkey! He will be against everyone, and everyone will be against him. Yes, he will live at odds with the rest of his brothers" (Gen. 16:12).

Notice that the angel of the Lord—who many Bible scholars believe was Jesus Himself—mentioned that her son would dwell in the presence of his brothers, plural. Since he would have only one brother, Isaac, this is clearly a prophetic passage about Ishmael's descendants. And the Arabs have been living "at odds" with the Jews since the time of Ishmael's birth.

The truth of that prophecy is contained in an oft-quoted Arab proverb today: "I against my brothers; I and my brothers against my cousins; I and my cousins against the world."[3]

God did honor Ishmael—He promised that Ishmael would be fruitful, the father of twelve rulers, and a great nation. But in His sovereignty, God established His covenant with Isaac, the child of promise. The title to the promised land of Israel passed from Abraham to Isaac, and then to Jacob.

You can imagine that more than a little competition existed in Abraham's household. That rivalry still exists today, but on a larger scale.

August 1929, prior to the formation of the State of Israel, a
up of secular Jews went to the Western Wall and raised a blue-
nd-white Zionist flag. Before leaving, they sang the Zionist
anthem, "Hatikvah."

The next day, Muslim protesters visited the same wall, beating
the Jewish worshipers there. The following Friday, thousands of
Muslims burst into the Old City streets. Eyewitnesses reported that
youths screamed, "O Jews, the faith of Mohammed is fulfilled with
the sword!" With clubs and knives, Muslims assaulted Jews in the
city, and within the hour Jews were under attack throughout
Jerusalem. By the time the attacks ended, a week and a half later,
133 Jews and 116 Arabs lay dead.[4]

"The accounts share this much," writes Gershom Gorenberg:

> Two national groups were wrestling for one piece of land. Unable to
> settle that conflict, the British would stumble out of Palestine in
> 1948, and Arab and Jew would continue fighting until, in the last
> quarter of the century, they began giving up some pieces of their
> dreams in return for some measure of peace, despite its fragility.
> Nineteen twenty-nine is a reasonable point for making when a dis-
> pute turned into a war.[5]

"There is no solution," wrote Israeli hero David Ben-Gurion.
"We want the country to be ours. They want the country to be
theirs."[6]

Two Disparate Religions

The conflict between Arabs and Jews goes deeper than disputes
over the lands of Palestine. The conflict is theological. It is Judaism
versus Islam, and Islam's theology insists that Islam triumph over
everything else. That's why when you visit an Arabic city, the
Islamic prayer tower is the highest point in the settlement.

The Arabs believe that Jesus, Moses, David, and several other Hebrews were prophets; however, Muhammad was the greatest prophet. Though Muslims revere the Bible, including the Torah, the Psalms, and the Gospels, they hold that the Quran (the Koran) is the absolute true word of God, revealed through the angel Jibraeel (Gabriel) to Muhammad. Muslims believe that Allah is God, that he has neither father nor mother, and that he has no sons.

Do not be confused into thinking that Allah is just another name for the same God worshiped by Christians and Jews. Allah is the moon god, married to the sun goddess, represented by the crescent moon that is visible on every mosque throughout the Muslim world. The Muslims ridicule the holy God of Israel, saying that He is "bloodthirsty, fickle-minded, harsh and greedy. He is pleased with imposture and deceit. He is loquacious and passionately fond of long speeches."[7]

Nor should you think that Arabs are as relaxed about religion as most Western people. Religion is the hub of an Arab's life. "Every activity, every thought, feeling, or custom is regulated by the laws of Islam," writes Ramon Bennett, "which are unquestioningly believed by minds that give unpledged allegiance. In this the Muslims are in 'sharp contrast with those who profess other religions.'"[8]

Muslims are so devout that they will not tolerate criticism of their religion. Remember Salman Rushdie? In 1989 his novel, *The Satanic Verses*, based upon verses Muhammad supposedly received from the devil, resulted in his death sentence. The novelist was forced into hiding when the Ayatollah Khomeini of Iran announced a $3 million reward to anyone who killed the writer.[9] In 1994 another writer, Taslima Nasrin, suggested that the Quran should be revised. The local Islamic leader announced a bounty of $2,500 to anyone who would kill her.[10]

Understand this: no matter what the Arabs say about peace, their religion demands that they defeat Christians and Jews. Islam proclaims a theology of triumphalism. Simply translated, Muslims believe that it is the will of Allah for Islam to rule the world.

Islamic law stipulates that to fulfill Muhammad's task, every "infidel domain" must be considered a territory of war. According to Moris Farhi, author of *The Last of Days*, Muslims believe that there can be no peace with Jews or Christians or any other non-Islamic people, and that if peace must be made, only a truce is permissible—and that "for a maximum of ten years as an expedient to hone our swords, whet our blood, and strengthen our will."[11] Muhammad made physical violence an invisible, yet integral, part of that faith.

Islamic theology boils down to one condition: the fundamentalist Arabs must destroy the Jews and rule Israel, or Muhammad is a false prophet and the Quran is not true. Such a thought is inconceivable! For that reason, the fundamentalist Arabs, who are the majority, must attack Israel and the Jews to be loyal to their prophet. The strategy of Islamic Jihad is as simple as it is satanic: "Kill so many Jews that they will eventually abandon Palestine."[12]

In his book *Philistine*, Ramon Bennett says,

> If leaders and lawmakers are to sufficiently comprehend the danger that Islam presents to both Israel and the West, in order to motivate them to action, they first need to know something about it. *Islam is the antithesis of biblical Christianity.* Christianity advocates love and compassion toward God and one's neighbor. Islam promotes hatred and cruelty—diabolical cruelty. Execution, crucifixion, the severing of hands, feet and tongues, the gouging out of eyes are all part of Islam's "submission to the will of Allah."[13]

The late Imam Hasan al-Bana of the Islamic resistance movement, Hamas, summed up their philosophy so well that his statement was included in their covenant: "Israel will exist and will continue to exist until Islam will obliterate it, just as it obliterated others before it."[14]

Who Are the Palestinians?

Most Arabs, though certainly not all, are Muslims who hold to the Islamic faith. Jordan, Syria, Iraq, Iran, Saudi Arabia, and Egypt are among the world's leading Arab and Islamic nations.

So who, exactly, are the Palestinians, and why are they intent upon making war upon Israel? They are Arabs at the mercy of Arab leadership, and they are being used as pawns in the ancient feud between the chosen people of God and their cousins.

Joseph Farah, a self-described "Arab-American journalist who has spent some time in the Middle East dodging more than my share of rocks and mortar shells," says that the Palestinian claims to a homeland, strife in Israel, and Muslim cries for control over holy sites are "phony excuses for the rioting, trouble-making and land-grabbing."[15]

He points out that prior to the 1967 Arab-Israeli war, there was no serious movement for a Palestinian homeland. The Israelis gained the West Bank and Old Jerusalem in that war, but they took those areas from Jordan's King Hussein, not Yasser Arafat.

"The truth," Farah writes,

> is that Palestine is no more real than Never-Never Land. The first time the name was used was in 70 A.D. when the Romans committed genocide against the Jews, smashed the Temple and declared the land of Israel would be no more. From then on, the Romans promised, it would be known as Palestine. The name was derived from the Philistines, a Goliathian people conquered by the Jews centuries earlier. It was a way for the Romans to add insult to injury.[16]

Farah goes on to note that there is no language known as Palestinian, there is no distinct Palestinian culture, and there has never been a land known as Palestine governed by Palestinians. Palestinians are Arabs, he says, "indistinguishable from Jordanians, Syrians, Lebanese, Iraqis, etc. Keep in mind that the Arabs control

99.9 percent of the Middle East lands. Israel represents one-tenth of 1 percent of the landmass.

"But that's too much for the Arabs. They want it all. And that is ultimately what the fighting in Israel is about today. Greed. Pride. Envy. Covetousness. No matter how many land concessions the Israelis make, it will never be enough."[17]

What about Islam's holy sites? Farah reminds us that the Al-Aqsa Mosque and the Dome of the Rock on the Temple Mount represent Islam's third most holy site, but in fact, the Quran says nothing about Jerusalem. Mecca is the holy city of the Quran. Medina is mentioned countless times. But Jerusalem is never mentioned, and there is no historical evidence to suggest Muhammad ever visited the Jews' holy city.

So why are the Palestinians so intent upon keeping their mosque on the Temple Mount? Muslims cite a vague passage in the Quran, the seventeenth sura, titled "The Night Journey." The story relates that in a dream or vision Muhammad was carried by night "from the sacred temple to the Temple that is most remote, whose precinct we have blessed, that we might show him our signs." Centuries ago, some Muslims decided that the two temples mentioned had to be in Mecca and Jerusalem, though Jerusalem had no Islamic mosque at the time.

"And," Farah adds, "that's as close as Islam's connection with Jerusalem gets—myth, fantasy, wishful thinking. Meanwhile, Jews can trace their roots in Jerusalem back to the days of Abraham."[18]

Muhammad never could have had the Al-Aqsa Mosque in mind when he wrote of the farthest mosque because it did not exist until generations after his death! Furthermore, Muhammad never considered Jerusalem a sacred city. When he was trying to encourage the Jews to accept him as a prophet, he kept the Jewish Sabbath and other laws, including prayer facing Jerusalem. But when it became obvious that the Jews would not convert, the angry prophet changed the direction of prayer by turning his back to Jerusalem and faced Mecca instead. He also dropped the Jewish Sabbath and chose to worship on Friday instead.[19] He flatly forbade his followers to face Jerusalem in prayer and issued a prohibition against it on February 12, 624.[20]

But the Palestinians would like to erase those facts from history. In an official pamphlet for tourists who visit the Al-Aqsa Mosque, Muslim officials write, "The beauty and tranquility of Al-Aqsa Mosque in Jerusalem attracts thousands of visitors every year. Some believe it was the site of the Temple of Solomon, peace be upon him . . . or the site of the Second Temple . . . although no documented historical or archaeological evidence exists to support this."[21]

Asked if he recognized the ancient Jewish historical link to the Temple Mount, Arafat's main negotiator, Nabil Shaath, replied, "I can recognize you have your beliefs, but I do not have to share them. And I don't."[22]

Indeed, Palestinians repeatedly assert that the Jews have no historic connection to the Temple Mount.

The "Day of Rage": October 6, 2000

The Islamic Hamas group designated October 6, 2000, as one of many "days of rage" against Israel, and despite peace talks, fighting raged on several fronts. Palestinians pledged to liberate Jerusalem from the Jewish "infidels," and Prime Minister Ehud Barak spoke for the first time in terms of war.

"With the same determination we had in leaving no stone unturned to find a way toward peace," he told an Israeli television reporter, "with the same determination . . . we will fight and defend our soldiers and our citizens, even if it is against the whole world."[23]

The day began with relative calm. Israeli police, in an effort to stem violence, pulled their men back from the Temple Mount. It was the first time in memory that police had left the area unguarded, with Muslims praying at the Al-Aqsa Mosque on top of the Temple Mount and Jews praying at the Wailing Wall below.

The morning prayers began without incident, then activists from the Palestine Liberation Organization moved in. Sheik Mohammed Hussein, the Muslim cleric who gave his daily sermon over loudspeakers, told his listeners, "You are the protectors of Al-Aqsa now. The occupiers have left. Don't give them an excuse to come back."[24]

But as soon as prayers ended, so did the restraint. Hundreds of Palestinian youths ran to the edge of the mount and attacked police below with a barrage of stones and bottles. Charging down the ramp from the mosque, the youths managed to push police back. At one point, they threw a tear gas canister into the police headquarters; then when the Israeli staff evacuated, protesters set fire to the building.[25]

On the same day, in Nablus, gunmen attacked the Israeli-controlled Joseph's Tomb outpost. In the Gaza Strip, Palestinian gunmen kept up attacks on the Netzarim settlement and besieged other Jewish neighborhoods.

While the violence swept through Israel, Yasser Arafat appeared in Tunis, the capital of Tunisia, to rally support for the Palestinians.

The Palestinian Leader, Yasser Arafat

Yasser Arafat was born in 1929 to a successful merchant father and religious mother. His birth name was Mohammed, but he was soon nicknamed Yasser, meaning "easy." Arafat's mother died when he was only four, and his father sent him to live with an uncle in Jerusalem.

As a teenager in the 1940s, Arafat became involved in the Palestinian cause. Before the British withdrew in '48, he was a leader in the Palestinian effort to smuggle arms into the territory.

After the war of '48, Arafat studied civil engineering at the University of Cairo, but his life's work would have nothing to do with engineering. He headed the League of Palestinian Students and soon became committed to the idea of forming a group that would free Palestine from Israeli occupation. In 1956 he founded Al Fatah, an underground terrorist organization. In 1967, when the Arabs lost the Gaza Strip, the Golan Heights, and the West Bank, the Arab nations turned to Arafat, perhaps because desperate times called for desperate measures. In 1968 he became the leader of the Palestine Liberation Organization (PLO), a position he has held since that time.

Of Arafat, Ariel Sharon said, "I don't know anyone who has as much civilian Jewish blood on his hands as Arafat since the Nazis' time."[26]

The PLO holds several records of dubious distinction:

- Greatest variety of targets: between 1968 and 1980, the PLO committed more than two hundred major terrorist acts in or against countries other than Israel. Their targets included forty civilian passenger planes, five passenger ships, thirty embassies, and economic targets such as fuel depots and factories.[27]

- The worst midair explosion: February 21, 1970. The Popular Front for the Liberation of Palestine (PFLP) blew up a Swiss airliner, killing thirty-eight passengers and nine crew members.[28]

- The most sustained terrorist campaign: between September 1967 and December 1980, the PLO carried out at least three hundred attacks in twenty-six countries. Total casualties: 813 killed, 1,013 injured.[29]

- The largest number of hostages held at one time: three hundred passengers were held hostage on four hijacked jets. The PLO demanded the release of terrorists held by Britain, Switzerland, and Germany. The plan worked.[30]

- The largest number of people killed and wounded by a single booby-trap bomb: July 4, 1975. Fifteen Israelis were killed and eighty-seven wounded by a PLO bomb planted in Zion Square, Jerusalem.[31]

- The wealthiest terrorist organization: although it is impossible to determine how wealthy the PLO is, in the early 1980s it was known that the PLO had an annual income of at least eight hundred million pounds sterling.[32]

I will never forget the hijacking of the *Achille Lauro*, the Italian cruise ship boarded by Palestinians on October 7, 1985. Members of the Palestine Liberation Front, a small guerrilla faction of the PLO, demanded the release of Palestinian prisoners in Israel. During the two-day standoff, the hijackers murdered and dumped overboard an invalid Jewish-American passenger, sixty-nine-year-old Leon Klinghoffer. Horrified Americans watched the story unfold on television.

For more than twenty years the PLO launched bloody attacks on Israel, fortifying Arafat's reputation as a ruthless killer. But by 1988 he had warmed to the international scene, and he began to ply the United Nations with diplomacy. The PLO would recognize Israel as a sovereign state, he said. The United Nations heaped praise upon his head, and, warmed by his reception, in 1993 he agreed to meet with his avowed enemies. Secret peace talks in Norway led to the Oslo Peace Accords with Israeli Prime Minister Yitzhak Rabin. This agreement granted limited Palestinian self-rule and earned Arafat, Rabin, and Israeli Foreign Minister Shimon Peres the 1994 Nobel Peace Prize.[33] Further talks advanced peace in greater degrees, with the Israelis pulling out of several areas and leaving them to Palestinian control.

We've seen several pretensions of peace in the last few years—Arafat shaking Yitzhak Rabin's hand in the White House Rose Garden, and Arafat signing the Oslo Peace Accords of 1993 and the Wye River Memorandum of October 1998. In the Wye River document, Arafat and the Arab Palestinian Authority promised to combat terrorism, confiscate illegal firearms, limit the number of Palestinian police, prevent hostile propaganda, and amend the PLO Charter in

Israel Today

Palestinian Control

Joint Control

Israeli Control

response to Israel's withdrawing from the West Bank city of Hebron.[34]

Israel has withdrawn from Hebron, but the Palestinian Authority has not yet remedied any of the cited violations. Most glaring is the halfhearted effort to amend and publicly repudiate the Palestinian National Charter, a thirty-year-old document that declares "the liberation of Palestine will destroy the Zionist and imperialist presence."[35]

Indeed, Arafat's own words demonstrate that he has no intention of amending the Palestinian Charter. To this date, the PLO has not rescinded any provisions of its charter that call for the destruction of Israel.

Newt Gingrich, touring Israel in 1998, told CNN, "No Palestinian official should talk about or threaten bloodshed, but yet it is a routine pattern in this region for the Palestinian Authority to, in effect, incite violence."[36]

But while Gingrich spoke, the Palestinian Authority's television station carried an interview with Ahmed Tibi, a personal adviser to Yasser Arafat. "We are here to state that we are the owners of this land," he said. "We are the rightful owners. This is our history, and we will never bend."[37]

On the same broadcast, scenes from a rally in Ramallah were shown where a crowd chanted, "Palestine is Arab; Netanyahu Binyamin, Nazi, son of Satan; the entire land is Palestine." Other shots showed a dais occupied by Arafat, who joined in another chant: "All of Jerusalem is Arab; the entire land is Arab."[38]

But the Palestinians do not tell the entire truth. Consider these facts:

- Immediately after Israel's reunification of Jerusalem in 1967, the city's Arab residents were offered full Israeli citizenship. Most declined to accept it.

- Those who did not accept citizenship retained the right to participate in municipal elections and enjoy all economic, cultural, and social benefits afforded to Israeli citizens, including Israel's health funds, social security services, and membership in Israel's Labor Federation.

- The civil right of Palestinian Arabs to maintain their own non-political humanitarian, educational, and social institutions was reiterated by Israel during the peace negotiations.[39]

- After the unification of Jerusalem, the neglected Jordanian sector was provided with basic water and sanitation utilities, so the standard of living in the Arab area rose dramatically.

- In short, Israel has not failed to offer any Palestinian citizen equal rights with Israeli citizens. But Yasser Arafat still is not satisfied.

What Does Arafat Want?

The following news excerpts give us an indication of Arafat's unrelenting goals:

The goal of our struggle is the end of Israel, and there can be no compromise. (Yasser Arafat, *Washington Post*, March 1970)[40]

Peace for us means the destruction of Israel. (Arafat, *El Mundo* [Caracas, Venezuela], February 1980)[41]

The jihad will continue . . . You have to understand our main battle is Jerusalem . . . It is not their capital. It is our capital. (Arafat, speech in Johannesburg, South Africa, May 1994)[42]

We are going to continue the Palestinian revolution until the last martyr to create a Palestinian state. (Arafat, speech in Gaza, January 1995)[43]

By Allah I swear . . . that the Palestinian people are prepared to sacrifice the last boy and the last girl so that the Palestinian flag will be flown over the walls, the churches, and the mosques of Jerusalem. (Arafat, *Jerusalem Post*, September 1995)[44]

What we have witnessed in the Palestinian territories these past few days obliges our negotiators to raise the level of demands in the negotiations. (Hani Al-Hassan, PLO Central Committee, 12 October 2000)[45]

Raise the level of their demands? We've already seen that Arafat and the PLO are the ones who are not willing to compromise.

Yasser Arafat, because he is Islamic, wants Israel's complete defeat. Because he is Palestinian, he wants full control over Jerusalem and the land of Israel.

In her book *My Life*, the late Israeli Prime Minister Golda Meir wrote, "I have never doubted for an instant that the true aim of the Arab states has always been, and still is, the total destruction of the State of Israel or that even if we had gone back far beyond the 1967 lines to some miniature enclave, they would not still have tried to eradicate it and us."[46]

Know this: in November 1947, the United Nations General Assembly passed Resolution 181, proposing that the city of Jerusalem be internationalized. The Arab nations rejected the resolution and promptly launched a war against Israel. Today Resolution 181 is null and void, but Yasser Arafat would like to resurrect it. When you hear about this, know that his proposal has nothing to do with making peace. It has everything to do with waging war against Israel's very existence.

What other tactics is Arafat using? Charles Krauthammer, writing in the *Washington Post*, laid out the Palestinian strategy:

- Use violence to bring international pressure on Israel.

- Keep Israel mobilized, draining its resources and exhausting its will.

- Bleed Israel as in Lebanon, but this time in the very suburbs of Jerusalem and Tel Aviv.

- Thus force Israel back to the negotiating table from a position of weakness.[47]

"Arafat doesn't oppose negotiations," writes Krauthammer. "He just opposes negotiations where he lacks the upper hand. The aim of the violence is to gain the upper hand, force Israel to sue for peace and then dictate the terms of a final settlement."[48]

Israel, you see, cares when its soldiers die. Islamic theology holds that martyrs in battle go straight to paradise. According to Islamic belief, upon death, the suicide bombers and other martyrs are placed on an enviable path to heaven. "Verily," the late King Ibn Sa'ud told a British guest, "the word of God teaches us, and we implicitly believe it, that for a Muslim to kill a Jew, or for him to be killed by a Jew, ensures him immediate entry into Heaven and into the august presence of God Almighty."[49]

Today on the Temple Mount when the Friday sermons are given, you will find Muslim clerics making frequent mention of the following verse of the Quran:

And slay them wherever ye find them, and drive them out of the places whence they drove you out, for persecution is worse than slaughter. And fight not with them at the Inviolable Place of Worship until they first attack you there, but if they attack you there then slay them. Such is the reward of disbelievers. (Quran 2:191)

What sort of persecution is this verse referring to? The Israelis have welcomed Arabs who wish to live in their midst and accept citizenship. No one has denied their civil rights.

But listen to how a Muslim cleric defines *persecution*:

The truth is simple: Israel is land confiscated from the Arabs, and they are trying to get it back . . . Jews and Israel are the reason for this endless cycle of violence. If the Jews have reasons in the Bible to get the land by hook or by crook, then the Muslims have the right to defend themselves and get back the land from where they have been driven out by any means.[50]

With this view, writes Louis Beres, Ph.D., the Muslim suicide bomber "is engaged in self-defense. The burning, disemboweling and dismembering of Jews is altogether agreeable and purposeful here because 'surely persecution is far worse than slaughter.' With this view is revealed the authoritative Arab perspective on the 'peace process.'"[51]

What do the Palestinians want? Mark it down: they want nothing less than the destruction and removal of Israel. And they will stop at nothing, even lying and dissembling, to get it.

The Oslo Accords of 1993 bound the PLO to relinquish the option of war against Israel. The May 1994 Gaza-Jericho Agreement stated that the "Palestinian Authority . . . shall . . . abstain from incitement, including hostile propaganda" against Israel.[52]

Yet, only a few months after the Oslo Accords were signed, Israel opened the archaeological tunnel near the Western Wall, and Arafat immediately claimed that a crime had been committed against Islamic holy places. Ordering Palestinian police not to stop crowds from "spontaneously" charging Israeli troops, Arafat declared that Jerusalem would be won with blood and fire. He incited the crowd with these incendiary words: "They will fight for Allah, and they will kill and be killed, and this is a solemn oath . . . Our blood is cheap compared with the cause which has brought us together and which at moments separated us, but shortly we will meet again in heaven . . . Palestine is our land and Jerusalem is our capital."[53]

In 1996, the Voice of Palestine radio station ran constant broadcasts calling for Palestinians to go into the street and battle against the Zionist enemy. The religious leader of the Palestinian police forces, Mufti Abdel-Salam Abu Shukeidem, urged his soldiers: "Our blessings to you, you who fight at the gates of the enemy and knock on heaven's door with his skull in your hands."[54]

But just as Ariel Sharon's visit did not actually provoke the unrest of autumn 2000, the tunnel opening did not actually provoke the unrest of autumn 1996. Six weeks before the tunnel opened, Arafat was quoted in the *New York Times* calling Israel a "demon" and urging Palestinians to use "all means" at their disposal to fight the Jewish nation.[55]

So what does Arafat want? The three things the Palestinian leader wants are part of the public record. If he succeeds in forcing

Israel to its knees by negotiation or forced settlement through an intermediary such as the United Nations, he'll ask for Jerusalem, a return of the land to the borders drawn by the 1947 UN commission for the partition of Palestine, and permission for descendants of Palestinian refugees to return to their original homes.

Do you know what this so-called refugee return would do to the nation of Israel? With a population of fewer than five million mostly Jewish citizens, adding another three to five million Arabs could mean the end of Israel as a Jewish state.

But I do not believe Israel will capitulate. I do not believe the nation will abandon the land granted to it by ancient and holy deed. I believe Israel will be attacked, it will suffer, but that nation will be saved by the strong and mighty hand of God in His perfect time.

Public PLO Pronouncements

PLO school textbooks continually deride the Jewish people. The PLO Teachers' Guides read, "The student should learn [that] racist superiority is the heart of Zionism, Fascism, and Nazism." Among the "important values" that should be taught is this: "Wrath to the alien thief [Israel] who obliterated the Homeland and dispersed its people."[56]

Listen to the highly quotable Arafat and other Palestinian leaders:

In May 1993, just after the signing of the first Oslo Accord, Faisal Husseini told his Arab audience: "Everything you see and hear today is for tactical and strategic reasons. We have not given up the rifle. We still have armed gangs in the areas, and if we do not get our state, we will take them out of the closet and fight again."[57]

On November 15, 1998, only a few weeks after the Wye River Accord, Arafat addressed a rally in Ramallah:

Our rifles are ready and we are ready to raise them again if anyone tries to prevent us from praying in holy Jerusalem . . . There are agreements and they better be carried out, because the "generals of the stones" [intifada rioters] are ready . . . For a hundred years we have faced this enormous global power [Zionism], and our people are still steadfast in Jerusalem.[58]

In March 1996, after an antiterrorism summit intended to signal a repudiation of violence from Palestinians, Nabil Shaath, Arafat's planning minister, said,

> But if and when Israel will say, "That's it, we won't talk about Jerusalem, we won't return refugees, we won't dismantle settlements, and we won't retreat from borders," then all the acts of violence will return. Except that this time we'll have 30,000 armed Palestinian soldiers who will operate in areas in which we have unprecedented elements of freedom.[59]

In a radio address in November 1995, Arafat said, "The struggle will continue until all of Palestine is liberated." In 1996 he told a group of Arab ambassadors that the PLO had plans "to eliminate the state of Israel [by making] life unbearable for the Jews."
He continued,

> We Palestinians will take over everything, including Jerusalem . . . We of the PLO will now concentrate all our efforts on splitting Israel psychologically into two camps. Within five years we will have six to seven million Arabs living on the West Bank and in Jerusalem . . . we [will] import all kinds of Arabs . . . You understand that we plan to eliminate the state of Israel and establish a purely Palestinian state . . . I have no use for Jews; they are and remain Jews. We now need all the help we can get from you in our battle for a united Palestine under total Arab-Muslim control.[60]

Can you sense the hatred behind the words? Arafat and others like him hate Israel because its people "are and remain Jews." The enmity goes far beyond the Israeli-Palestinian conflict over land. It goes back to Abraham, when two brothers vied for their father's attention. At the root of this rivalry is the simple human sin of envy: the Jews, descended from Isaac, are the chosen people of God. The Arabs, though blessed by God, are not the people of promise. As a gentile American, I am not part of the chosen people, either, but I respect God's sovereignty and am content to bless the Jews.

But the Arab jealousy of the Jews continues. An article published in November 2000 quotes the final words of a Muslim cleric's sermon in Jerusalem: "Say: O ye who are Jews! If ye claim that ye are favored of Allah apart from (all) mankind, then long for DEATH if ye are truthful!"[61]

In September 1996 Arafat announced,

> We will be willing to die as martyrs until our flag flies over Jerusalem. No one should believe they can frighten us with weapons. We have much stronger weapons, the weapon of belief, the weapon of sacrifice, the weapon of jihad . . . We shall continue the jihad, the long jihad, a complex jihad, a jihad of attrition, of holy death. Warfare is our only way to victory. The path of glory, the path of jihad.

A month later, he proclaimed, "We know only one word: jihad, jihad, jihad . . . We have a long struggle ahead of us. I call upon each and every one of you to bring into this world at least twelve children and to give me ten of them in order to continue the struggle."[62]

On July 1, 1998, an Arafat speech was broadcast on official Palestinian television: "The battle for Jerusalem is a battle of life or death, life or death, life or death."

On May 14, 1998, Arafat led Palestinian marchers in a chant: "With our soul and blood we will redeem you, O Palestine!"

This message on April 16, 1998, marked the tenth anniversary of the slaying of PLO leader Abu Jihad: "My colleagues in struggle and in arms, my colleagues in struggle and in jihad . . . Intensify the revolution and the blessed intifada. Reinforce the strong stance and strengthen the faith. We must burn the ground under the feet of the invaders."[63]

Palestinian television continually blasts Israel, referring to cities in disputed areas as "colonies" and "settlements," or as "cities of occupied Palestine." The State of Israel is called by names that indicate a complete unwillingness to recognize it, such as "the Zionist entity," "the Zionist enemy," "the occupation," and "the Tel Aviv government."[64]

You may read in the press, as I have, that Arafat the peacemaker is not in control of the terrorists in Jerusalem. Don't you believe it! When he issued an unambiguous cease-fire in September 1996, his Palestinian Authority soldiers immediately stopped shooting, then acted as a restraining force to quell any further unrest. According to Israeli military intelligence, Arafat is in full control of the current unrest and has given the go-ahead for terrorist acts in order to achieve the goal of the war he is fighting against Israel.

Israeli military intelligence officers see that another of Arafat's goals is to "balance the account of blood with Israel." He was taken by surprise at the responses the Israel Defense Forces prepared for the Palestinian violence in the fall of 2000, and intends to inflict as many casualties as possible on Israel to reduce the "victims gap." In particular, notes one report, "he wants to increase the number of Israeli children who are victimized in order to demonstrate to his people that he is avenging the deaths of the Palestinian children and teenagers in the Intifada."[65]

Violence is a crucial part of Arafat's plan. He intends to kill, then he needs the Israelis to launch severe reprisals, which will have serious repercussions in the international arena. Arafat *wants* the United Nations to become involved; he *wants* to draw the attention of other Arab-Muslim nations. He has become an expert deceiver, and at this moment much of the world's media is painting him in sympathetic colors.

Will the Negotiators Ever Achieve Peace?

Former Israeli Prime Minister Yitzhak Shamir's famous world-weary cry resonates today: "The sea is the same sea; the Arabs are the same Arabs."[66]

Believe it, my friend: as long as humans are negotiating for the peace of Jerusalem, real peace will not come. The Temple Mount stands in the way. The "be converted or be destroyed" creed of Islam will not allow it.

Another former Israeli prime minister, Bibi Netanyahu, explains why:

> It is important to understand that we're on the seamline between two very different cultures . . . We're part of a western, liberal democratic ethos, which respects political freedom and individual rights. On the other side is another culture and there cannot be a western-style peace because our partners are not part of the western culture. It is impossible to have a warm peace . . . but a cold peace is . . . better than a hot war.[67]

At Cornerstone Church, during our annual "Night to Honor Israel," Netanyahu explained that there are two kinds of peace: the peace of democracies and the peace of dictatorships. The former is an automatic, self-sustaining peace. People who rule themselves don't want to send their children to war, so there's an internal brake against aggression, evidenced by the electorate.

But dictatorships have no electorate. Dictators practice aggression against their own people and their neighbors. Since there is no internal brake on aggression, there has to be an external brake. And that can be provided only by the democracies of the world, who unite in a league of nations, such as NATO, and have the *strength* to enforce peace.[68]

Israel is the only democracy in the Middle East. It must make peace through careful negotiations and from a position of strength.

Israel must have a partner for peace, and as yet the Arabs are not willing to meet the Israelis on level ground. The people of Israel have established countless programs intended to bring Arabs and Israelis together to help change the image they have of each other. The following list is only a sampling of the many programs established by the Jewish people:

- A Bridge for Peace
- A Bridge to the Present Through the Study of the Past
- A School Community of Difference
- Afternoon workshops for Jewish and Arab children
- Arab-Jewish Cooperation for Cleaning up the Galilee Landscape
- Arab-Jewish Dance Troupe
- Arabic-Hebrew-English Language Learning Center Programs
- Beyond Words: Enhancing Dialogue in Israel Through Dance and Movement Therapy
- Bilingual Education in Israel
- Building a Common Language
- Calansuwa-Ramat Hasharon
- Camping and Wilderness Survival Combined with Social Activities for Physically and Emotionally Challenged Children and Youth of the Arab Sector
- Coexistence and Tolerance: An Educational Approach
- Continuing Employment of an Arabic Speech Therapist
- Dialogue: The Name of the Game
- Education Against Racism
- Encounter for Peace

- Teachers in Arad and Kseife
- ERAN Emergency Hotline in Arabic
- Festival for Local Creativity
- General Support and Annual Progress Report
- Good Neighbors Summer Programs
- Jewish-Arab Youth Circus
- Just Do "Shalom"
- Learning to Mainstream
- Living with Conflict
- Making Music in the Galilee
- Meet the Neighbors
- Music as a Language to Promote Coexistence
- Muslim Scout Movement
- Outreach to Arab Women
- School Pairing Project
- Teenagers Speak Peace
- Tennis 2000
- The Folklore of the Other
- The Image of Abraham
- Through Art We Communicate
- Through the Camera
- Tolerance Training for Israel's Border Police
- Understanding Ourselves, Understanding Each Other

The list goes on and on; it's too long to include in its entirety. But now that I've listed a few of the organizations founded by

Israelis to help their Arab neighbors, let me list the organizations founded by Arabs to help them understand their Jewish cousins:

• . . .

That's right—there are none, at least none at the time of this writing. There has been no reciprocity from the Arab side. Israel does not even exist on Arab maps studied by schoolchildren, members of the Arab media are still markedly anti-Semitic, and Arab children still attend mosques where "holy men" encourage them to rise up and kill the Jews. No Jewish child has ever gone to synagogue and heard that he is supposed to kill Arabs.

In the last days of the Clinton administration, President Clinton let it be known that he was not happy with the progress of the peace talks. In a last-ditch effort to leave a meaningful foreign policy legacy for his name, he tried to get the Palestinians and Israelis to settle their differences.

But why are we pressing the Israelis to enter into a treaty with people who have sworn to kill them? Washington can afford to be wrong about Arafat, but Israel cannot.

Former Prime Minister Netanyahu has realized what Ronald Reagan understood in the early 1980s—when dealing with a strong enemy, the best defense is a strong offense. Likewise, the Israelis must remain strong and remain committed to the defense of their people and their territory if they are to maintain control of their God-given land. Unfortunately, the Arabs will continue to needle them, provoking bullets with bottles and stones. Arab mothers send their sons to throw rocks at the Israelis, believing that paradise waits for those who die in what they consider a holy war.

A reporter for the *New York Times* went into Gaza in late October 2000, during the time of upheaval. He spoke with Hyam Temraz, a Muslim woman who stood holding her two-year-old son. "Tell the man what you want to be," the mother prodded through the slit in her black veil.

The little boy looked up at the reporter. "A martyr," he said.[69]

Everywhere in Gaza the walls are plastered with posters of men who have died in recent clashes with the Israelis. Many are pictured holding a gun, with the onion-shaped golden Dome of the Rock in the background. Remarkably, the pictures were taken long before the fighting broke out—they are a traditional pose, like our standard high school senior picture.

Writer Michael Finkel recently spent several days with Arab teenagers who skip school to throw rocks at Israeli soldiers at Karni crossing in Gaza. While he was there, a fifteen-year-old boy named Ahmed was killed.

At Ahmed's funeral, his mother remarked:

> What a grand celebration. Thanks be to God. Did you see how his face shone? Oh, he is still alive! I will give all my children, if that's what it takes to get our homeland back. All of them can become martyrs. It will be a dignity to me. [70]

Ahmed's family will soon be moving into a larger house. When a Palestinian is martyred in the intifada, no matter what his age, the Palestinian National Authority issues a payment of $2,000 to the family, followed by regular monthly payments of $150 that continue until the last child has left the home. The Red Crescent, an Islamic relief organization, provides an additional $2,500. Finally, the government of Iraq, through the largesse of Saddam Hussein, donates $10,000 to every martyr's family.[71]

Nazar Rayyan is a theology professor at Islamic University. His grandfather and great-uncle were killed in the 1948 war. His father, who settled in the Jabalya refugee camp in Gaza, grew up with bitterness, then passed it on to his son and grandchildren. His brother-in-law was a suicide bomber who blew up an Israeli bus in

1998. Today his sons, ages twelve, fifteen, and sixteen, daily join the boys who throw rocks at Israeli soldiers. All of them, he says, yearn to be martyrs for Palestine. He adds, "I pray only that God will choose them."[72]

How can Israel stand against such a philosophy? How could any nation? Years ago, former Israeli Prime Minister Golda Meir said, "We can forgive them for killing our children. But we can never forgive them for making us kill theirs."[73]

Four

Israel: A House Divided

We have to work out an arrangement to enable Palestinians to live their lives on these hills, but it is not going to be a solution where we kick them out or they kick us out. Between the Jordan and the sea is a very small stretch of land, two peoples are going to have to live side by side, no one is going to drive the other out.

—*Binyamin Netanyahu, former Israeli prime minister*[1]

We Palestinians will take over everything, including Jerusalem . . . We of the PLO will now concentrate all our efforts on splitting Israel psychologically into two camps. Within five years we will have six to seven million Arabs living on the West Bank and in Jerusalem.

—*Yasser Arafat, PLO chairman* [2]

In each of the four Gospels, Jesus told His followers: "Every kingdom divided against itself is brought to desolation, and a house divided against a house falls" (Luke 11:17). This is common wisdom, recognized by Abraham Lincoln during the Civil War, and by Yasser Arafat in the intifada of 2000. He would like to divide Israel, physically and governmentally. The task before him would be no challenge at all if God were not the ultimate authority guiding events in the Middle East.

A little background is in order. The Israeli form of government is more like the British model than the American. The State of Israel does have a president, though his position is largely ceremonial. Power is more directly wielded through the prime minister and the 120-member Israeli parliament, known as the Knesset.

Both the United States and Israel are democratic governments, governed by a body that represents the people. In that body you find the most striking difference between our countries. America's system tends to revolve around two political parties, the Republicans and the Democrats. Each of our traditional parties defines a platform that varies only slightly over the years, and most of our politicians tend to gravitate to one party or the other, subtly streamlining their messages to fit the platform of their choice.

The United States, melting pot that it is, is still far more stable and homogeneous than Israel, a tiny nation that welcomes citizens from around the world. In fact, "[Israel] is less a melting pot than a boiling pot," says Carol Clark, a writer for CNN. "Arabs and ultra-Orthodox Jews, settlers and secularists and waves of immigrants from Europe, North Africa, and the Middle East are all vying to project their vision of Israel."[3]

As a result of Israel's diverse population, there are diverse political parties, many of which seem to spring up overnight and vanish almost as quickly. In the 1999 Israeli elections, for instance, *thirty-three* political parties vied for the 120 seats in the Knesset.

One party in that election named itself after its founder, cosmetics queen and model Pnina Rosenblum. She failed to win a seat. Also losing out was the Green Leaf Party, which ran on a platform of legalizing marijuana and other so-called soft drugs. In its campaign ads, the party featured an Israeli flag with a green marijuana leaf in place of the Star of David.

By the time the 1999 votes were counted, sixteen political parties and four individual members had won seats in the Knesset.

Among the political groups are the One Israel Party, led by Ehud Barak; the Likud, who are known as hard-liners for not wanting to trade land for peace; the Yisra'el Ba'Aliya, composed of dissident Russian Jews; the Arab Democratic Party; the Shas Party, composed of ultra-Orthodox religious Jews; and Yisra'el Beiteinu, another party composed mostly of Russian immigrants.

Because no leader can effectively lead so many splinter groups, each with its own agenda, the prime minister must form a coalition among several groups—a fairly frustrating system of checks and balances. The government requires the Knesset's confidence—the support of at least sixty-one of its members. All Israeli governments, therefore, are coalitions with cooperating political parties. If a prime minister leads in a direction others cannot support, the Knesset can bring down the government by voting for a motion of no-confidence in the prime minister.

The Multifaceted Israeli Government

"Although weary from 52 years of nationhood without peace, realistic Israelis understand the causation behind this correlation: today Israel has the most accommodating diplomacy in its history, and is in the most perilous position in its history," commented George Will.[4]

Will is absolutely right when he says Israel is in the weakest position of its lifetime as a state, and I'm afraid things may get worse. In 1948, when every shred of human logic tells us that Israel should have been swept into the sea, the hand of God preserved and sheltered it as a nation. In 1967, when Egypt mobilized, Israel defended itself, then stood in open-mouthed wonder as God restored Jerusalem and the Temple Mount. And in 1973, when attacked by Arabs, Israel stood tall, drew upon its strength of resolve, and defeated its enemies.

For years Israel has survived through strength and the conviction that some things are nonnegotiable. But now, in the vain pursuit of peace, the nonnegotiable has suddenly become open to discussion.

Writes Will,

> Barak's attempt to satiate Arafat with a feast of Israeli retreats has even produced the idea of giving the U.N., that nest of anti-Israeli regimes, control of the Temple Mount. The consequence of all this may be the fulfillment of the undisguised aim of Israel's "partner in peace," the Palestine Authority, whose maps, textbooks, TV broadcasts and public places treat Israel as non-existent.[5]

George Will believes Barak risks forfeiting his nation's existence, but I believe God is stronger than any blunder any politician might make. The Almighty has purposes for Israel and for Jerusalem, and He will keep His promises.

When I opened my newspaper at breakfast in December 2000, on the front page I saw the news that Ehud Barak had just told the Knesset that he would be willing to set a date for new elections—a remarkable statement, considering that regularly scheduled elections were still two years away. In short, Yasser Arafat has brought Barak to this place.

Since September 2000, more than three hundred people have died in Intifada 2000, and Israeli hard-liners said Barak has been too soft on the Palestinians. Others strongly disapproved of Barak's latest peace plan offer to "swap neighborhoods" in Jerusalem and let the Arabs and Jews share the capital city. Beginning in July, key allies abandoned Barak.

Barak may have suggested that Jerusalem be divided into two halves, but Israelis themselves are divided into two camps—those who would trade land for peace, and those who believe that the land belongs to Israel by divine decree and should never be surrendered. Former Israeli Prime Minister Shimon Peres is of the former group, and on an American news program he recently said, "Nobody can kill the peace process because we need it like air." Besides, Peres went on, Arafat no longer runs "a terroristic organization. He is responsible for an administration which is 120,000 people strong . . . It is one thing to be a head of a revolution, and it is another thing to be a head of a state in being."[6]

Ha! What if the "state in being" is desperate to destroy Israel? I will not believe Arafat has cut his ties to terrorism until I hear he's lying in state somewhere in Israel.

Other Divisions

The majority of Jerusalem's 620,000 residents are either Arab (30 percent) or ultra-Orthodox Jews (25 percent). The reins of power, however, are firmly held by the secular and modern Orthodox Jews, who make up about 45 percent of the city's population.[7]

Lest we forget, Jerusalem is torn not only by Arab-Jewish strife, but also by disagreements between religious and secular Jews. The Haredi, or ultra-Orthodox, Jews accounted for nearly 33 percent of the Jewish population of Jerusalem in 1996, and that figure is expected to reach 40 percent by 2010 (Orthodox women have three times as many children as their secular counterparts).[8]

Secular and religious issues affect every aspect of life in Israel. Elevators do not operate on Saturday. Theaters do not open on the Sabbath. McDonald's won't serve a bacon McMuffin, but you can get a cheeseburger, though kosher dietary laws prohibit the mixing of meat and milk. Since bread is not permissible during Passover, McDonald's will serve your cheeseburger in a potato flour bun during the holiday.[9]

"Many secular Israelis regard their ultrareligious compatriots, who encompass a range of political views, as strange or dangerous zealots, not much different from the Muslim fundamentalists lined up against them," note *Newsweek* reporters.[10]

By and large, Israelis identify themselves as secular, Orthodox, or ultra-Orthodox. The Ashkenzai, secular Jews from Europe, were the architects of the state in the early 1900s; the more traditional Oriental Jews from the Eastern Hemisphere came later. A gulf exists between the two branches, and many Ashkenzai Jews hold a barely disguised contempt for the Orthodox Jews.

But many factions have managed to come together for Israel's sake. Although the Likud Party is nonreligious, in the past the members have cooperated with religious leaders in order to avoid trading land for peace. The religious leaders wanted to keep the land because God gave it to them. The nonreligious secularists wanted to keep the land for reasons of national security. Together, they were a strong force.

Political Revolt Known as Post-Zionism

Yoram Hazony has written a shocking and provocative book, *The Jewish State: The Struggle for Israel's Soul.* In it he describes the disturbing cultural and political revolt known as *post-Zionism,* whose aim is to dismantle Israel's legal and moral standing as the state of the Jewish people. He offers the first in-depth analysis of the "new historians" seeking to revise the story of Israel's founding, the revolution in the new Israeli public school curriculum, and other shocking aspects of the "new Israel" that have made headlines around the world.

Natan Sharansky, interior minister of the State of Israel, says,

Fifty years after the birth of the State of Israel, the greatest challenge facing the Jewish state is not securing it from external enemies, but rather preventing its internal disintegration. An ascendant "post-Zionism" threatens Israel's very foundations as a Jewish state and its central role in the lives of the entire Jewish people. In tracing the intellectual roots of "post-Zionism" and showing its pervasive influence in Israeli society, Yoram Hazony's book is invaluable for anyone who wants to understand this heart-wrenching inner challenge. [11]

Hazony examines those who envision Israel not as a state, but as a state of mind. Those who support the post-Zionist movement would say that having a state and all its attendant problems is more trouble than it is worth. Why deal with the problems of the State of Israel when its citizens can be Jewish without it?

This dangerous philosophy rises from an intellectual community representing an extreme minority. Zionism is predicated upon the belief that every Jew in the world has the right to return to Israel, but post-Zionism would disagree with that assertion. This philosophy, still in a nascent state, could rip the nation apart in the years to come.

Orthodox and Ultra-Orthodox Jews

A casual observer may find it difficult to discern the difference between Orthodox and ultra-Orthodox Jews. Both strictly observe the law, avoiding anything that would make them impure. The men keep their heads covered and pray at least three times a day. Everyone follows kosher dietary laws and abstains from work on the Sabbath, from sundown on Friday to sundown on Saturday.

You can often determine the degree of orthodoxy by studying the clothing of a Jewish person living in Jerusalem. The ultra-Orthodox men wear large black hats and large black skull caps beneath them, while their wives are literally kept under wraps, with only face and hands showing. Orthodox Jews, on the other hand, wear more Western clothing.

Many of the ultra-Orthodox actually opposed the State of Israel in the early days of the nation. They disagreed with Zionism, preferring to let God rather than the United Nations establish His people. Most ultra-Orthodox groups tend to exhibit contempt for the state of modern Israel and resist serving in the military. They argue that praying for the strength of Israel is as important as fighting for it.[12] As you might expect, this attitude reaps a matching contempt from secular Jewry toward the ultra-Orthodox. Meanwhile, the Orthodox Jews—who have managed to combine religion and nationalism—walk in the middle, often being condemned by groups to the right and the left.

Russian and Oriental Jewry

Religious Jews from Asian and African countries do not fit comfortably into the groups we've already discussed. They tend to form their own groups. One leader, Rabbi Ovadia Yosef, founded the Shas political party, which today controls nearly 10 percent of seats in the Knesset.

And since 1990, hundreds of thousands of Jews from Russia have poured into Israel. We'll discuss this in more detail in a later chapter, but we cannot underestimate the impact these Russian Jews have had on Jerusalem. You'll see Cyrillic shop signs in Jerusalem and hear the Russian language spoken. They, too, have formed a political party, Yisra'el Ba'Aliya, and gained at least seven seats in the Knesset. Many of these Jews are nonobservant, but they are generally highly educated. The newcomers are not always Zionists. Many qualify for Jewish citizenship on the basis of having one Jewish grandparent, but do not meet the Orthodox requirement of having a Jewish mother. So they are not likely to come to Israel for religious reasons. Many have come to seek greater economic opportunities.

The latest wave of immigrants represents more than 20 percent of the Jewish population. "Undoubtedly," writes Norman Atkins in his book about Jerusalem, "they and their children will assimilate Zionist norms of allegiance to the state, service in the army, and fluency in Hebrew. In parallel, influenced by the secularism of these immigrants, Israel is likely to move further away from traditional Judaism."[13]

Ethiopian Jews

The dramatic rescue of Ethiopian Jews from Communist rebels in the early 1990s caught the world's attention. Presently there are approximately 70,000 Ethiopian Jews living in Jerusalem.

The origin of Ethiopian Jews remains a mystery, but there are a couple of good possibilities. Some say they are the remnants of the tribe of Dan, one of the ten "lost tribes." The Ethiopians themselves believe they are descended from Solomon, sons of the queen of Sheba, who visited Solomon to view his glory and left after he had given her what her heart desired (1 Kings 10:13; 2 Chron. 9:12). A son? Many Bible scholars think so.

The Ethiopian royal chronicles record that Prince Menelik I of Ethiopia was the son of Solomon. According to researcher Grant Jeffrey, Prince Menelik grew up in Solomon's palace in Jerusalem. While being educated by the priests of the temple, he became a strong believer in the true God.[14]

In 1935, Leo Roberts published an article in *National Geographic* called "Traveling in the Highlands of Ethiopia." He spoke with many people in the land and heard a remarkably consistent story:

> Solomon was a doctor, a healer, a learned man who had the power to cure, a *hakim*. And the Queen [of Sheba] suffered from a short, distorted right foot. Her journey to Jerus Alem was made to see whether Hakim Solomon could help her, and naturally she carried presents to him. The child that was born to them was Menelik I. Solomon educated the lad in Jerus Alem until he was 19 years old, when the boy returned to Ethiopia with a large group of Jews, taking with him the true Ark of the Covenant.[15]

Whether or not the true ark did reside with the Ethiopians is debatable, but their story rings true. Solomon was known as a learned man, and Scripture tells us that God granted him wisdom (2 Chron. 1:11). As an added benefit, God told Solomon:

> Wisdom and knowledge are granted to you; and I will give you riches and wealth and honor, such as none of the kings have had who were before you, nor shall any after you have the like. (2 Chron. 1:12)

Though the Ethiopian Jewish community was cut off from world Jewry for two millennia, the people sustained traditions remarkably similar to those of mainstream Judaism. They had the five books of Moses and the stories of the prophets, but they had no knowledge of the oral law, which was codified only after the fall of the second temple in A.D. 70.[16]

Driven out by a Marxist regime, all but several hundred Ethiopian Jews have now left Africa and live in Israel.

Christians in Jerusalem

Yes, there are Christians in Jerusalem—residents as well as tourists! Since the city is filled with sites significant to those who follow Jesus Christ, centuries-old churches are sprinkled throughout the city.

In Jerusalem you will find churches of every denomination, including Greek Orthodox, Russian Orthodox, Roman Catholic, Syrian Catholic, Maronite (the Christian Uniat Church of Lebanon), Greek Catholic, Armenian Catholic, Chaldean Catholic, Armenian Orthodox, Syrian Orthodox, Copt, and Ethiopian Orthodox. You will also find represented Anglicans, the Church of Scotland, Seventh-day Adventists, Pentecostals, the Church of Christ, Baptists, the Brethren, the Mennonites, Jehovah's Witnesses, and Lutherans. In short, nearly everybody.

The founding of Israel provoked unease among the Christians in Jerusalem, says writer Norman Atkins, who were uncertain what to expect from the new Jewish state and were deeply suspicious of Jewish intentions (the Vatican still does not recognize Israel). Nevertheless, Israel's Declaration of Independence spelt out the state's attitude to the diverse faiths within its borders, pledging to "guarantee the freedom of religion, conscience, education and culture [and] safeguard the holy places of all religions."[17]

It is worth noting that many of Jerusalem's Arabs are Christians and belong to mainline churches in the city. There are also about two thousand messianic Jews in Jerusalem.[18]

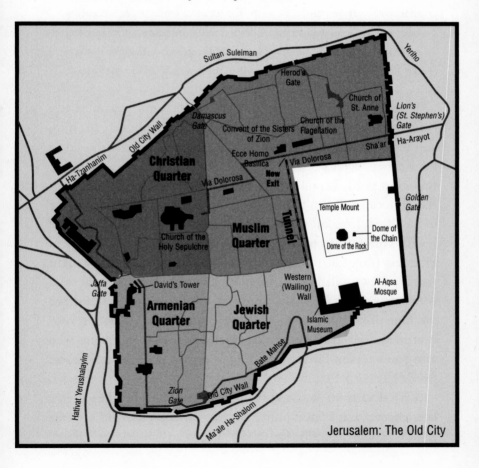

Jerusalem: The Old City

Many Israelis look with suspicion upon the rise of Christian Zionism. As Bible-believing Christians, we see the birth of the State of Israel as fulfilled prophecy. I thoroughly believe it is my duty as a Christian to bless Israel and pray for the nation. I do not believe Israel has been usurped or supplanted in God's plan.

While many Israelis are grateful for Christian support, they tread lightly and fear that Christians want only to convert them from Judaism to Christianity. Gershom Gorenberg explains,

> Virtually all Jews, including the most secular, reject the evangelical view that you can remain a Jew in the ethnic sense while accepting Christianity—indeed, the Israeli Supreme Court based a 1960s ruling on that consensus. To "support Israel" while actively seeking to convert the Jews is, in Jewish eyes, to couple a caress with a stab in the back.[19]

Listen, my friend: if you have a Jewish friend, you must live before him as a representative of Christ. Love him, care for him, and let the light of your faith shine to him. The Jewish people have experienced the hatred of Christianity for more than two thousand years, beginning with the Crusades and evolving into the Holocaust of the twentieth century. They have not seen the unqualified love of God from Christianity. It's time for the Jewish community of the world to experience practical acts of kindness from Christians without a hidden agenda. Paul taught that the Jews will be provoked to jealousy (Rom. 11:11), and when they ask you about your faith, you then may fulfill the teaching of Peter, which says, "But sanctify the Lord God in your hearts, and always be ready to give a defense to everyone who asks you a reason for the hope that is in you, with meekness and fear" (1 Peter 3:15).

We'll discuss the Jews and their concepts about the Messiah in a later chapter, but I felt it important for you to understand how the Jewish people typically feel about Christian missionary efforts.

Michael Arnold, writing from Israel, observes that many Jews have shunned the figure of Jesus because of the anti-Semitic persecution carried out in His name.[20] He has a point, one I thoroughly discussed in my book *Final Dawn Over Jerusalem*. For too long, too many Christians have committed acts of hate against the Jewish people, and it must stop. Anti-Semitism is sin, and as sin, it damns the soul.

Even today, says Ron Kronish, a Reform rabbi in Israel, many Orthodox Jews refuse to say Jesus' name, referring to Him only as "that man." "How many Jews have ever opened the New Testament, except for a few who went to college in the West and had to read parts in a humanities class?" he asks. "Many Israelis still think you can be converted just from touching the page."[21]

Interest in the historical and Jewish Jesus is flourishing—on a decidedly low-key level. David Flusser, a professor of Judaic studies at Hebrew University and an Orthodox Jew, refers to Jesus as "my teacher"[22] and studies the life of Christ in an effort to understand Jewish life in Jesus' day. Though for most Israelis the figure of Jesus remains taboo, others are overcoming the prejudices of their forefathers, who identified Jesus with Christian anti-Semitism.

And thousands of Christians are eager to understand the Jewish people. Chana Safrai, a professor of Jewish thought at Hebrew University, notes that "almost all good Christians today are trying to re-root or channel themselves to Judaism in one way or another. No serious scholar today, unless he's Ku Klux Klan, even questions the Jewish roots of Jesus."[23]

Interestingly enough, one reason Jews are taking another look at Jesus is that Yasser Arafat has claimed that Jesus, an observant Jew, was the world's first Palestinian. Bethlehem lies in Palestinian territory, and Arafat would like Christians to support the Palestinian cause. While modern Jews don't necessarily want to claim Christ, they don't want Arafat to claim him, either.[24]

Israeli Arabs

Not all the Arabs living in Palestine fled in the war of 1948. Many remained where they were, and today their numbers have grown. Half of Israel's Arab population lives in the cities and villages of Galilee. There are sizable Arab communities in Nazareth, Haifa, Ramla, Jaffa, and Jerusalem.[25]

The Arabs who remained in Israel have prospered. Arab illiteracy stood at 95 percent in 1948, but is only 5 percent today. Today six thousand Arabs are studying at Israeli universities.[26]

The Arabs have enjoyed social benefits too. Israeli laws granting equal rights for women have helped liberalize attitudes toward women in Arab society.

Seventy-seven percent of Israeli Arabs are Muslim, 13 percent are Christian, and the remainder are Druze and Bedouin. The only legal discrimination against Arabs in Israeli society is that they are not required to serve in the military. (The Druze community is subject to the draft, but the members requested to be included.)[27]

Although the Arab and Jewish Israeli citizens possess equal rights under the law, not everyone considers the situation "equal." Racial tension, much like that between races in the United States, bubbles beneath the surface of modern life. An Arab party is represented in the Knesset, yet no Arab party has ever participated in a governing coalition, and no Arab member of the Knesset has ever headed a government ministry.[28]

"We are Israeli citizens when they want us to be," says Falastin Isma'il, director of a Haifa-based media center for the Palestinian population of Israel. "The rest of the time we have problems with jobs, land, houses, and education."[29]

Polls now show that two-thirds of Jewish Israelis consider the current Arab protesters traitorous. Israeli Knesset member Michael Kleiner says the protests of autumn 2000 destroyed the illusion that Israel's Arabs were loyal citizens.[30]

Though Arab Israelis have ostensibly lived in peace for many years, dissatisfaction, coupled with racial and religious strife, may prove to be a volatile combination. "If they will not solve this issue [of discrimination and mutual distrust between Jews and Arabs inside Israel]," says Isma'il, "it will explode."[31]

Palestinians

After 1967, when Israel occupied the West Bank, East Jerusalem, and the Gaza Strip, most Arabs enjoyed a honeymoon period with the new government. A free press was established, universities founded, and elections held for local municipalities. "The Arabs," writes Norman Atkins, "for their part, were beguiled by Israeli liberalism and other Western ways."[32]

Israel hoped the Arabs of the West Bank would adapt as easily as the Arabs who had remained in the land in 1948, but the Arabs of Gaza and the West Bank identified strongly with Palestinian nationalism. When given the right to take Israeli citizenship, the 150,000 Arabs of East Jerusalem refused the offer to a man.[33]

In the 1970s and 1980s, PLO activity relied heavily upon terrorism. By 1987 the intifada, or uprising, had begun. The occasional clash with stones and bottles soon became an orchestrated campaign designed to make Israel's Western allies uncomfortable with photos of Palestinian women and children standing helpless before the powerful Israeli army. Comparisons to David and Goliath—with Israel pictured as the cruel, godless giant—began to appear in every media report.

Yasser Arafat has had his share of failures—he backed Saddam Hussein, who was soundly defeated in the Gulf War, and he lost his "superpower" patron when the Soviet Union collapsed.[34]

But Arafat is not finished. And if he should fall tomorrow, someone will rise to step into his place. The conflict between the Jews and the Arabs is not predicated on land, rights, or citizenship. It springs from jealousy born of hatred, and that hatred springs from supernatural sources.

Satan hates everything God loves. And though God loves all people, He has a special place in His heart for the descendants of Abraham and Isaac, the heirs to His promise.

Listen to the words in the book of Zechariah:

> And it shall come to pass
> That just as you were a curse among the nations,
> O house of Judah and house of Israel,
> So I will save you, and you shall be a blessing.
> Do not fear,
> Let your hands be strong. (8:13)

The Flag of Israel and the Name of God

I don't know whether you've ever had a chance to examine a prayer shawl. I have one, and it is one of my most treasured possessions. No, I don't believe you have to own or wear one for your prayers to reach heaven, but the Hebrew prayer shawl is a visible reminder of who and what God is.

Moses wore a prayer shawl to his funeral, where God buried him. Daniel wore one in the lions' den. Jesus was given one on His thirteenth birthday and wore it every day of His life. He will wear it when He comes again with the saints of heaven.

The directions for a prayer shawl came from God Himself:

Speak to the children of Israel: Tell them to make tassels on the corners of their garments throughout their generations, and to put a blue thread in the tassels of the corners. And you shall have the tassel, that you may look upon it and remember all the commandments of the LORD and do them, and that you may not follow the harlotry to which your own heart and your own eyes are inclined. (Num. 15:38–39)

God designed the prayer shawl, called a *tallit*, and He commanded all Jews of every generation to wear it. The border of blue was a reminder that God is in heaven. The first color in the tabernacle was blue, and the first line in the Lord's Prayer is "Our Father, who art in heaven." We are never to forget that God is above us, watching our comings and goings, caring about every aspect of our lives.

The fringes, or *tzitzit* in Hebrew, are a very important part of the prayer shawl—indeed, the wearing of *tzitzit* is considered to be equal to all the other commandments together. "The threads," says Alan Unterman, "bind man to God."[35]

Using the practice of gematria, in which each letter of the Hebrew alphabet corresponds with a number, we discover that the *tzitzit* upon a prayer shawl represent the name of God. The numbers of coils spell out *Yud, heh, vav,* and *heh.* Put them all together and you have *Yud heh vav heh,* which equals *Jehovah.*

If you look at the fringes on a prayer shawl, you will be reminded of the names of God:

- *Jehovah Rophe*—the God who heals

- *Jehovah Shalom*—the Prince of Peace

- *Jehovah Jireh*—the God who supplies

- *Jehovah Rohi*—the Lord is my shepherd

- *Jehovah Tsidkenu*—Righteousness

- *Jehovah M'Keddish*—Holiness

- *Jehovah Nissi*—the Lord our Banner in war

The knots in the *tzitzit* represent 613 commandments of the Word of God. They are to remind the wearer of the Word of the Lord, but it is not enough just to remember. We must also *do it.*

The prayer shawl was every Jewish man's tabernacle. The wilderness tabernacle was only eighteen feet by forty-five feet, not large enough to hold two million worshiping people. And so every Jewish man put his prayer shawl over his head while quoting Psalm 104:1–2:

> Bless the LORD, O my soul!
> O LORD my God, You are very great:
> You are clothed with honor and majesty,
> Who cover Yourself with light as with a garment,
> Who stretch out the heavens like a curtain.

The Hebrew prayer shawl is now the flag of Israel. The prophet Isaiah wrote,

> He will set up a banner for the nations,
> And will assemble the outcasts of Israel,
> And gather together the dispersed of Judah
> From the four corners of the earth. (11:12)

God has gathered the Jewish people from the gentile nations to the promised land under His flag. He designed it, and the Jews have worn it for generations.

The prayer shawl appears in Scripture on several occasions. Remember the story of the woman with an issue of blood? She reached out to touch the edge of Jesus' garment. The word we translate "hem" in Matthew 9:20 (*kraspedon*) is actually a Greek word for "fringe." She was reaching for the *tzitzit*. She was reaching for the *name of God*.

Jesus said, "If you ask anything in my name, I will do it." (John 14:13).

Notice the last appearance of a prayer shawl in Scripture:

> Now I saw heaven opened, and behold, a white horse. And He who sat on him was called Faithful and True, and in righteousness He

judges and makes war. His eyes were like a flame of fire, and on His head were many crowns. He had a name written that no one knew except Himself. He was clothed with a robe dipped in blood, and His name is called The Word of God . . . And He has on His robe and on His thigh a name written:

KING OF KINGS
AND LORD OF LORDS. (Rev. 19:11–13, 16)

The name on His thigh is the *tzitzit* of the prayer shawl around His shoulders. Jesus will return to earth just as He left it . . . as a rabbi. He will come wearing the name that is above all names, and every eye shall see Him coming in power and glory.

On Jesus' last day in Jerusalem before His crucifixion, He stood on the slopes of the Mount of Olives and, weeping, looked over the city. "O Jerusalem, Jerusalem," He cried, "the one who kills the prophets and stones those who are sent to her! How often I wanted to gather your children together, as a hen gathers her chicks under her wings, but you were not willing!" (Matt. 23:37).

Through the long lens of foreknowledge, Jesus saw the coming Roman invasions: Titus in A.D. 70, and Hadrian in A.D. 130. He saw the city surrounded by Roman legions, starving citizens, Jews being captured and crucified.

He saw what historians later told us—that the Romans crucified as many as 500 Jewish residents at a time. They slaughtered citizens in the streets until blood flowed like water. Hadrian's troops killed more than 500,000 Jewish people in his attack on the city.

Jesus saw the crusaders who would come in His name, robbing, raping, and ravaging the Jewish people from Europe to Jerusalem.

He saw Jerusalem conquered and reconquered thirty times, with millions of His people, the Jews, being slaughtered.

He saw the horror of the Holocaust, and He sobbed, "O

Jerusalem, Jerusalem." And then He said, "Your house is left to you desolate; and assuredly, I say to you, you shall not see Me until the time comes when you say, 'Blessed is He who comes in the name of the LORD!'" (Luke 13:35).

The city of Jerusalem still waits, but the time of waiting is drawing to a close.

Five

Jerusalem in the Terminal Generation

The air over Jerusalem is saturated with prayers and dreams like the air over industrial cities. It's hard to breathe.

—*Yehuda Amichai, poet* [1]

I f there's any place in the world where belief in the End is a powerful force in real-life events," writes Gershom Gorenberg in his book *The End of Days*, "it's the Holy Land. The territory today shared and contested by Jews and Palestinians is the stage of myth in Christianity, Judaism, and even Islam. When a great drama is played out here, the temptation to match events with the script of the Last Days can be irresistible."[2]

Gorenberg is right when he says the entire world looks to Jerusalem for signs of the latter days. But there are other proofs, too, and they are not based on mere myth. They are based on the infallible, rock-solid Word of God.

An Explosion of Knowledge

The first proof that we are living in the earth's terminal generation is found in Daniel 12:4: "But you, Daniel, shut up the words, and seal the book until the time of the end; many shall run to and fro, and knowledge shall increase." The literal translation of this Scripture indicates that a vast increase in knowledge will occur in the last days.

Such an explosion occurred in the last century, which any schoolchild can demonstrate. Visited the Internet lately? A wealth of information is available at your fingertips with the click of a few keys and a mouse. Entire multivolume encyclopedias are available on single DVDs, and gigantic databases are open and accessible for anyone with a modem or cable connection. We are living in the information age, just as Daniel foresaw.

From the Garden of Eden until A.D. 1900, men walked or rode horses just as King David and Julius Caesar did. In the span of a few years, however, mankind invented the automobile, the jet plane, and the space shuttle. Today you can fly from New York to Paris in three hours.

Our technology has also increased exponentially. While not necessarily advancing wisdom in the average man or woman, technology has made fathomless depths of knowledge and information available to us. You can receive faxes in your car, take a message on your cell phone, and drown in information from your Web TV.

In the last two generations, we have put men on the moon and redefined both death and life. Medical science has learned how to clone animals and plants, while geneticists have created glow-in-the-dark bunnies. Premature infants weighing less than one pound can survive, and unborn babies now routinely undergo surgery while within the womb.

All this knowledge ought to be a good thing, but we're not always the wiser for it. Our information explosion has not produced utopia or a more unselfish society; we have created instead a generation of well-informed people who know more about rock stars than relevant history. Our "enlightened society" seeks freedom and self-expression, but is enslaved by drugs, perversion, and the forces of darkness.

We have turned God's natural order upside down. We favor death for the innocent and mercy for the guilty. We grant women the right to choose while denying their unborn children the right to live. Our government leaders void the ballots of Americans who are serving their country in the military while counting "pregnant chads" and "dimples" in the hope that their candidate will prevail at the ballot box.

Why? Because knowledge without God produces intellectual barbarians, smarter sinners. Hitler's Nazis threw living Jewish children into the ovens. Many Nazi soldiers were educated men, but their education was accomplished without the acknowledgment or the knowledge of God.

We are the terminal generation, "always learning and never able to come to the knowledge of the truth" (2 Tim. 3:7) because we seek truth apart from God. You can't think your way to truth. You can't philosophize your way there. You can't think happy thoughts and reach nirvana. The only way you will ever find eternal, ultimate truth is by seeking and finding God.

In Jeremiah 8:9, we read,

> The wise men are ashamed,
> They are dismayed and taken.
> Behold, they have rejected the word of the LORD;
> So what wisdom do they have?

And Proverbs 26:12 tells us, "Do you see a man wise in his own eyes? There is more hope for a fool than for him."

If you reject truth, the only thing left to accept is empty knowledge based upon falsehood. America has rejected the truth of God's Word. We have rejected God Himself, and all we have left is a devilish lie.

The Rebirth of Israel

Another proof that we are the terminal generation is the State of Israel's existence.

I remember very clearly the day when I was eight years old, sitting at our kitchen table with my father, a quiet man with a brilliant mind. The date was May 15, 1948, an ordinary day in Texas, but far from ordinary for the rest of the world.

Dad and I were quietly listening to the radio. I'd propped my arms on the kitchen table and was watching my dad—he was listening to the radio and reading a book at the same time. Dad loved books and the study of prophecy, and although he didn't say much, people tended to listen when he did speak.

The radio broadcaster made a startling statement: "The United Nations has today announced that the members have formally recognized the State of Israel."

My father put down the book he was holding and said nothing for a long moment, but I knew from the distant look in his eye that he'd been profoundly moved. Then he shifted his gaze to me and said, "We have just heard the most important prophetic message that will ever be delivered until Jesus Christ returns to earth."

I've forgotten many episodes from my childhood, but I never forgot my father's words that night. And today I know how right he was: biblical prophecy unequivocally states that Israel must experience a rebirth before the coming of Messiah.

The Bible also prophesies that the nation will be born in a day:

"Who has heard such a thing?
Who has seen such things?
Shall the earth be made to give birth in one day?
Or shall a nation be born at once?
For as soon as Zion was in labor,
She gave birth to her children.
Shall I bring to the time of birth, and not cause delivery?" says the
    LORD.
"Shall I who cause delivery shut up the womb?" says your God.
"Rejoice with Jerusalem,
And be glad with her, all you who love her;
Rejoice for joy with her, all you who mourn for her." (Isa. 66:8–10)

Once the disciples came to Jesus and asked Him for the signs of the end of the age. "Tell us," they said, "when will these things be? And what will be the sign of Your coming, and of the end of the age?" (Matt. 24:3).

Jesus responded by saying,

Now learn this parable from the fig tree: When its branch has already become tender and puts forth leaves, you know that summer is near. So you also, when you see all these things, know that it is near—at the doors! Assuredly, I say to you, this generation will by no means pass away till all these things take place. (Matt. 24:32–34)

In Bible prophecy Israel is often pictured as a fig tree. Jesus said, "When its branch has already become tender and puts forth leaves." His meaning is clear: when Israel is a young tree, reborn and growing, putting forth leaves, it should be obvious to all that the latter days are at hand.

Jesus said, "This generation will by no means pass away till all these things take place" (v. 34). The generation that sees the rebirth of Israel is the terminal generation.

The Jews Return Home

Since A.D. 70, when the Romans attacked Jerusalem, destroyed the temple, and set into motion a series of events that resulted in the Diaspora, the Jewish people have been scattered throughout the entire world. They were not in control of their own destiny, nor did they dwell in a homeland of their own until May 15, 1948.

The Israeli Declaration of Independence, passed on May 14, 1948, contains the country's immigration policy: "The State of Israel is open to Jewish immigration and the Ingathering of Exiles." The Law of Return, enacted July 5, 1950, extends to every Jew in the world the right to immigrate to Israel. As recently as 1996, the Israeli government voiced its continuing commitment to increase immigration and strengthen the bond of Jewish heritage and Zionism.[3]

The prophet Jeremiah wrote,

> "Therefore, behold, the days are coming," says the LORD, "that they shall no longer say, 'As the LORD lives who brought up the children of Israel from the land of Egypt,' but, 'As the LORD lives who brought up and led the descendants of the house of Israel from the north country and from all the countries where I had driven them.' And they shall dwell in their own land." (23:7–8)

More than 750,000 Russian Jews, from what Jeremiah called "the north country," returned to Israel between 1988 and 1996. A Conservative News Service bulletin from March 1999 reports that the number of Russian Jews immigrating to Israel doubled in the first two months of 1999 and was expected to continue to increase in the coming months. Compelled to leave Russia by acts of anti-Semitism, including ransacked synagogues, bombings, cemetery desecration, and anti-Jewish statements by political leaders, the Russian Jews have been streaming toward the promised land.

Our own ministry has given more than $1.8 million to bring Russian Jews to Israel. We have seen them on CNN, disembarking from planes in Tel Aviv. We have read their stories in every form of print media. They do now live in their own land, just as Jeremiah predicted. Their return to their homeland is another sign of the terminal generation.

Jerusalem Under Jewish Control

Another proof that we are the terminal generation is found in Jesus' words that Jerusalem would be "trampled by Gentiles until the times of the Gentiles are fulfilled" (Luke 21:24). Jerusalem was under Gentile control from A.D. 70 until the Six-Day War of 1967.

I ran across an interesting story the other day. In the temple, the Levites had a particular psalm they sang for each day of the week. The second temple, the one where Jesus worshiped, was destroyed on a Saturday night—and yet, says a rabbinic legend, that night the Levites inexplicably sang the song for Wednesday. Why?

Perhaps they caught a prophetic vision of the future. For on Wednesday, June 7, 1967, Israel's troops retook the Temple Mount, and God's chosen people once again ruled the mount of God. That day marked the birth of a new era and offered another proof that we are living in the latter days.[4]

Instant International Communication

In the book of Revelation, John wrote,

And I will give power to my two witnesses, and they will prophesy one thousand two hundred and sixty days, clothed in sackcloth . . . When they finish their testimony, the beast that ascends out of the bottomless pit will make war against them, overcome them, and kill them. And their dead bodies will lie in the street of the great city which spiritually is called Sodom and Egypt, where also our Lord was crucified. Then those from the peoples, tribes, tongues, and nations will see their dead bodies three-and-a-half days, and not allow their dead bodies to be put into graves. And those who dwell on the earth will rejoice over them, make merry, and send gifts to one another, because these two prophets tormented those who dwell on the earth. (11:3, 7–10)

We'll discuss these two men in greater detail later, but the two witnesses will appear on the earth during the Tribulation. They will wear the traditional clothing of mourning, and they will call men to repent.

Prophecy tells us that the entire world will be able to see the two witnesses in the streets of Jerusalem. My grandfather's generation could not explain that. Neither could my father's. How could people in the United States see people in Jerusalem at the same moment people in Africa watched the same scene? It was a mystery.

Then came television, followed by international satellites and wireless communication. In this generation we can watch any major news story unfolding anywhere on the globe within seconds of the event.

This was impossible in 1900.

It was impossible even in 1960.

It is possible today because ours is the terminal generation. One day the world's population will see the two witnesses' bodies lying untouched in the streets of Jerusalem.

Deception on a Global Scale

The advent of global communication has only made it easier for evil to spread its lies over the face of the planet. In Matthew 24, Jesus warned, "Take heed that no one deceives you" (v. 4). Bible prophecy declares that deception will be epidemic in the terminal generation.

Jeremiah 9:5 paints another portrait of the widespread web of deceit:

> Everyone will deceive his neighbor,
> And will not speak the truth;
> They have taught their tongue to speak lies;
> They weary themselves to commit iniquity.

Truth has become such a casual thing. In this country we have had a president who made lying an art form, quibbling about shades of word meanings when a three-year-old could see through his lies. We buy into public relations stories and spin doctors' myths and don't even want to know the real truth about our movie stars and folk heroes.

Our government leaders have lied to us. Can we forget the egregious lie presented to the Florida Supreme Court as Vice President Gore attempted to change the results of the Florida vote in the presidential election? Speaking on behalf of Al Gore, lawyer David Boies submitted a sworn affidavit from Michael LaVelle testifying that "dimpled" ballots were upheld in an Illinois court case and counted in an election. But when LaVelle was presented with evidence to the contrary, he quickly changed his story and filed an amended affidavit the next day. "Interestingly," noted an editorial in the *Washington Times*, "there is no evidence that Democrats have filed the revised affidavit either with the Florida canvassing boards or with Florida courts, who have been making decisions based on Mr. Boies' misinformation to them."[5]

Lying exists in the highest courts of our land! Politicians in the highest offices think nothing of twisting the truth to suit their own aims!

But lying crouches in the home too. We teach our children to lie, telling them to tell callers that "Mommy isn't home" when, in truth, Mommy doesn't want to be interrupted while she's watching her favorite TV show. We tell our children's school administrators that Johnny was sick when, in truth, we wanted to spend the day at the beach.

Truth is no longer *told*—it's manipulated, massaged, painted, glossed over, varnished, camouflaged, spun by spin doctors, and hidden between the lines.

Deception will continue its rampant reign. Deceit will be the cardinal quality of the terminal generation, and though lies have always been with us, the coming Antichrist and his PR man, called the False Prophet, will elevate deception to new levels. Even the appellation of the coming Antichrist, "man of peace," is a bald-faced lie.

You can't find truth in the world's lies. What God wants you to know about life and about the future is written in His Book, not in the latest New Age bestseller. Run from those who tell lies, and keep your tongue and mind set on God's truth, lest your senses become dull like others of the terminal generation.

Signs in the Heaven and Earth

Jesus told us that the latter days would be marked by "famines, pestilences, and earthquakes in various places. All these are the beginning of sorrows" (Matt. 24:7–8).

Another translation calls these signs "the beginning of birth pains" (NIV). Famine, pestilence, and earthquakes are like the pains a woman begins to feel when she's about to give birth. When she feels those pains, she knows the end of her pregnancy is approaching.

The Jewish people have a teaching about these birth pangs. Hebrew eschatology, called *acharit ha-yamin*, describes the premessianic era as one of great upheavals and wars, known as "the birth pangs of the Messiah." The Talmud describes this era as the "footprints of the Messiah"—a time when arrogance will increase. The government will turn to heresy, and there will be no one to rebuke its wrongdoing. Young people will shame their elders; a person's own family will become his enemies.[6]

Earthquakes are another sign of the last days. Many theologians believe that earthquakes are increasing as the latter days approach, but scientific data do not support this supposition—we are able to detect earthquakes far more easily than we used to.

The following chart indicates how many times the earth trembles in an average year. Notice that there are approximately nine thousand very minor quakes per day.

Frequency of Earthquakes Worldwide[†]

Descriptor	Magnitude	Annual Average
Great	8 or higher	1
Major	7–7.9	18
Strong	6–6.9	120
Moderate	5–5.9	800
Light	4–4.9	c. 6,200
Minor	3–3.9	c. 49,000
Very minor	2–3	c. 1,000[†]
Very minor	1–2	c. 8,000[*]

[†]Since 1900. [*]Per day.

Source: National Earthquake Information Center, U.S. Geological Survey.[7]

What I'd like you to notice, however, is that Jesus said the earth would quake in the latter days, and I believe He meant it would quake as it did in the past when God moved in the affairs of men.

The Bible records at least thirty-three instances of God using earthquakes to communicate with the spiritual hard of hearing. The earth quaked at Mount Sinai when Moses received the Ten Commandments (Ex. 19:18); God used an earthquake in Jerusalem at the Crucifixion to split the veil of the temple from top to bottom (Matt. 27:51). He used an earthquake at the Resurrection to roll the stone from the borrowed tomb—not to let Jesus out, but to let others in! (Matt. 28:2) He used a temblor to set Paul and Silas free from the jail at Philippi (Acts 16:26). And He will announce the coming of Israel's Messiah with an earthquake:

And he said:
"The LORD roars from Zion,

And utters His voice from Jerusalem;
The pastures of the shepherds mourn,
And the top of Carmel withers." (Amos 1:2)

At the coming of the Messiah, the Dome of the Rock in Jerusalem (if it is still standing) will collapse when the Mount of Olives splits in half.

The nearly constant trembling of the earth beneath us is God's voice speaking through nature, reminding us that we are the terminal generation.

Worldwide Evangelism

Jesus told His disciples, "This gospel of the kingdom will be preached in all the world as a witness to all the nations, and then the end will come" (Matt. 24:14).

Despite the best efforts of dedicated missionaries, never in the world's history has it been possible for the gospel to be preached in *all* the world, to *all* nations, until today.

Technology has made the difference. Television and radio reach into every home, and dedicated Christian broadcasters are spreading the word throughout civilized countries.

Even uncivilized nations, however, are hearing the gospel in a way they can understand. Consider, for instance, the incredible work of the people dedicated to the Jesus Film Project, sponsored by Campus Crusade for Christ. The Jesus Film Project seeks to give everyone in the world the chance to hear the gospel in his native language. So whether a person speaks Swahili, French, or a language whose name is extremely difficult for most to pronounce, he can encounter the life and message of Jesus in a language "of the heart."

As of October 1, 2000, more than 3.9 billion people had viewed the film, with more than 121 million decisions for Christ. The film, which explains the gospel of Jesus Christ in the native tongue of an unreached group, is available in 624 language translations, with another 282 in the translation process. And notice this: *the film has been shown in 233 of the 234 countries of the world.*[8]

The gospel is being spread throughout the globe, just as Jesus said it would.

Nuclear and Biological Warfare

My father's generation could not understand several prophetic passages of Scripture. One incomprehensible passage was Zechariah 14:12–15:

And this shall be the plague with which the LORD will strike all the people who fought against Jerusalem:

Their flesh shall dissolve while they stand on their feet,
Their eyes shall dissolve in their sockets,
And their tongues shall dissolve in their mouths.
It shall come to pass in that day
That a great panic from the LORD will be among them.
Everyone will seize the hand of his neighbor,
And raise his hand against his neighbor's hand;
Judah also will fight at Jerusalem.
And the wealth of all the surrounding nations
Shall be gathered together:
Gold, silver, and apparel in great abundance.
Such also shall be the plague
On the horse and the mule,
On the camel and the donkey,
And on all the cattle that will be in those camps.
So shall this plague be.

Zechariah didn't know how to describe his troubling vision, so he called the gruesome results a plague. Given the reality of biological warfare, he might have seen the results of a disease, or he might have witnessed the result of massive radiation and nuclear warfare.

Years ago, I watched a docudrama about Hiroshima that contained a reenactment of the bombing that ended World War II. Watching the program, I saw flesh literally melting off the bones of victims before the corpses could hit the ground. Suddenly I understood that Zechariah could have been describing the destruction of an atomic bomb.

The atomic bomb that devastated Hiroshima was awful, but mankind has progressed to weapons far worse. A one-megaton nuclear blast (a mere firecracker compared to the massive H-bomb) instantly atomizes everything within a two-mile radius. Within an eight-mile radius, everything instantly ignites in flame. The land itself becomes a raging inferno, a literal hell on earth.

In November 1999, the sheikh of Al-Azhar, Dr. Muhammad Tantawi, called upon the Arabs and Muslims "to acquire nuclear weapons as an answer to the Israel threat." According to Dr. Tantawi, one of the first Muslim commanders, Abu Bakr, instructed his followers, "'If they fight you with a sword, fight them with a sword; if they fight you with a spear, fight them with a spear.' If Abu Bakr had lived today, he would have said, 'if they fight you with an atomic bomb, you must fight them with an atomic bomb.'"[9]

Tantawi continued,

Islam welcomes any force to serve the right and to defend the people's honor . . . If Israel has nuclear weapons, it will be the first to be defeated because it lives in a world in which there is no fear of death. We are not afraid of the Israeli nuclear weapons. What we are afraid of is the [possibility] that we will not rise up and that we will not advance.[10]

Zechariah's plague might be the result of an atomic bomb, but it could be the result of a biological weapon. After the First World War, several countries began experimenting with anthrax, tularemia, plague, and yellow fever. In 1989, the CIA learned that a vast complex of buildings in the heart of Russian Siberia was the center of what is called black biology. The program is called Vector, and it contains a bank of 10,000 viruses, including 140 strains of smallpox and three kinds of Ebola, the disease that literally causes your internal organs to hemorrhage and disintegrate. A former Russian scientist told journalist Diane Sawyer that the Russians may have engineered a deadly genetic merger—a marriage of smallpox and Ebola. The mortality rate of such a virus would be 90 to 100 percent, and there are no treatments.[11]

The Rise of Perversion and Immorality

Jesus gave us yet another sign of the end days. He told His disciples,

> But of that day and hour no one knows, not even the angels of heaven, but My Father only. But as the days of Noah were, so also will the coming of the Son of Man be. For as in the days before the flood, they were eating and drinking, marrying and giving in marriage, until the day that Noah entered the ark, and did not know until the flood came and took them all away, so also will the coming of the Son of Man be. (Matt. 24:36–39)

What characteristics marked the days of Noah? Genesis tells us that man's wickedness on the earth was very great and that "every intent of the thoughts of his heart was only evil continually" (6:5).

Can America descend any lower into the cesspool of immorality? Sometimes I doubt it, then I open yet another newspaper or magazine and realize I was wrong. Not long ago I opened *Newsweek*, a reputable news magazine, and read,

> Television has finally created a man who can go toe-to-naked-toe with the bed-hopping ladies of "Sex and the City." His name is

Brian, a Pittsburgh advertising executive with a sexy grin, smoldering brown eyes and pheromones that never miss. Brian goes home
with a different person every night, even when he's seduced a client
into an office tryst earlier in the day. With that kind of irresistible
charm, perhaps it's not surprising that his lesbian friends ask him to
father their baby. Nor is it surprising that Brian misses the birth
because he's too busy bedding a 17-year-old . . . . The men on
Showtime's "Queer As Folk" all sleep with men.[12]

The *New York Times* declares that "redefining wholesome is part
of the series' point . . . This series is intended to jolt a mainstream
audience, and it does, with language that is largely unquotable and
sex scenes so intimate that the squirm factor for most viewers will
be high."[13]

In the last few years, we have witnessed the rise of an aggressive
homosexual society. Lesbian couples adorn the covers of magazines;
now television gives us gay promiscuity in prime time. The
Newsweek reporter goes on to say,

It's been a huge year for gays on television, and we mean that literally. John Goodman is in a sitcom about a large gay man in Ohio.
Richard Hatch took off his clothes, survived "Survivor," and
became the most overexposed celebrity in America. The skinny
actors on "Will & Grace" did their part, too, by winning the Emmy
for best comedy.[14]

What passes for *openness* and *tolerance* in this generation has not
produced liberty. Our *license* has produced a generation dying
with AIDS.

We have murdered another generation through the so-called
freedom to choose—abortion!

This "enlightened generation" deals daily with drive-by shootings,
rape, child abuse, incest, and the collapse of the traditional family.

I have a solution for those who are living in the hell created by drug addiction, AIDS, homosexuality, pornography, and satanism—and that answer is Jesus Christ. He is the answer!

He can turn your sorrow into joy.

He is a friend who sticks closer than a brother.

He is El Shaddai, the Bread of Life, the Living Water.

He is the Prince of Peace to the tormented mind.

He is strength to the weary, and light to those who walk in darkness.

He is hope to the hopeless.

Try Him. Love Him. Serve Him.

And you'll discover that He never fails.

He is the answer, the only answer, to the needs of this terminal generation.

Six
America's Economy and Israel

The price of oil, which is already slowing western economic growth, is sensitive to events in Israel and anti-American sentiment is rising across the Arab world because of its perceived support of Israel.

—*Matthew Fisher,* Ottawa Sun, *November 24, 2000*[1]

Washington's pro-Israel bias has led to rising anti-Americanism as far afield as Pakistan and Indonesia. U.S. forces are on alert throughout the Middle East for stepped-up terrorist attacks. And Saudi Arabia has taken the rare step of threatening to use its oil muscle. It could cost us heavily at the pump.

—*Holger Jensen,* Denver Rocky Mountain News, *November 2, 2000*[2]

Money is an exciting topic. If you don't think so, just try taking twenty dollars away from the next person you meet on the street. Jesus tried to teach us about dealing with money—sixteen out of thirty-eight parables deal with the topic of possessions. Five hundred verses in the New Testament are concerned with prayer, less than five hundred discuss faith, and more than two thousand touch on how to handle our possessions.

Wall Street is headed for trouble, don't you doubt it. Despite the optimistic predictions flowing from policy makers in our nation's capital, America's economy is teetering on a razor-thin edge. In the November 4, 2000, issue of the *National Journal*, John Maggs claimed that one man, more than any other, will determine whether the current surge in oil prices will negatively impact the American economy. Who is this man? No, it's not an American president. No, it's not Alan Greenspan. No, it's not even the head of an American oil company. Maggs says the man is Saddam Hussein, the "last person that the next American president is going to want holding the cards."[3] He continues,

> Since the United Nations' easing of the Gulf War sanctions, Iraq has been exporting 2.5 million barrels of crude oil a day, more than any giant oil company and more than all but a handful of countries. Yet Iraq's government has been regularly threatening since March to reduce or eliminate its exports . . . More recently, Saddam has tied the threats to the outbreak of violence between Israelis and Palestinians. Those threats are not just words, either. Saddam moved a force of five divisions to western Iraq, not far from his border with Jordan, and as close to Israel as he can get.[4]

Maggs asserts that the world economy will pay a high price should Saddam make good on his threat. Not only the world, but the United States in particular. "Several Arab nations," he notes, "have threatened to withhold oil to punish Europe and the United States for their support of Israel. In addition, two weeks ago, the oil minister of Iran, the world's third-largest oil exporter, threatened to cut off oil supplies unless Israel withdraws troops from Palestinian areas."[5]

Don't doubt it, my friend. A state of war in the Middle East could dramatically disrupt our oil supply. And without oil, we would have no gasoline. Without gasoline, the trucking industry would close down, the airlines wouldn't fly, mail delivery would come to a halt, and people would be unable to get to their jobs.

With industry out of commission, the stock market would crash. Within a matter of weeks, America would be severely disabled.

But what about our strategic oil reserves? Patrick Clawson, of the Washington Institute for Near East Policy, told me that the United States has only a two-month supply of oil. If Saddam Hussein decided to turn off the oil in March, by May our economy would be devastated.

A report from the James A. Baker Institute for Public Policy states that at the time of Iraq's invasion of Kuwait, oil markets experienced a major supply glut that included excess commercial oil stockpiles as well as tens of millions of barrels of unsold crude oil afloat in tankers. But these surpluses do not exist today.[6]

"We are just one event away from a real crisis," says Philip Verleger, a respected economist who advises major oil companies. "Iraq or some other sudden cutoff in supply could be that event."[7]

Oil has tripled in price since the spring of 1999, moving from $10.90 a barrel to $33.92 exactly one year later. Our planet isn't running out of oil, but we are growing more and more vulnerable to those who control the spigots.

John Maggs reports that oil prices have played a crucial role in the past three U.S. recessions, going back to 1973.[8] The roaring U.S. economy of the past several years may come skidding to a halt, then collapse.

"With timing and luck," writes Maggs, "Saddam or some other force in the world could trigger a new oil crisis with long-term effects for the United States and the world economy. And there won't be much that the White House, or economists, can do about it."[9]

Even without considering the threat of an oil shortage, economic troubles loom before us. John Makin, senior economist at the American Enterprise Institute, is now forecasting a recession in the United States in 2001. "The recession will be sharp," he maintains. And he warns that a U.S. recession could become a global recession.[10]

Makin is not alone in forecasting economic trouble for the coming year. Stephen Roach, chief economist of Morgan Stanley Dean Witter, has warned his clients to "remain on maximum alert for a global hard landing in the first half of 2001."[11]

And in his book *The Coming Internet Depression*, Michael Mandel warns that the stock market boom will crash, causing widespread economic pain in the form of canceled investments, bankruptcies, and layoffs.[12]

The Day the Dollar Dies

The apostle James wrote of the future economy:

> Come now, you rich, weep and howl for your miseries that are coming upon you! Your riches are corrupted, and your garments are moth-eaten. Your gold and silver are corroded, and their corrosion will be a witness against you and will eat your flesh like fire. You have heaped up treasure in the last days. (James 5:1–3)

Stored money will be worthless when the economy crashes. The worldwide economic crash could create the chaotic platform upon which the Antichrist will appear.

Perhaps you remember President Clinton's celebration of the so-called budget surplus of 1998. After the announcement of this "leftover money," debate raged in Congress and the national media about how we should spend the supposed windfall. No one, however, talked about the solid truth underlying all the political hyperbole. The truth, simply put, is this: *there is no extra money.* Despite Washington's claims that the Clinton administration wiped away thirty years of red ink, the national debt continues to grow. As of September 2000, the national debt—the total amount of outstanding Treasury bonds, bills, and notes our government owes—stood at $5,677,647,064,339.47.[13] That's more than $5 *trillion*.

How many is a trillion? If you went into business the day Jesus Christ was born, stayed open 365 days a year, and lost $1 million every day, you'd have to work through today and for another 700 years before you'd lose $1 trillion.

One million dollars can be contained in a stack of one-thousand-dollar bills four feet high. You'd have to stack one-thousand-dollar bills sixty-seven *miles* high before you'd have a trillion.

"The growing national debt is an unwelcome guest at today's surplus party," said Concord Coalition National Policy Director Robert L. Bixby. "But politicians who energetically boast about surpluses today will have a difficult time explaining to their constituents in a few years why they need to raise the debt limit."[14]

An editor for *Countryside & Small Stock Journal* recognizes that individuals can appear to live high on the hog by using credit cards, but "their day of reckoning will come. It's no different for nations."[15]

The editor adds that extraordinary economic and political efforts have propped up our economy. This is comparable to the practice of putting out small fires in national parks, even though small fires are natural and beneficial:

> But when they're extinguished by man, the fuel on the forest floor builds up, leading to conflagrations such as the Yellowstone burn of 1988. By putting out the smaller fires, the managers of the economy didn't prove us early whistle-blowers wrong; they merely set the stage for a finale that will be much worse than even the grimmest of us foresaw back in the 1960s.[16]

Debt Disaster

The growing national debt will ultimately murder the American dollar. Proverbs 21:20 (NIV) tells us, "In the house of the wise are stores of choice food and oil, but a foolish man devours all he has." America has devoured not only all it has, but also all its children will have! By God's accounting system, our nation's spending policy is formulated by fools. We are spending all we have and all we can borrow from Europe and Japan.

The other day a man told me that Congress raised taxes so they could pay off the national debt. That's a myth! Two years ago the national media featured shots of Clinton and various members of Congress celebrating the budget surplus. Lots of people made a big fuss about extra money, but all that hoopla was only wool being drawn over the eyes of the American people.

Let me explain: in 1998, America experienced a year of economic stability. Unemployment was at a peacetime low. Inflation was negligible. President Clinton announced a $39 billion budget surplus, while the Congressional Budget Office estimated that it might run as high as $63 billion. People celebrated, Democrats clapped themselves on the back, and Republicans began pushing for tax cuts.

It was all Cinderella talk.

The explanation lies in history. In 1968, to pay for the war in Vietnam, President Lyndon Johnson decided—for the first time—to include Social Security in the national budget. Social Security, by necessity, takes in more money than it pays out, so the Social Security surplus helped LBJ balance his books.

Today, the Social Security surplus is at least $100 billion a year, and it alone accounts for the federal budget surplus. If you separated Social Security from the national budget, as in pre-LBJ days, the budget wouldn't show a surplus at all. It would show a *deficit* of more than $37 billion.

A deficit budget can be a good thing, for it curtails government spending. But when you start talking about a surplus, politicians begin dreaming up new ways to spend money we don't really have. Because while the politicos in Washington are arguing over the perception of deficit versus surplus, none of them are talking about the national debt.

The national debt is about 67.4 percent of our U.S. gross domestic product (GDP). Eric Black, a staff writer for the *Minneapolis Star Tribune*, explains why this is important:

> Imagine a family that is borrowing money every year, never paying off any of the debt, and therefore paying more interest every year. It's not healthy. But in assessing the magnitude of the problem, you'd certainly want to know whether the family's income was rising fast enough to enable them to pay their growing interest costs without invading the grocery or mortgage money. Expressing the debt as a percentage of GDP indicates which is growing faster . . . Between 1981 and 1996, the GDP grew by 250 percent, a healthy pace. During the same period, however, the national debt grew 500 percent—twice as fast as the economy.[17]

Black goes on to explain that the percentage of national debt to GDP did decline slightly in 1997, but it could easily begin to grow again. "One way to think about the phenomenal growth of the national debt is to consider it as the price we pay for putting off a visit to the dentist," says Lawrence Malkin, an economic columnist. Postponing the visit never eases the pain, but only makes it worse.[18]

Again and again in America's history, national debt was created during wartime and paid during peacetime, but after World War II, the government decided not to pay off the debt. The debt to GDP ratio in 1945 was more than 100 percent.[19]

Our nation is simply digging itself deeper and deeper into a ditch with sides so steep that we'll have a difficult time getting out. If we are to survive, we must send a shocking message to our elected officials—stop spending this nation into poverty! Stop sending our children and grandchildren into debtors' prison.

Someday the dollar will die because it has no basis, no real value.

What Is a Dollar Worth? Less and Less

Have you ever stopped to consider the worth of a single dollar?

The world's first system of exchange was the barter system. If I wanted something from you, I would offer some tobacco, a cow, or a couple of chickens in exchange. Precious metals became the next system of monetary exchange, then banks were created and paper receipts represented the value of gold stored in a bank's vault. The American mint printed dollars to represent the gold stored in Fort Knox, but when America was taken off the gold standard in 1933, the dollar in your pocket lost value.

Under the gold standard, the supply of dollars was determined by the supply of gold. Gold must have a fixed dollar value, x dollars per ounce, and if the supply of gold increased, then the money supply could grow by x dollars. Under this system, inflation cannot take hold, for the government cannot manipulate the money supply. The supply of gold—and money—was limited by the amount of gold mined. Without a gold standard, governments print money at their own discretion, and the free flow of dollars ultimately cheapens the value of goods. When an item is plentiful, its value falls.

America abandoned the gold standard in the midst of the Great Depression, and the world went off the international gold standard in 1971. These days, exchange rates fluctuate freely, and the United States Federal Reserve, headed by Alan Greenspan, controls the American economy. Don't think for a moment that our economy is controlled by Congress or the president.

The Federal Reserve has no elected officials. The board of governors is composed of seven members appointed by the president for fourteen-year terms.

The Federal Reserve has never been audited.

The Federal Reserve sets the rate of interest that determines what your money is worth. It's a shocking fact, but true: the value of your dollar is controlled by an organization that is not controlled by America.

If someone tells you, "You look as sound as a dollar," well, you'd better start looking for a casket.

We Are "Entitling" Our Way to Disaster

The American economy will die because of entitlements. Did you know that before 1930 it was considered unconstitutional for the government to tax one citizen and give his money to another? For one hundred years the Supreme Court had voted against such programs. But Franklin Delano Roosevelt packed the Supreme Court with liberal judges who voted in favor of entitlements, and the floodgates flew open. The American people discovered that the United States government was willing to provide handouts.

More than two hundred years ago, Professor Alexander Tyler wrote about a powerful Greek society that had fallen two thousand years earlier:

A democracy cannot exist as a permanent form of government. It can only exist until the voters discover they can vote themselves money from the [public] treasury. From that moment on, the majority will vote for the candidate promising the most benefits from the public treasury, with the result that a democracy always collapses over loose fiscal policy and is always followed by a dictatorship.[20]

In 1964, in his State of the Union Address, Lyndon Baines Johnson announced an "unconditional war on poverty," proclaiming, "One thousand [dollars] invested in salvaging an unemployable youth today can return $40,000 or more in his lifetime." Fueled by Johnson's belief in the Great Society, Congress enacted an unprecedented amount of legislation instituting poverty reduction programs.

Today, more than thirty years later, we have spent more than $5.4 trillion, but America's poverty rate has not budged. In fact, the poverty rate in 1966 was 14.7 percent. By 1993, after spending billions of dollars, the poverty rate had actually increased to 15.1 percent.

How does this translate into everyday reality? In 1993 alone, American taxpayers spent more than $324 billion on eighty different welfare programs—that exceeds $3,300 from each tax-paying household.

With the $5.4 trillion we've spent in fighting the War on Poverty, we could have purchased every factory, all the manufacturing equipment, and every office building in the United States. Even after these purchases, we would have enough money left over to buy every airline, railroad, trucking firm, commercial maritime fleet, telephone company, television and radio company, power company, hotel, and every retail and wholesale store in the nation![21]

Welfare has become one of the government's largest categories of spending. By 1994, after adjusting for inflation, welfare spending was six and one-half times greater than at the beginning of Johnson's War on Poverty.[22] William Lauber observes:

> In welfare you get what you pay for. Ever since President Johnson and Congress enacted the Great Society programs, our government has paid for nonwork and out-of-wedlock births. And, consequently, it has achieved huge increases in both . . . By offering benefits to people without regard to character or behavior, the entitlement system has helped destroy the character and resolve of the poor.[23]

What is the biblical solution to poverty? "Six days you shall labor" (Ex. 20:9). America is the land of equal opportunity; everyone can work and pay taxes. The Bible says, "If anyone will not work, neither shall he eat" (2 Thess. 3:10). Nothing in your life will work until you do!

The Word of God makes provision for the man or woman who cannot work because of poor health or advanced age. In Israel, the farmers were forbidden to cut the grain in the corners of the field so widows and orphans might glean grain for their needs. The limbs of fruit trees could be flayed only once, so the remaining fruit could be harvested by the poor. It is the responsibility of the church and society to provide for people who legitimately cannot work.

Why Would God Allow an Economic Crash?

God will allow an economic crash to affect America and the world because America's number one false god is the god of money. Don't believe me? Consider these facts:

We sacrifice our health to the god of mammon (money). We ruin our health to get wealth, then spend all our wealth to regain our health! This is madness. America's hospitals and doctors' offices are filled with patients suffering from stress-related illnesses. Why so much stress? Because we're spending all we have and borrowing more to keep up with the Joneses. It's time for most Americans to consider plastic surgery—cut up those credit cards and get out of debt!

We sacrifice our marriages and our children in the mad pursuit of money. How much time did you spend talking to your children yesterday? How much time did you spend at work? The average father in America talks to his children forty-eight seconds per day. Make sure you value your priceless human relationships above your career.

Banks are America's new cathedrals of worship. The next time you enter one, look at the lavish furniture, and notice how the typical customer goes in to talk to a loan officer. Nine times out of ten, he will enter with a solicitous and almost reverent manner. If we honored God like that, revival would sweep America. Banks aren't the source of our wealth—God is!

Some of you have sold your soul to the god of mammon. You

can't tithe for the love of money. You can't give, can't live, and can't love. But hear me! The god of America will fall.

In Deuteronomy 28:17–18, God announced the curses that will fall upon the nation that does not obey Him: "Cursed shall be your basket and your kneading bowl. Cursed shall be the fruit of your body and the produce of your land, the increase of your cattle and the offspring of your flocks." The basket (for gathering produce), the kneading bowl (for making bread), the produce of the land, the increase of cattle and offspring of flocks—all have to do with a nation's economy. Men may *think* they control the economies of nations, but they do not. God does.

God will allow an economic crash because such a scenario fits into His prophetic plan. The coming Antichrist's economy will be a cashless society in which every financial transaction is electronically monitored. John, writer of the book of Revelation, described the situation: "He causes all, both small and great, rich and poor, free and slave, to receive a mark on their right hand or on their foreheads, and that no one may buy or sell except one who has the mark or the name of the beast, or the number of his name" (Rev. 13:16–17). I'm going to save the complete discussion of the Antichrist's future economic system for a later chapter, but know this: in the resulting confusion of a worldwide economic crash, the man of sin will rise to prominence just as Hitler rose to power because of Germany's economic crisis.

God Almighty will topple America's false god, mammon. He says to us, "I am the Lord your God, and there is none other beside Me. I am your shield, your buckler, your high tower, your provider."

Remember, America, the power to gain wealth does not come from Alan Greenspan, the rest of the Federal Reserve, the president, Congress, or Wall Street. God rules in the affairs of men!

God will topple our economy because our national conscience is dead. American society, founded upon the principles of faith and freedom, has left its moral underpinnings and chased after the wind. We are like King Solomon, who said,

> Whatever my eyes desired I did not keep from them.
> I did not withhold my heart from any pleasure,
> For my heart rejoiced in all my labor;
> And this was my reward from all my labor.
> Then I looked on all the works that my hands had done
> And on the labor in which I had toiled;
> And indeed all was vanity and grasping for the wind. (Eccl. 2:10–11)

America is a soulless mockery of what it once was. Our society, like ancient Rome's, is headed for destruction, but I've got good news. God's kingdom is rock solid and will never fall! Jesus prayed, "For Yours is the kingdom and the power and the glory forever" (Matt. 6:13).

Of His kingdom there shall be no end, and His economy will never fail. Amen!

Seven

Winds of War over Jerusalem

An end must be put to Zionism. If they [the PLO]
cannot, then Iraq alone is able to do so. Let them give
us a small adjacent piece of land and let them support
us from afar only. They will see how we put an end to
Zionism in a short time.

—*Saddam Hussein, October 3, 2000*[1]

Iraq, which has not been heard from lately, has been
taking a ferocious stand against Israel, unmatched by
any state in the region. Iraqi Foreign Minister
Mohammed al-Sahhaf referred to Israel as a "midget
entity, a usurper and a claw of colonialism . . . Iraq does
not, and will not, recognize this usurper entity."

—*Cal Thomas, October 11, 2000*[2]

Make no mistake—at some moment in the future, Russia,
together with its Arab allies, will lead a massive attack upon the
nation of Israel that will probably involve nuclear weapons. The
prophet Ezekiel clearly described the coming battle, which I believe
will take place just before the Antichrist steps forward to take his
place on the world stage.

Even today, Arafat is courting help from Russia and the European
Union. A report from the *Star*, a Jordanian newspaper, printed just

125

after the failed Camp David talks in the summer of 2000, painted a picture of a courageous Arafat fighting for truth alone:

> Camp David has succeeded in focusing negotiations on the crucial issues that could make or break an agreement between Palestinians and Israelis . . . We can only sympathize with Arafat who had to endure Clinton's coercive measures. But we also join millions of Arabs who cheered him for standing by his position and for refusing to compromise on Palestinian rights in Jerusalem. If anyone was courageous at Camp David it was definitely the Palestinian leader . . . What was indeed painful is to see Arafat fighting the Jerusalem battle single-handedly. He is now asking Arabs and Muslims to take up their responsibility and make their position clear and send that message to both Israel and the U.S. The question is, will they dare do this?[3]

The November 26, 2000, edition of the *New York Times* contained the article "Russia Backs European Plan for New Force." The subhead: *Moscow likes a military plan that excludes America.*

I read the article with interest, and I was only half surprised to learn that Russia is now ready to cooperate with the new 60,000-member military force being established by the European Union (EU). Russia is not part of the EU, but for some reason that nation feels compelled to help create this new army. According to the *New York Times,* "a day after President Vladimir V. Putin of Russia received the Palestinian leader, Yasser Arafat, in Moscow, Mr. Ivanov also called for the European Union to be more involved in Middle East Peace Talks."[4]

According to the Russian Foreign Minister Igor Ivanov, "Russia, as a cosponsor of the Middle East peace process, believes that the European Union should take a more active role in its international mediation. The very proximity and approaches on these questions between Moscow and Brussels allows us to act in tandem and if necessary, in a joint effort."[5]

The players are lining up, my friends. The Russians and the Arabs are aligning, and the European Union, which I believe will produce the Antichrist, waits in the wings with a supportive military army. The horrific battle of Gog and Magog is practically on the drawing table.

When Will the Battle Begin?

To be perfectly honest, I cannot be dogmatic about this event's occurrence after the Rapture—the instant in which Christ will appear in the clouds to take the church to heaven (1 Thess. 4:13–18). We know this battle over Israel will occur, and I believe it will result in the Antichrist's stepping in to offer Israel and its enemies a seven-year peace treaty. We also know the church will be taken away *before* the Antichrist is revealed. However, we cannot unequivocally say whether the church will be snatched up before or after Russia's attack upon Israel.

I can't gloss over an event as significant as the Rapture in a single sentence. Jesus said, "Of that day and hour no one knows, not even the angels in heaven, nor the Son, but only the Father" (Mark 13:32). Despite the thousands of people who would like to predict the exact year, month, day, or hour of Christ's return to gather His church, Jesus said that no man knows. But the Father knows when He will send Jesus to fetch His bride home. And although we do not know the day and hour, we know by prophetic Scripture that the Rapture is very near.

Due to the astounding popularity of end-times books like the *Left Behind* series, I doubt there are many Christians who don't have at least a rudimentary knowledge of the Rapture. But if your memory needs refreshing, the Rapture will occur like this: without warning, Jesus Christ will appear in the heavens in a burst of dazzling light. Instantly the trump of God will sound, announcing the appearance of royalty, for Jesus is the Prince of glory, the

King of kings, and the Lord of lords. The voice of the archangel shall summon the dead from their resting places, and all over the earth graves will explode as their occupants soar into the heavens in new, supernatural bodies.

In the next moment, empty cars will careen down the highway, their drivers and occupants absent. Homes of believers will stand empty with supper dishes on the dining table, food bubbling in the microwave, and water running in the sink. The occupants of those homes will have been snatched from this vale of tears to a land where there is no crying, no parting, and no death. There we will celebrate the marriage supper of the Lamb of God and His radiant bride, the church, without spot or blemish!

The next morning, headlines will scream, "MILLIONS MISSING!" The church of Jesus Christ—which includes every born-again believer—will be completely absent from the earth. A few politically correct pastors, New Age church members, and secular humanist religious leaders will remain, and they will be hard-pressed to explain why they didn't vanish with the true saints of God. Over the next few months, churches will be packed with weeping people who will have realized, too late, that God's Word is infallible, and that the world stands on the brink of a time known simply as the *Tribulation.*

Either right before or right after the Rapture, another earth-shaking event will occur—war in the Middle East, a battle known to Bible scholars as the advance of Gog and Magog. John Wesley White believes this war might occur very soon after the Rapture—the Rapture might even trigger it.

"The Americas," he writes, "with their multitudes of born-again people suddenly raptured away from the distinguished posts of leadership which they occupy, would provide an opportune moment for the [Russians] to make their move . . . What would hinder the Russians and their Islamic satellites from launching what Hitler called a 'final solution' to the Jewish problem?"[6]

Let's take a look at the biblical basis for this prophecy.

The Valley of Dry Bones

In chapter 37 of Ezekiel, the prophet was caught up by the Spirit of God and taken to a valley of dry bones. Some Bible scholars believe Ezekiel was taken bodily to the ruins of Jerusalem, where those who had died in defense of the city lay unburied outside the walls. In any case, Ezekiel looked at a multitude of dry bones, scattered by wind, rain, and wild animals, and wondered what God had in mind by bringing him to such a place.

God then asked the prophet a strange question: "Son of man, can these bones live?"(v. 3)

Nonplussed, Ezekiel lifted his brows. Perhaps it was a trick question because those bones had been dead a long time, but with God anything is possible. The prophet, ever a diplomat, gave a careful answer: "O Lord GOD, You know" (v. 3).

God then told Ezekiel to prophesy to the valley of dry bones, and as Ezekiel spoke, the bones began to clatter and clack. An arm bone rushed to join its mate; a thigh bone snapped to a leg bone. Broken ribs came together; crushed skulls curved to their original state. And then, as the prophet watched, sinews, or ligaments, grew over the bones, then skin appeared to cover them over. In moments, the bones were miraculously changed into human bodies, complete and whole, but they did not move or breathe.

Then God spoke again. "Prophesy to the breath," He told Ezekiel, "prophesy, son of man, and say to the breath, 'Thus says the Lord GOD: "Come from the four winds, O breath, and breathe on these slain, that they may live."'" (v. 9).

So Ezekiel obeyed, and breath came into the bodies, and they opened their eyes and lived. They stood, an exceedingly great army of men.

And God said to Ezekiel:

Son of man, these bones are the whole house of Israel. They indeed say, "Our bones are dry, our hope is lost, and we ourselves are cut off!" Therefore prophesy and say to them, "Thus says the Lord GOD: 'Behold, O My people, I will open your graves and cause you to come up from your graves, and bring you into the land of Israel. Then you shall know that I am the LORD, when I have opened your graves, O My people, and brought you up from your graves. I will put My Spirit in you, and you shall live, and I will place you in your own land. Then you shall know that I, the LORD, have spoken it and performed it,' says the LORD."

The prophecy is concerned not with Israel as individuals, but with Israel as a nation. The Jewish people were scattered throughout the world like the bones in the valley, but God brought them back together in 1948. J. Vernon McGee noted, "They have a flag, they have a constitution, they have a prime minister, and they have a parliament. They have a police force and an army. They have a nation, and they even have Jerusalem. They have everything except spiritual life."[7]

At this moment, the Israelis can be compared to the bodies who lacked the breath of life in Ezekiel's vision. They are physically complete, but they are lacking the breath of spiritual life itself. They have not recognized their Messiah, but they will, at an appointed time after the battle described in the next chapter of Ezekiel.

Gog and Magog Are Drawn to Israel

In Ezekiel 38, the prophecy continues: "Now the word of the LORD came to me, saying, 'Son of man, set your face against Gog, of the land of Magog, the prince of Rosh, Meshech, and Tubal, and prophesy against him'"(vv. 1–2).

The leader is Gog, and his kingdom is Magog. Magog is referred to as one of the sons of Japheth in Genesis 10:2 and in 1 Chronicles 1:5.

Who is Gog? He is called the prince of "Rosh, Meshech, and Tubal," provinces of Asia Minor. However, that geographical area is today occupied by Iran, Turkey, and the southern provinces of the CIS, the Commonwealth of Independent States. The CIS, which originally consisted of three former Soviet republics—Belarus, Ukraine, and Russia—grew to include eight other republics two weeks after the commonwealth's establishment in December 1991. The Republic of Georgia joined in 1993, bringing the total of former Soviet republics to twelve. The CIS states operate much like the American states—they are responsible to a central organization while governing themselves, but they are far from stable.

The CIS has been characterized by infighting among member states from its inception. Ethnic and regional hostilities that had been restrained by decades of central Soviet authority have reemerged in bloody civil wars. More important, a fundamental disagreement has arisen over the goals and purpose of the CIS. One camp, led by Russia and Kazakstan, envisions the CIS as a vehicle for closer economic and political integration; another camp, led by Ukraine, visualizes the CIS as a transitional organization preparing individual republics for complete independence.[8]

Moscow is the capital and largest city in Russia, one of the founding members of the CIS. I believe that Rosh of Ezekiel 38 is a combination of Russian states. Seeking long-lost power and glory, the Russian states, headed by a military leader from Moscow, will learn that strength lies in unity.

Linguistics reinforce the geographic identification of Gog and Magog as Russian states. Many people believe Rosh is related to the modern word *Russia,* and Meshech and Tubal, respectively, are variations of the spellings of *Moscow* and *Tobolsk,* an area in the Ural section of Russia. The name *Russia* does not appear in Scripture, but this detailed description of the invader of Israel clearly fits that now unstable nation.

A great military movement under the leadership of Gog, the prince or leader of Rosh, is described in Ezekiel 38:4: "I will turn you around, put hooks into your jaws, and lead you out, with all your army, horses, and horsemen, all splendidly clothed, a great company with bucklers and shields, all of them handling swords."

Next God identifies the invaders that will join Russia—Persia, Ethiopia, Libya, Gomer, and Togarmah (vv. 5–6).

Persia is easily identified as Iran. Ethiopia and Libya refer to the Arab Islamic nations of the Arabian Peninsula. I believe that when Ezekiel spoke of Persia, Ethiopia, and Libya, he was referring to the contemporary Arab states that are constantly calling for holy war to exterminate Israel. Gomer and Togarmah most likely refer to the region now occupied by the nation of Turkey. Since Israel is the fourth greatest military power on the face of the earth, there is no way the Arabs could defeat Israel by themselves. So they will enter into an agreement with Russia, which will be more than willing to share military organization, know-how, and weapons in return for access to the Persian Gulf.

In brief summation, it is reasonable to assume Russia will lead a massive Pan-Islamic military force to invade Jerusalem. Russia's motive is to control the oil-rich Persian Gulf, which will bring America and the West to their knees. The fundamentalist Muslims have a burning passion to control Jerusalem. This Russian–Pan-Islamic union is an unholy alliance that will lead to holy war.

Israel, the Key to End Times

It is not possible to understand Bible prophecy without understanding Israel's past, present, and future. Israel will be the epicenter of the earth's shuddering travails in the last days, and all pivotal events will center on the Holy Land and the people of Abraham.

Israel was founded by a sovereign act of God. God said to Abraham,

> Get out of your country,
> From your family

132

And from your father's house,
To a land that I will show you. (Gen. 12:1)

Upon Abraham's arrival in the promised land, God repeated this promise: "To your descendants I will give this land" (v. 7).

There are presently two controversies concerning Israel. The first states that God's promise to Abraham was not a promise of literal land, but a promise of heaven. Those who embrace this position teach that Israel has lost favor with God through disobedience and the church is now Israel. The second controversy holds that the promise to Abraham and his descendants is literal, but conditional, based upon Israel's obedience to God.

This common confusion is instantly corrected by clear and obvious teaching found in the Word of God. In Genesis 22:17, God told Abraham, "Blessing I will bless you, and multiplying I will multiply your descendants as the stars of the heaven and as the sand which is on the seashore."

God mentioned two separate and distinct elements: stars and sand. The "stars of the heaven" represent the church. Stars, as light, rule the darkness, which is the commission of the church. Jesus told His followers, "You are the light of the world" (Matt. 5:14). Jesus is the "Bright and Morning Star" (Rev. 22:16). And Daniel 12:3 tells us,

> Those who are wise shall shine
> Like the brightness of the firmament,
> And those who turn many to righteousness
> Like the stars forever and ever.

Stars are heavenly, not earthly. They represent the church, Abraham's *spiritual* seed.

The "sand of the seashore," on the other hand, is earthly and represents an earthly kingdom with a literal Jerusalem as its capital city. Both stars and sand exist at the same time, and neither ever replaces the other. Just so, the nation of Israel and the church exist at the same time and do not replace each other.

The Bible clearly teaches that God's promise to Abraham was *literal* and *unconditional.* Let's examine the Scripture to verify beyond any doubt that God intended Abraham and the Jewish people to possess a literal land.

In Genesis 13, God told Abraham,

Lift your eyes now and look from the place where you are—northward, southward, eastward, and westward; for all the land which you see I give to you and your descendants forever . . . Arise, walk in the land through its length and its width, for I give it to you. (vv. 14–15, 17)

Genesis 15:18 records, "On the same day the LORD made a covenant with [Abraham], saying: 'To your descendants I have given this land, from the river of Egypt to the great river, the River Euphrates.'" Then God listed the heathen tribes living in that area at that time. This is a very literal land. Heaven is not described, even allegorically, as the area between the river of Egypt (the Nile) and the Euphrates.

God told Abraham,

Know certainly that your descendants will be strangers in a land that is not theirs, and will serve them, and they will afflict them four hundred years. And also the nation whom they serve I will judge; afterward they shall come out with great possessions. (Gen. 15:13–14)

Israel's departure from the promised land was literal because the people physically left and journeyed into a literal Egypt. After four hundred years they became a nation of two to three million people, and they physically left a literal Egypt for a literal promised land. The books of Exodus, Leviticus, Numbers, Deuteronomy, and

Joshua deal with Israel's return to a literal promised land—not heaven.

The title deed to the promised land was passed to Isaac from Abraham. God said to Isaac, "Dwell in this land, and I will be with you and bless you; for to you and your descendants I give all these lands, and I will perform the oath which I swore to Abraham your father" (Gen. 26:3).

The title deed to the promised land was then passed to Jacob from Isaac. In Genesis 28:13, God told Jacob, "I am the LORD God of Abraham your father and the God of Isaac; the land on which you lie I will give to you and your descendants." You have to be in a very literal land to lie upon it!

Was God's promise to Abraham conditional? Those who believe God's promise depended upon Abraham's obedience simply do not understand the blood covenant.

In the Old Testament, there were three kinds of covenants: a shoe covenant, a salt covenant, and a blood covenant. In the blood covenant, the most solemn and binding, the contracting parties would agree on the terms of the covenant. Then they would take an animal or animals, kill them, split the carcasses in half down the backbone, and place the divided parts opposite each other on the ground, forming a pathway between the pieces.

The two would then join hands, recite the contents of the covenant, and walk between the divided halves of the slain animals. The blood covenant meant they were bound until death, and if either party broke the terms of the covenant, his blood would be spilled just as the blood of the animals that had been killed. A blood covenant was a permanent and unconditional promise. God gave to Abraham, Isaac, Jacob, and their descendants an unconditional promise of a promised land in which they were to live literally and forever by blood covenant.

In Genesis 15, God commanded Abraham to take a heifer, a female goat, a ram, a turtledove, and a pigeon. All were split in half except the birds. Because no man can look upon God and live, God placed Abraham in a deep sleep as He prepared to enter a blood covenant with him.

In his sleep, Abraham saw "a smoking oven and a burning torch that passed between those pieces" of the slain animals (Gen. 15:17). In the Old Testament, the burning lamp signified the presence of the shekinah glory of God. God was binding Himself by blood covenant to Abraham and his descendants forever, saying, "To your descendants I have given this land." Never did God suggest the covenant was conditional. Exactly the opposite is true; this covenant depends only on the faithfulness of God, and He is ever faithful.

Psalm 89:30–37 confirms this unconditional promise. God said,

If his [David's] sons forsake My law
And do not walk in My judgments,
If they break My statutes
And do not keep My commandments,
Then I will punish their transgression with the rod,
And their iniquity with stripes.
Nevertheless My lovingkindness I will not utterly take from him,
Nor allow My faithfulness to fail.
My covenant I will not break,
Nor alter the word that has gone out of My lips.
Once I have sworn by My holiness;
I will not lie to David:
His seed shall endure forever,
And his throne as the sun before Me;
It shall be established forever like the moon,
Even like the faithful witness in the sky.

God clearly said He will not break covenant with Israel, David's sons, even though Israel disobeys Him. He also said that the moon is a witness of this covenant. When you walk out at night and see the moon shining in the heavens, you see God's eternal witness speaking to all men in all languages that His covenant with Israel is forever and unconditional.

Could a Peace Treaty Be Effective?

Every other week you can pick up your local paper and read something about the peace process currently occupying the Israeli government. From the concerned look on Yasser Arafat's face during press conferences, you might believe he has wanted nothing more than peace with Israel throughout his entire life.

But even if a peace accord is signed, keep in mind that Arafat frequently compares previous peace accords to the Khudaibiya agreement made by the prophet Muhammad with the Arabian tribe of Koreish. That pact, slated to last for ten years, was broken within *two* years when Arab forces, having used the time of truce to grow stronger, defeated the Koreish tribe. Comparing the peace accords to the Khudaibiya pact is tantamount to stating they are only temporary arrangements.[9]

As recently as November 15, 1998, just weeks after the October 1998 Wye River Accord, Arafat told a rally, "We chose the peace of the brave out of faith in the prophet, in the Khudaibiya agreement."

Understand this: Islamic fundamentalists, led by terrorist groups such as Hamas, believe that what Muhammad taught was truth—that it is Allah's will for them to rule the earth. As long as breath remains in their bodies, they will fight Israel to the death.

They want to control Jerusalem, and to control Jerusalem, they must conquer Israel. Holy war is coming, no matter how much Arafat or Putin or members of the United Nations talk of peace. The previously signed peace accords are as useless as gasoline in a fire extinguisher.

Saladin was a Muslim leader who, after a cease-fire, declared a holy war against the crusaders and captured Jerusalem. Chairman

Arafat once told an audience of Egyptian TV viewers that Muhammad was able to sign a treaty he did not intend to keep by not including his title "messenger of Allah" in the agreement. "Then," Arafat continued,

> Omar bin Khatib and the others referred to this agreement as the "inferior peace agreement." Of course, I do not compare myself to the prophet, but I do say that we must learn from his steps and those of Salah-a-Din [Saladin]. The peace agreement which we signed is an "inferior peace" . . . We respect agreements the way that the prophet Muhammad and Salah-a-Din respected the agreements which they signed.[10]

Jerusalem, the city of God, is caught in a supernatural crossfire. Trading land for peace will not bring rest to that troubled city. Giving Yasser Arafat and the PLO part of Jerusalem to establish a Palestinian city or a Palestinian state will not bring permanent peace.

Why Would Russia Want to Attack?

Why would Russia decide to invade Israel? There are several likely reasons.

First, instability within the CIS might lead to such an invasion. The Russian economy is dangerously weak, but the country has valuable assets: military weapons, knowledge, and organization. Why not offer these assets to the Arab nations that desperately need them?

Second, although Russia is rich with oil reserves and other natural resources, the resources tend to be located in remote areas difficult to access. Therefore, Russia must establish alliances with the countries that sit upon and control the world's vast oil fields—the Arab nations surrounding the Persian Gulf.

To transport that oil—and engage in military defense and shipping—Russia desperately needs a warm-water seaport. You need only to look at a map of Russia to see that its seaports are primarily located in the frozen Arctic Ocean and to the east. Russia needs a western seaport that opens into the Mediterranean Sea. Currently Russian ships must travel through the Black Sea, then through the narrow Bosporus, then through the Sea of Marmara and the Aegean before reaching the Mediterranean. Israel, however, is located right on the Mediterranean—prime shipping territory.

Third, six of ten republics in Russia today are controlled by Islamic fundamentalists, and the Soviet Union stored its nuclear arsenal in one of these republics. Muslims, who are concentrated mostly in the ethnic Republics of Chuvashia and Bashkortostan in the middle Volga region, and in the Republics of Chechnya, Ingushetia, Alania (North Ossetia), Kabardino-Balkaria, and Dagestan, today form the second largest religious group in Russia.[11]

The signs are already appearing. Listen to the words of Uri Dan and Dennis Eisenberg, writers for the *Jerusalem Post:*

> The thunderous roar of U.S. missiles raining down earlier this month [September 1996] on military targets in southern Iraq provoked hostility among most European and Middle-Eastern Arab countries. In sharp contrast, the action taken by Bill Clinton was warmly welcomed by Britain and Israel. This positive attitude was underlined by [then] Prime Minister Binyamin Netanyahu, who told this column minutes before seeing the American president . . . that he had emphasized to his host the dangers to peace in the Middle East posed by Iran, Iraq, and other countries. In all probability Netanyahu singled out Russia, which has reverted to the policies of the former Soviet Union and is aiming to become a dominant power in the Middle East once again. The Russian bear has already hugged Iran in a honeyed embrace by building a nuclear reactor for the mullahs of Teheran. It is also working hard to take Syria back into its bosom, holding out modern arms for Damascus as bait. But Iraq is clearly the prize maiden being wooed by Moscow.[12]

The writers go on to explain that Russia is offering Iraq, a leading Arab state, an all-out effort to get the UN to lift the oil embargo that prohibits the sale of Iraqi oil to world markets, as well as $2 billion worth of high-tech equipment for enhancing the flow of oil from Iraq to Russia. "Though the situation isn't as dangerous as it was when the Soviet Union was a superpower," Dan and Eisenberg write, "the Israeli government is aware of the problem of an increasingly hostile Russia as the Kremlin woos Mideastern Arab states primarily for their oil. Israel will have to learn to handle the way the Kremlin operates."[13]

In 1996 Moscow signed energy agreements with Iraq worth up to $10 million that are to go into effect once UN sanctions are lifted. And it has reached agreement with Iran on delivery of defense-related goods (read—weapons!) totaling $4 *billion* over the next four to five years.[14]

Why is Russia wooing the Arab nations of the Middle East? Contemporary observers see one overwhelming reason:

The real factor driving Russian interest [in the Middle East] is a geopolitical or strategic one. Economics enters in a big way only when it is a question of selling arms. Here the Russian defense industry exerts tremendous pressure to enter the Middle East regardless of any strategic consequences, even by low-balling other competitors and selling at what appear to be dumping prices to anyone who will buy.[15]

In other words, Russia is so eager to have a presence in the Middle East that it will practically give weapons away. Russia needs economic partners, it needs a strategic port, and in the light of the crumbling economy, it does not want to become a "welfare nation." One writer comments, "We err if we underestimate how deeply Russian elites fear becoming a Western economic colony."[16]

When the Islamic nations, which despise Israel, join forces with Russia, they will greatly benefit from the strength of Russia's armed forces. The Islamic nations have oil and cold, hard cash. Russia has military knowledge and the organizational skills necessary to launch a military invasion. Together, they will make a treaty guaranteeing mutual support.

Russia will say to the Islamic nations, "You want Jerusalem and the Temple Mount as a holy site. We want the Persian Gulf oil. Let's join forces to rule the world!" Russia is already friendly with the Islamic nations. Its leaders protested loudly when the United States began bombing Saddam Hussein's military installations in Iraq.

The final and most compelling reason for Gog and Magog to invade Israel is the "hook" God will put in Gog's jaw. Regardless of the human or economic reasons, God will inexorably draw Gog and his forces toward Israel.

The end result? A massive Pan-Islamic military force led by Russia's high command will come against Israel "like a cloud, to cover the land" (Ezek. 38:16).

The Guardian of Israel Never Sleeps

As is the case with so many things, what man intends for evil God intends for good. This monumental battle between Israel and the coalition of Islamic nations and Russia is no exception. For while this dread army believes it has devised this battle of its own accord to serve its own ends, in fact God the Father has been at work.

Ezekiel 38:4–6 records God's words:

I will turn you around, put hooks into your jaws, and lead you out, with all your army, horses, and horsemen, all splendidly clothed, a great company with bucklers and shields, all of them handling swords. Persia, Ethiopia, and Libya are with them, all of them with shield and helmet; Gomer and all its troops; the house of Togarmah from the far north and all its troops—many people are with you.

In Ezekiel 38:16, we see again that the Lord has orchestrated this battle: "It will be in the latter days that I will bring you against My land."

Gog will not see the hand of God; he will see only Israel, "the land of those brought back from the sword and gathered from many people on the mountains of Israel, which had long been desolate; they were brought out of the nations, and now all of them dwell safely" (Ezek. 38:8). As a result of the treaties with the Palestinians in which Israel has traded valuable strategic territory for peace, Israel will appear to be more vulnerable than ever—a "land of unwalled villages . . . a peaceful people, who dwell safely, all of them dwelling without walls, and having neither bars nor gates . . . and against a people gathered from the nations, who have acquired livestock and goods, who dwell in the midst of the land" (Ezek. 38:11–12).

As a result, the coalition will "come from [its] place out of the far north, [it] and many peoples with [it], all of them riding on horses, a great company and a mighty army. [The coalition] will come up against My people Israel like a cloud, to cover the land" (Ezek. 38:15–16).

When Israel is dwelling in its ancient land, when old enmities are cloaked and smoldering beneath plastic smiles, the Russians will gather their allies and look toward the Holy City. But what the invaders do not realize is that God has sworn by His holiness to defend Jerusalem. Since God created and defends Israel, the nations that fight against Israel fight against God Himself.

The invaders will find an easy entry into the promised land. With gratefulness to Allah (or the Russian military commander), they will embark on their plan of plunder and genocide.

The vast majority will never know what hit them. Their defeat will be sudden, horrible, and complete.

God's Response to the Threat

God says that when Gog sweeps down from the north, "My fury will show in My face" (Ezek. 38:18). King David said, "Behold, He who keeps Israel shall neither slumber nor sleep" (Ps. 121:4). After watching the Jews of the Holocaust walk into the gas chambers, after seeing the "apple of His eye" thrown into the ovens and their ashes dumped by the tons into the rivers of Europe, after seeing the "land of milk and honey" run red with Jewish blood in five major wars for peace and freedom, God will stand up and shout to the nations of the world, "Enough!"

First, He will send a mighty earthquake so devastating that it will shake the mountains and the seas, and every wall shall fall to the ground:

> Surely in that day there shall be a great earthquake in the land of Israel, so that the fish of the sea, the birds of the heavens, the beasts of the field, all creeping things that creep on the earth, and all men who are on the face of the earth shall shake at My presence. The mountains shall be thrown down, the steep places shall fall, and every wall shall fall to the ground. (Ezek. 38:19–20)

Second, almighty God will send massive confusion to the multinational fighting force, and "every man's sword will be against his brother" (Ezek. 38:21). This is exactly what God did when He commanded Gideon to blow the trumpets and break the pitchers. The Philistines became divinely confused and turned their swords on each other. Gideon won a great military victory without one casualty. God will do it again in defense of Israel.

Third, the Lord of hosts will open fire with His divine artillery:

> I will bring him to judgment with pestilence and bloodshed; I will rain down on him, on his troops, and on the many peoples who

are with him, flooding rain, great hailstones, fire, and brimstone. (Ezek. 38:22)

This passage could be interpreted in two ways. First, the "fire and brimstone" might refer to Israel's release of nuclear weapons in a last-ditch attempt to prevent annihilation. "Pestilence" might refer to cheaper, more nefarious implements of war; Russia and Iraq have the world's largest store of chemical and biological weapons. I can easily imagine a scenario where they fire biological weapons upon Israel, but God miraculously turns the anthrax-laden missiles or causes them to misfire, so that the invaders are destroyed by their evil intention!

The second interpretation is that this event is a repeat of Sodom and Gomorrah. God will blast Israel's enemies into oblivion by raining fire and brimstone from heaven. In either case the results are equally catastrophic.

Nuclear Doomsday?

Ezekiel 39:6 presents a possible scenario that I find interesting in light of today's technology. Let's look at the verse: "I will send fire on Magog and on those who live in security in the coastlands. Then they shall know that I am the LORD."

When God says He will "send fire," I have to wonder whether He is referring to actual fire and brimstone, like what fell upon Sodom and Gomorrah, or whether He is referring to nuclear war. Sometimes God acts in miraculous ways; at other times He uses men to accomplish His purposes. I believe that the fire that fell on Sodom was real and from heaven; I believe that the walls of Jericho fell because the people shouted and God worked, not because the sound of so many trumpets caused an unsteady wall to crumble.

Most important, I believe that God's intervention on Israel's behalf in this battle will be of obvious supernatural origin. Scripture tells us that the world will know God intervened on Israel's behalf. Tiny Israel could not defeat a Russian-Arab coalition without God's help, for though Israel has nuclear weapons, so does Russia.

God could certainly use man's implements to work His will, however, and this verse about "fire" from the sky falling upon people who "live in security in the coastlands" deserves another look.

Consider this scenario: Israel has said it will never be the first to introduce nuclear weapons into the Middle East,[17] but it may feel forced to use them if a gigantic Russian-led military force descends on it from the north. Stan Goodenough, a writer for the *Jerusalem Post*, points out that with every inch of territory Israel gives away in the name of peace, it is being backed into a corner from which it would have no choice but to defend itself with nuclear weapons:

> The smaller Israel becomes, the more its defensive options will be restricted to the non-conventional [weapons]. In simple terms, a 1967-size Israel will find itself almost impossibly limited in terms of the time and space it needs to mobilize for a conventional war. As long as Judea and Samaria and Gaza and the Golan Heights are under Israeli control, attacks by the Arab states can be better anticipated and more easily repulsed by conventional means . . . Confronted by an Arab onslaught without these vital pieces of land, however, Israel would have virtually no choice but to go the non-conventional route, or risk immediate and complete annihilation.[18]

Goodenough also points out that it would take only three Hiroshima-type bombs on Tel Aviv to completely decimate the country. Casualty estimates are more than 400,000, and Israel could never survive such a blow.[19]

Suppose Israel decided to launch a nuclear attack on Russia in a desperate attempt to halt the approaching Russian-Arab army . . .

Will Nuclear Bombs Fall on the United States?

When I had dinner recently with former Prime Minister Netanyahu, he told me that Russian scientists have been working with Iran to produce medium- and long-range nuclear missiles. The medium-range missiles are capable of hitting Jerusalem, and the long-range missiles are capable of hitting New York City and other American coastal cities.

There's something else you should know about the old USSR. During the height of the cold war, Soviet scientists designed and built a doomsday machine, which they named Dead Hand. The Russian military maintains it to this day. According to Dr. Bruce Blair of the Brookings Institution, this doomsday machine, with backups and fail-safes aplenty, was designed to detect any attack on Russia and automatically send a message to a complex of communications rockets. Assuming that Russian commanders had been wiped out by an American first strike, the Dead Hand would feed orders into the rockets, which would launch automatically. From space, these communications rockets would relay orders to nuclear-armed warheads, which would fire out of their silos or off their mobile trucks and zoom toward their preassigned targets.[20]

Unfortunately, the preassigned targets set up in Soviet cold war days were American cities.

Are we the people "living in security in the coastlands" upon whom the fire will fall? I found it interesting that a July 2000 report in *USA Today* declared that nearly 55 percent of the American population now lives within fifty miles of a coastline.[21]

The nuclear doomsday that Americans have dreaded since the beginning of the cold war could come upon us quite by accident. Though in 1991 the Bush administration took our long-range nuclear bombers off alert, and in 1994 the Clinton administration made the oceans instead of Russia the standby aim points for our intercontinental ballistic missiles on alert, Washington still has more than three thousand strategic warheads on land- and submarine-based missiles that can be launched within minutes.[22] If missiles begin to fly at us, I think it's a pretty safe bet that our people would give the order to launch as well.

We will certainly sustain damage from this war, for God says, "All men who are on the face of the earth shall shake at My presence. The mountains shall be thrown down, the steep places shall fall, and every wall shall fall to the ground" (Ezek. 38:20). Whether this devastation arises from nuclear war, hydrogen bombs, a massive earthquake, a combination of all three, or something else altogether, every living person on the face of the planet will tremble as God wreaks destruction upon Israel's enemies.

During the 1980s United Press International disseminated a story about the dreams—reportedly occurring on the same night—of three distinguished Jewish rabbis. Each man dreamed that the Gog-Magog war was not far away. The UPI report noted, "The chief rabbi of the Wailing Wall in Jerusalem's Old City is sure Israel will confront the Soviet Union in a battle over the holy city. 'And it will be a nuclear war,' they contended, drawing in both superpowers."[23]

Gog and Magog Are Annihilated

Ezekiel's graphic account of the battle's aftermath makes clear just how thorough and disastrous is the defeat of this Russian-Muslim coalition. The prophet opened chapter 39 by stating, "I am against you, O Gog." As the news cameras of the world survey millions of bloated bodies lying in the hot Middle Eastern sun, this comment will go down in history as one of the greatest understatements of all time.

Why is God against Russia? I can think of several reasons, including the fact that Soviet leaders imposed atheism upon millions of people for most of this century. For years during the cold war, we watched atheism emanate from Moscow and infiltrate scores of countries around the world. Tim LaHaye says,

No nation in the history of the world has destroyed more flesh than Russia through the spread of Communism . . . but her greatest sin has not been the destruction of flesh, as serious as that is. Her greatest sin has been the soul damnation caused by her atheistic ideology . . . No nation has done more to destroy faith in God than Communist Russia, thereby earning the enmity of God.[24]

The most crucial reason God is set against Gog, I believe, has to do with the fact that God promised Abraham, "I will bless those who bless you and curse those who curse you." For years, Russia has cursed and persecuted the Jews.

The Russian word *pogrom*, which pertains to the massacre of a helpless people, passed into the international lexicon after the devastation of Russian Jews in the Ukraine in 1903. The Russian nation has been persecuting Jews since the time of the czars. In the span of time between the two world wars, the entire Jewish population of the Russian Western War Zone—including older people, sick people, and children—were forcibly evacuated into the interior of the country on twelve hours' notice.

The blood of more than 500,000 innocent Jews cries out for justice, and God will deliver it in His battle against Gog and Magog.

The Aftermath of the Battle

Ezekiel did not tell us how many will die in the battle; he told us how many will be left alive: only a "sixth part" (39:2 KJV). The casualty rate for this battle will be 84 percent, an unheard-of figure in modern warfare.

The prophet's narrative of the end results continued. Ezekiel said the bloated bodies of the enemies of Israel will be a banquet for buzzards. The beasts of the field will have a feast unlike anything since dogs ate the body of Jezebel.

"And as for you, son of man, thus says the Lord GOD, 'Speak to
every sort of bird and to every beast of the field:
"Assemble yourselves and come;
Gather together from all sides to My sacrificial meal
Which I am sacrificing for you,
A great sacrificial meal on the mountains of Israel,
That you may eat flesh and drink blood.
You shall eat the flesh of the mighty,
Drink the blood of the princes of the earth,
Of rams and lambs,
Of goats and bulls,
All of them fatlings of Bashan.
You shall eat fat till you are full,
And drink blood till you are drunk,
At My sacrificial meal
Which I am sacrificing for you.
You shall be filled at My table
With horses and riders,
With mighty men
And with all the men of war," says the Lord GOD. (Ezek. 39:17–20)

According to Peter C. Craigie, the participation of beasts in the
demise of the invaders stresses the finality of the event. Human
beings who were to have been the masters and stewards of the earth
have, in the pursuit of evil, become victims of the natural order.[25]

The people of Israel will set about burying the dead in a mass
grave eerily reminiscent of the huge trenches the Nazis used to bury
Jewish dead in the Holocaust:

"It will come to pass in that day that I will give Gog a burial place
there in Israel, the valley of those who pass by east of the sea; and it
will obstruct travelers, because there they will bury Gog and all his
multitude. Therefore they will call it the Valley of Hamon Gog. For

seven months the house of Israel will be burying them, in order to cleanse the land. Indeed all the people of the land will be burying, and they will gain renown for it on the day that I am glorified," says the Lord GOD. "They will set apart men regularly employed, with the help of a search party, to pass through the land and bury those bodies remaining on the ground, in order to cleanse it. At the end of seven months they will make a search. The search party will pass through the land; and when anyone sees a man's bone, he shall set up a marker by it, till the buriers have buried it in the Valley of Hamon Gog. The name of the city will also be Hamonah. Thus they shall cleanse the land." (Ezek. 39:11–16)

Some Bible scholars believe this valley of the dead might be in modern-day Lebanon. It is a country of mountains that run from north to south, with a valley in between two mountain ridges, and a logical path for a Russian-led attack on Israel. The prophet Habakkuk mentioned Lebanon in a passage dealing with the last days: "For the violence done to Lebanon will cover you" (2:17), and Zechariah 11:1 declares, "Open your doors, O Lebanon, that fire may devour your cedars."

The dead bodies of the invaders will be strewn in the fields and mountains surrounding Israel, and the seven-month burial detail will involve all Israeli citizens. Every last bone shall be buried. *Hamon-Gog* is a Hebrew word for "the multitude of Gog," which is to become the name of this vast cemetery for the invaders of Israel.

Not only will there be tremendous carnage, but the weapons left by the devastated forces will provide fuel for Israel for seven years— through the years of the Tribulation.

"Then those who dwell in the cities of Israel will go out and set on fire and burn the weapons, both the shields and bucklers, the bows and arrows, the javelins and spears; and they will make fires with them for seven years. They will not take wood from the field nor cut down any from the forests, because they will make fires with the weapons; and they will plunder those who plundered them, and pillage those who pillaged them," says the Lord GOD. (Ezek. 39:9–10)

Can you imagine weapons burning for seven years? I was in Israel during the Peace in Galilee War led by General Ariel Sharon back in the eighties. I personally saw Israeli eighteen-wheel trucks bringing back the spoils of war in a convoy that stretched farther than my eye could see. The trucks, bumper to bumper coming out of Lebanon, were carrying loads of war booty back to Israel. The supplies had been stored in Lebanon by the Soviet Union and were said to be enough to keep 500,000 men in combat for six months. As great as those spoils were, it was only a matter of days before the Israeli army collected and stored them. But Ezekiel described a conflict so vast it will take seven years to gather and dispose of the weapons of war.

Israel will derive an unexpected benefit from this. The prophet said the war booty from this massive invasion will provide Israel with fuel for seven years, and because of this, the forest will be spared. In that verse alone, we find proof that this will occur in the latter days—even contemporary times. Prior to the State of Israel's establishment in 1948, the land was almost entirely deforested, a desert wasteland. But the Israelis have worked hard to make the promised land bloom again.

It has been my pleasure over the years to plant a tree each time I go to Israel. Each time we visit we add to a "Night to Honor Israel" plot in an Israeli forest. I'm glad to know that the invading armies will leave such a massive amount of fuel that "our" trees will survive the war.

This Is Not Armageddon

Though the world will reel at the damage sustained in this battle, this is not Armageddon, the battle that is to come later on God's prophetic "doomsday clock." This battle will involve only a select group of nations, while Armageddon will involve "all the kings of the earth," a true world war. In this battle, Gog's armies will be arrayed in the open field (Ezek. 39:5), while at Armageddon the enemy armies will enter the city of Jerusalem. Christ will appear at the end of Armageddon to establish His millennial kingdom, but at the end of this war, Israel will turn its eyes back to the God of Abraham, Isaac, and Jacob.

Israel Acknowledges the Hand of God

Why does God allow the nations to make war upon Israel? There is only one answer: for His glory. Ezekiel wrote, "So the house of Israel shall know that I am the LORD their God from that day forward . . . I will magnify Myself and sanctify Myself, and I will be known in the eyes of many nations. Then they shall know that I am the LORD" (39:22; 38:23).

Mankind worships a pantheon of so-called gods. Some worship Buddha, others Allah, some Satan, some gods of their own making, but who is the almighty God? When the God of Abraham, Isaac, and Jacob finishes mopping up the enemies of Israel on the mountains (notice that Jerusalem and the cities are saved), there will be no doubt that Jehovah God is the almighty God. God said, "It will be in the latter days that I will bring you against My land, so that the nations may know Me, when I am hallowed in you, O Gog, before their eyes" (Ezek. 38:16).

Truly the only way we can understand the significance of this incredible defeat is to accept it as an act of God. The defeat of Gog and Magog will accomplish the purpose of glorifying God before Israel and the world. Ezekiel wanted the world to know that God will supernaturally neutralize the enemies of Israel and destroy them that His name might be glorified.

A second reason for this great display of God's power is to testify to His beloved Jewish people that He alone is their God. Through their miraculous deliverance, the hearts of the Jewish people will begin to turn again to the God of Abraham, Isaac, and Jacob:

"So the house of Israel shall know that I am the LORD their God from that day forward. The Gentiles shall know that the house of Israel went into captivity for their iniquity; because they were unfaithful to Me, therefore I hid My face from them. I gave them into the hand of their enemies, and they all fell by the sword. According to their uncleanness and according to their transgressions I have dealt with them, and hidden My face from them." Therefore thus says the Lord GOD: "Now I will bring back the captives of Jacob, and have mercy on the whole house of Israel; and I will be jealous for My holy name—after they have borne their shame, and all their unfaithfulness in which they were unfaithful to Me, when they dwelt safely in their own land and no one made them afraid. When I have brought them back from the peoples and gathered them out of their enemies' lands, and I am hallowed in them in the sight of many nations, then they shall know that I am the LORD their God, who sent them into captivity among the nations, but also brought them back to their land, and left none of them captive any longer. And I will not hide My face from them anymore; for I shall have poured out My Spirit on the house of Israel," says the Lord GOD. (Ezek. 39:22–29)

Israel, the spiritually dead body of Ezekiel's vision, will know beyond all doubt that God orchestrated its victory in this attack. This may be the impetus needed for officials to begin construction of the third temple on the Temple Mount, quite possibly alongside the existing mosque. I don't know exactly how it will happen, but I do know that Israel will build the third temple, and it is logical to assume Israel's spiritual reawakening will be the result of seeing God's mighty hand acting in the nation's defense.

Please note very carefully that at this point the Jewish people as a group have yet to accept Jesus as their Messiah. The Bible is very clear that this will happen at the end of the Tribulation, a time yet to come on God's prophetic clock. Because of this cataclysmic battle on the soil of the Holy Land, the nation of Israel will begin to turn toward the most high God, but some of them will be distracted by a newcomer on the world stage, a charismatic man who comes to Israel with outstretched arms, promising peace and safety.

Eight

The Antichrist Conquers Jerusalem

> What Arafat is really after in Russia and other European capitals isn't so much new ideas to get the peace process going again as support for his plan for an international force to keep Israelis and Palestinians apart.
>
> —Edmonton Sun, *November 24, 2000*[1]

> The Palestinians have been pushing for a bigger European role in the Middle East peacemaking, accusing the United States—the main mediator—of being biased toward Israel.
>
> —Washington Times, *November 2, 2000*[2]

> The European Union on Monday took its first major step to turn itself into a military power, as its defense ministers pledged troops and equipment to create a 60,000 member force by 2003 . . . The force could be sent into the field within 60 days and could stay as long as a year, under the European Union's plans.
>
> —Tampa Tribune, *November 21, 2000*[3]

My friend, as unrest in the Middle East increases, don't let your heart be troubled by talk of war. We've had wars in the past, and we'll continue to have them until the end of time. Jesus can carry you through the day of turmoil.

Look at what the psalmist wrote: "May the LORD answer you in the day of trouble; may the name of the God of Jacob defend you" (Ps. 20:1).

Some spiritual space cadets piously say, "If you were spiritual, you'd never have trouble." By that standard, Jesus wasn't spiritual, for all His days were flooded with trouble.

- Herod slaughtered thousands of babies when Jesus was born. His parents had to run into Egypt to save their lives.

- He was born into a hated minority, the Jews.

- The legitimacy of His birth was questioned.

- The established religious leaders called Him a heretic.

- The established government branded Him a traitor and political insurrectionist.

- His closest friends denied Him during His trial.

- He was crucified with criminals and buried in a borrowed tomb.

And what was His reaction to all this trouble?

"Be of good cheer," He told us, "for I have overcome the world."

Is someone always raining on your parade? Get over it!

Do you feel that if you inherited General Motors, someone would outlaw automobiles? Smile!

Do you feel the only way to wake up with a smile on your face is to go to bed with a coat hanger in your mouth?

Have you suffered great reversals? Be of good cheer!

If you are going through a great trial, be of good cheer!

If your marriage is under attack, be of good cheer!

If your friends have become your accusers, be of good cheer!

Jesus did not protest when He encountered trouble. He proclaimed the gospel. He did not defend; He declared. My friend, if you are a fellow Christian, you don't need to defend the Word of God to a mad-dog world in the day of trouble. We must declare it, proclaim it, and release its power.

Jesus did His duty. He did what the Father sent Him to do. The church has been sidetracked in a day of trouble. We've let our focus shift to trivial side issues, and we've forgotten to do our duty—to preach the gospel and win the lost, cast out demons and heal the sick, be filled with the Spirit, pull down the strongholds of sin and Satan, demolish the strongholds of witchcraft, satanism, and pornography.

We are to declare victory over the world, the flesh, and the devil. We are more than conquerors through Christ—and conquering is our duty!

Some years ago a shipwreck occurred off the coast of the Pacific Northwest. A crowd of fishermen from a nearby village stood on the shore to watch the ship as it foundered on the rocks. A lifeboat was sent out to rescue the ship's crew, and after a terrific struggle through the raging surf, the rescuers came back with a boatload of survivors and a message: one young man remained in the ship. There'd been no room for him in the lifeboat.

"I'll go get him," one fisherman said, gripping the edge of the lifeboat.

Just then, a little gray-haired mother cried out, "No! Don't go, Jim. Your father drowned at sea, your brother, William, sailed away, and you're all I have left. If you're lost, I'll have no one."

Jim looked at his mother and gave her a tender smile. "Mother, I must go. It's my duty."

The crowd fell silent as the lifeboat emptied, and Jim climbed in and grabbed the oars. Through the pounding surf he rowed, pushing the craft beyond the breakers, toward the disintegrating wreck on the rocks beyond. On the sand, Jim's mother wept silently and hugged her arms beneath her thin sweater.

"He ain't gonna make it," someone said, squinting toward the small craft, a frail shell bobbing atop the angry waves.

For a few breathless moments the little boat disappeared, then they saw it again, moving back through the surf toward them. At last it drew close enough for them to see two figures inside the boat, Jim and another sailor. Both were soaked to the skin.

"Did you get him?" one of the men called out, dashing into the wavewash. "Did you get the last man?"

"Aye, I did," Jim called back. "And tell Mother I've found him. William, my brother, has come home."

My friend, miracles occur when Christians do their duty! The church needs to hear more about duty, discipline, and devotion. We are soldiers of the cross, and we serve a risen King. The intifada in the Middle East is only a shadow of the real fight, the war between the forces of God and the forces of the devil.

When you hear of trouble in the Middle East, or when it knocks on your front door, be of good cheer. Lift high the blood-stained banner of Jesus Christ, and tell the kingdom of darkness that the victory is and forever will be God's!

The Supernatural Battle for Jerusalem

More than three thousand years ago, King David conquered the Jebusites and made Jerusalem the capital of Israel. We know that David was no saint. In his lifetime he committed murder, adultery, and a host of other sins. So why did God love him so dearly and favor him so much? Because he was a warrior with spiritual insight. He loved the Word of God. He was an ordinary man, but because he drew near to God, God drew near to him.

We've all heard the story of David versus Goliath. It's one of the first stories you learn in Sunday school, and children warm to the idea that it's not size that matters, but courage and commitment.

There's another aspect to the story you may not have considered. David versus Goliath was a supernatural battle. David's brothers and 40,000 Israelite soldiers were terrified of Goliath, but David wasn't.

He saw the battle for what it was: Satan's attack upon the people of God and their right to control their God-given land! And so he picked up five stones and marched out to face the enemy, comforted and sustained by the confident trust that he was following the will of God.

Then David said to the Philistine,

"You come to me with a sword, with a spear, and with a javelin. But I come to you in the name of the LORD of hosts, the God of the armies of Israel, whom you have defied. This day the LORD will deliver you into my hand, and I will strike you and take your head from you. And this day I will give the carcasses of the camp of the Philistines to the birds of the air and the wild beasts of the earth, that all the earth may know that there is a God in Israel." (1 Sam. 17:45–46)

Ah, my friend, the same God who sustained and protected and strengthened David in the battle with Goliath will sustain and protect and strengthen Israel in its time of trouble. Don't you doubt it!

Scripture records another situation where David faced supernatural warfare. As he approached Jerusalem, ready to do battle with the Jebusites, the occupiers of the holy mount looked out upon the approaching ragtag crew and laughed. They said, "'You shall not come in here; but the blind and the lame will repel you,' thinking, 'David cannot come in here'" (2 Sam. 5:6).

But David turned and told his men, "Whoever climbs up by way of the water shaft and defeats the Jebusites (the lame and the blind, who are hated by David's soul), he shall be chief and captain" (2 Sam. 5:8).

For years no one could understand what this verse meant. Was the king of the Jebusites thinking that even his weakest people could defeat David? Why, then, would David give an honor to anyone who struck down helpless people, and why would he hate them with his very soul?

The riddle was solved when Israeli archaeologist Yigael Yadin discovered clay tablets from the Hittite era that explained that parading "lame and blind" people was an act of witchcraft, a curse upon the enemy. By leading out the lame and blind, a king was saying, "May the first man that strikes these lame and blind people become as lame and blind as they are!"

That's why David hated them. They represented what Goliath represented, the occultic, satanic empire!

David attacked and drove out the Jebusites, and Jerusalem was conquered in the name of God. God loved David for his fearless heart. David single-handedly drove God's enemies out of Israel and Jerusalem.

Mark this down, friend: the supernatural battle for Jerusalem is not over. The battle of Islam versus Judaism is the same supernatural struggle David faced—the power of the destroyer, Satan, against the true God of Israel.

Jesus said, "The thief does not come except to steal, and to kill, and to destroy. I have come that they may have life, and that they may have it more abundantly" (John 10:10).

Which religion advocates destruction and death and spreads through the conquering of nations? The answer should be clear.

Mark down another fact: the Antichrist wants to rule the world from the city of Jerusalem *because* it has been promised to Jesus Christ, the Messiah. Islam did not begin in Israel. The prophet Muhammad never visited the Temple Mount, except in his "vision." But because the Temple Mount is holy to the Jews, because it is the future throne of the Messiah, Satan wants it. The Antichrist will want it, and he will have it . . . for a limited time.

For a complete picture of the satanic prince who is to come, we must turn to the books of Revelation in the New Testament and Daniel in the Old Testament. Journey with me as we delve into a study of who the Antichrist is and what he intends for Jerusalem.

The First Seal: The Rider on the White Horse

John the Revelator, who once walked with Jesus, was allowed a glimpse of the end times during his exile on Patmos. In his glimpse into heaven, he saw a scroll sealed with seven seals in the right hand of Him who sits on the throne of heaven—Jesus Christ. A voice proclaimed, "Who is worthy to open the scroll and to loose its seals?" John wept when no one in heaven or on the earth or under the earth was able to open the scroll (Rev. 5:1–4).

But one of the elders comforted him: "Do not weep. Behold, the Lion of the tribe of Judah, the Root of David, has prevailed to open the scroll and to loose its seven seals" (v. 5).

While John watched, Jesus Christ came forth, looking like a Lamb that had been slain. While the elders and the raptured church watched, the perfect sacrificial Lamb came forward before the host of believers numbering "ten thousand times ten thousand, and thousands of thousands" out of every tribe and to tongue and people and nation. While the redeemed church sang praises to Him, Jesus Christ opened the scroll (Rev. 5:6–6:1).

After the breaking of the first seal, John saw a white horse: "He who sat on it had a bow; and a crown was given to him, and he went out conquering and to conquer" (Rev. 6:2).

The man on the horse is the Antichrist, a master imitator. Because prophecy tells us Jesus will return on a white horse at His second coming (Rev. 19:11), this man rides a white horse, but he is no savior. He is given a bow, a weapon of war, and a crown. He goes forth to conquer the world.

He will be successful.

The first and most noticeable sign of the Tribulation's advent is the rise of a global personality, a man whose name will be on everyone's lips. I don't know his name and wouldn't hazard a guess, but I believe he is alive at this moment and knows his satanic assignment.

Is the Antichrist a literal man? Listen to this quote from the *Dallas Morning News:*

Many scholars argue that the Bible's authors never intended their work to be interpreted as literal prophecy. The Antichrist in Revelation, for example, alludes to the Roman emperor Nero, who represented evil to early Christians. The passage predicting Armageddon, scholars say, refers to the final victory of good over evil, not a literal battle. The Rapture, mentioned in 1 Thessalonians, is an expression of the apostle Paul's confidence that Christians will spend eternity with Jesus.[4]

My reaction to this? Poppycock! First of all, any so-called scholar who talks about the Bible's "authors" doesn't understand how the Bible was written. You could talk about the Bible's "writers," "scribes," "amanuenses," or even "secretaries," but you don't dare talk about the Bible's "authors." An author is one who writes words he has pulled out of his mind or imagination. The Bible was *authored* by the Holy Spirit of God, not by man. Men recorded the words of God under the absolute control of the Holy Spirit so that the finished product was simply the Word of God!

Second, the men who wrote what the Holy Spirit dictated were not creating allegories or fables. John the Revelator wasn't trying to tactfully describe the Roman emperor Nero, nor was he being metaphorical when he described Armageddon with great and vivid detail. And if Paul merely wanted to reassure Christians that they would spend eternity with Jesus, why didn't he just say so? No, my friend. The Rapture is literal, Armageddon is an actual battle, and the Antichrist is a living, breathing person whom the Bible calls the chief son of Satan (2 Thess. 2:3).

John wasn't the only biblical writer to mention the Antichrist. Daniel was exposed to him not once, but three times. Let's look at the story beginning in Daniel's tenth chapter.

Daniel's Fasting and Prayer

In the third year of Cyrus, king of Persia, a message was revealed to Daniel, also called by his Babylonian name, Belteshazzar. The year was about 534 B.C., about four years after Daniel received the vision of the seventy weeks. Daniel was very old, still respected, though probably retired from public service.

In the first few verses of the tenth chapter of his book, Daniel told us that he had been in mourning for three full weeks: "I ate no pleasant food, no meat or wine came into my mouth, nor did I anoint myself at all, till three whole weeks were fulfilled" (v. 3).

Something had shaken Daniel to his core, rocked him so severely that he didn't take a bath or comb his hair for three full weeks! We're not told why Daniel was in mourning, but we can hazard a guess. Since Daniel told us it was the third year of Cyrus's reign, and we know that in his *first* year Cyrus proclaimed a decree allowing any willing Hebrew to return to the land, Daniel might have been upset because so few of his people returned to Jerusalem. (That was still prior to the time when Nehemiah and his colaborers formed a committee to rebuild the walls.)

Daniel also might have been in mourning because he realized he would not return to his beloved Jerusalem, God's holy city. He was at least ninety, and perhaps he realized he could be of more use to his people in his powerful palace position.

After deciding to seek the face of God, Daniel fasted and prayed and sought the Lord for three full weeks. After twenty-one days, he went outside to the banks of the Tigris River, and there he saw a vision unlike any he had ever seen. Some Bible scholars believe he saw the transfiguration of Jesus Christ.

> I lifted my eyes and looked, and behold, a certain man clothed in linen, whose waist was girded with gold of Uphaz! His body was like beryl, his face like the appearance of lightning, his eyes like

torches of fire, his arms and feet like burnished bronze in color, and the sound of his words like the voice of a multitude. And I, Daniel, alone saw the vision, for the men who were with me did not see the vision; but a great terror fell upon them, so that they fled to hide themselves. Therefore I was left alone when I saw this great vision, and no strength remained in me; for my vigor was turned to frailty in me, and I retained no strength. Yet I heard the sound of his words; and while I heard the sound of his words I was in a deep sleep on my face, with my face to the ground. (Dan. 10:5–9)

Daniel's description of this heavenly visitor is strikingly similar to that of John, who saw Jesus and recorded his impression in Revelation. John saw "One like the Son of Man, clothed with a garment down to the feet and girded about the chest with a golden band. His head and hair were white like wool, as white as snow, and His eyes like a flame of fire; His feet were like fine brass, as if refined in a furnace, and His voice as the sound of many waters" (Rev. 1:13–15).

Though others were with Daniel, they did not see the vision, but they were frightened enough to retreat and hide in the bushes along the river. The apostle Paul had a similar experience on the Damascus Road. He saw Jesus and heard His voice, while his frightened companions saw nothing. But on the Damascus Road and by the Tigris River, the supernatural power of God was clearly evident.

Overcome with the power and significance of what he had seen, Daniel, already weak from fasting, fainted dead away.

Suddenly, a hand touched me, which made me tremble on my knees and on the palms of my hands . . . Then he said to me, "Do not fear, Daniel, for from the first day that you set your heart to understand, and to humble yourself before your God, your words were heard; and I have come because of your words. But the prince of the kingdom of Persia withstood me twenty-one days; and behold, Michael, one of the chief princes, came to help me, for I had been left alone there with the kings of Persia. Now I have come to make you understand what will happen to your people in the latter days, for the vision refers to many days yet to come." (Dan. 10:10, 12–14)

If the man Daniel saw at the first part of the vision was Jesus, the man speaking now definitely is not, for Jesus would not need help from the archangel Michael. This nameless angel—who most believe to be Gabriel, with whom Daniel had spoken before—explains that he was hindered by the prince of Persia, the satanic ruler over the kingdom of Persia for Satan, the god of this world. The holy angel was given his marching orders on the first day of Daniel's fasting and prayer, but was blocked for twenty-one days by this demonic prince. We are not given a name for this being, but he was a high-ranking principality assigned by Satan to control the demonic activities in the kingdom of Persia, where Daniel lived.

The devil, you see, has a host of fallen angels under his command, just as God has a host of angels. Both demons and angels are organized into hierarchies, and the mighty prince of Persia was able to hinder this messenger until Michael, the archangel, arrived to help clear the way. Demons are earthbound creatures who walk the earth (Matt. 12:43) and crave the habitation of a body. When Jesus cast the demons out of the demoniac (Matt. 8:28–34), they begged to be permitted to enter the swine. Angels fly in the heavens and have bodies that are fully described in Scripture. Therefore, fallen angels are not demons. They are two different satanic battalions with the same commander in chief, Satan himself.

Why would Satan want to block an angel from appearing to Daniel? God wanted to give Daniel important prophetic information, but Satan didn't want Daniel to have it. In sharing this information about Satan's restraint and struggle via the prince of Persia, the heavenly messenger lifted the curtain on the invisible warfare going on all around us. Paul wrote, "For we wrestle not against flesh and blood, but against principalities, against powers, against the rulers of the darkness of this world, against spiritual wickedness in high places" (Eph. 6:12 KJV). A *principality* in Satan's high command is a chief ruler of the highest rank (Eph. 1:21; Col. 2:10).

Interestingly enough, before he left, the angel told Daniel, "And now I must return to fight with the prince of Persia; and when I have gone forth, indeed the prince of Greece will come . . . (No one upholds me against these, except Michael your prince. Also in the first year of Darius the Mede, I, even I, stood up to confirm and strengthen him.)" (Dan. 10:20–11:1).

There's a wealth of assurance in the angel's parenthetical comment. "It was I," the angel confided in a daring whisper, "who strengthened King Darius after you were thrown into the lions' den. Do you remember how distraught he was? He spent a sleepless night worrying about you and beseeching God, so it was I who gave him the strength to trust that God would save your life."

The angel also mentioned that soon he would encounter not only the prince of Persia again, but also the prince of Greece. Why? Because the prophecy the angel related concerns Greece.

The angel began his prophecy by explaining that it had to do with Daniel's people, the Jews: "Now I have come to make you understand what will happen to your people in the latter days, for the vision refers to many days yet to come" (Dan. 10:14).

What follows is the most detailed account of history in all the Bible, yet it was prophetic when written. The angel's words cover events from approximately 529 B.C. to 164 B.C., and we will see how they were exactly fulfilled. They also cover just-as-certain events, which will be fulfilled in the seven-year Tribulation to come.

The Law of Double Reference

As we look at the next passage in Daniel, we need to understand the prophetic *law of double reference*. This very important principle means simply that two events, widely separated as to the time of their fulfillment, may be brought together into the scope of one prophecy. "This was done," says Dwight Pentecost, "because the prophet had a message for his own day as well as for a future time. By bringing two widely separated events into the scope of the prophecy, both purposes could be fulfilled."[5]

R. B. Girdlestone explains it this way:

> Yet another provision was made to confirm men's faith in utterances which had regard to the far future. It frequently happened that prophets who had to speak of such things were also commissioned to predict other things which would shortly come to pass; and the verification of these latter predictions in their own day and generation justified men in believing the other utterances which pointed to a more distant time. The one was practically a "sign" of the other, and if the one proved true the other might be trusted. Thus the birth of Isaac under the most unlikely circumstances would help Abraham to believe that in his seed all the families of the earth should be blessed.[6]

Daniel's vision in chapters 10–12 is a prophecy of double reference. It pertains to what will come in the near future as well as what will come to pass in the latter days. Chapter 11 contains a remarkable example of prewritten history. The angel explained exactly what would happen in Greece, Egypt, and Syria during the years between the Old and New Testaments. When you read Daniel's prophecy and compare it to world history, you'll see why prophecy should never be confused with allegory or metaphor.

Many Bible scholars speak of the intertestamental period as a time of silence, but God was not at all silent about this time period. He predicted the course of human events, described the nations that would oppress the children of Israel for generations to come, and foretold the rise of a ruler, Antiochus Epiphanes, who would be a picture or "type" of the prince spoken of in Daniel's vision of seventy weeks. Antiochus Epiphanes, however, was by far the lesser of two evils.

These two antichrists mentioned in Scripture are perpetually confusing to the evangelical community. Antiochus Epiphanes is the first antichrist about which Daniel wrote, making his appearance on the stage of world history from 175 to 164 B.C. The second antichrist to which Daniel referred is the Antichrist who will appear in the latter days following the rapture of the church. This illustrates the prophetic law of double reference.

Because we are primarily concerned about events of the Tribulation, let me summarize the now historical events included in this vision:

Four additional Persian kings would rule after Cyrus, and the fourth would be the richest of them all (Dan. 11:2). This actually happened, and Xerxes, the king who married Esther, was the wealthiest of the four.

"A mighty king" shall stand up (v. 3). This was Alexander the Great of Greece.

This king would be uprooted, and his kingdom divided into four pieces and given to people not of his posterity (v. 4). Alexander died at age thirty-two, and his kingdom went to his four generals.

"The king of the South shall become strong, as well as one of his princes" (v. 5). One of the generals, Ptolemy, began a dynasty in Egypt, while Seleucus did the same in Syria.

"They shall join forces" (v. 6). Egypt and Syria made an alliance in 250 B.C., after both generals had died. Ptolemy II gave his daughter Berenice in marriage to the grandson of Seleucus, Antiochus II. Two years later, however, Ptolemy II died, and Antiochus II divorced

Berenice and remarried his former wife, Laodice. Laodice then poisoned Antiochus and had Berenice killed. She appointed her son, Seleucus II, to the throne.

"But from a branch of her roots one shall arise in his place" (v. 7). Back in Egypt, Berenice's brother, Ptolemy III, now ruled. He invaded Syria and revenged his sister's death by executing Laodice. To save his own neck, Seleucus II ran away from the trouble.

"And he shall also carry their gods captive to Egypt" (v. 8). Ptolemy III carried away tons of Syrian plunder, including 4,000 talents of gold, 40,000 talents of silver, and 2,500 golden idols.

"The king of the North shall come" (v. 9). Seleucus II attempted to counterattack Egypt, but was killed. He was succeeded by his son Antiochus III.

"And the king of the South shall be moved with rage" (v. 11). The next few verses describe continuing warfare between Egypt and Syria. In 198 B.C. Antiochus III won control of Palestine at a battle outside Sidon. In 193 B.C. Antiochus gave his daughter Cleopatra (not the famous Cleopatra) in marriage to Ptolemy V. He hoped Cleopatra would foster Syrian interests in Egypt, but Cleopatra turned out to be a loyal wife—just as Daniel had predicted (v. 17).

"After this he shall turn his face to the coastlands" (v. 18). Antiochus III joined with Hannibal and together they invaded Greece, but in 188 B.C. Roman warriors drove them out of their newly acquired territory.

"There shall arise in his place one who imposes taxes" (v. 20). Seleucus IV ruled in his father's stead, but was soon murdered by his own prime minister.

Antiochus Epiphanes, a Picture of the Antichrist

Antiochus Epiphanes was the youngest son of Antiochus III, and the angel told Daniel that he was a "vile person." He would take the throne with an agenda of peace, the angel predicted, and "seize the kingdom by intrigue" (v. 21). Let's look at the complete scriptural portrait of this historical character:

> And in his place shall arise a vile person, to whom they will not give the honor of royalty; but he shall come in peaceably, and seize the kingdom by intrigue. With the force of a flood they shall be swept away from before him and be broken, and also the prince of the covenant. And after the league is made with him he shall act deceitfully, for he shall come up and become strong with a small number of people. He shall enter peaceably, even into the richest places of the province; and he shall do what his fathers have not done, nor his forefathers: he shall disperse among them the plunder, spoil, and riches; and he shall devise his plans against the strongholds, but only for a time. (Dan. 11:21–24)

Harold Willmington tells us that Antiochus Epiphanes was nicknamed *Epimanes*, a word meaning "madman," by those who knew him best. Apparently he pretended to be a second-century Robin Hood, stealing from one party and doling plunder out to others.[7]

> He shall stir up his power and his courage against the king of the South with a great army. And the king of the South shall be stirred up to battle with a very great and mighty army; but he shall not stand, for they shall devise plans against him. Yes, those who eat of the portion of his delicacies shall destroy him; his army shall be swept away, and many shall fall down slain. Both these kings' hearts shall be bent on evil, and they shall speak lies at the same table; but it shall not prosper, for the end will still be at the appointed time. (Dan. 11:25–27)

In 170 B.C., Antiochus Epiphanes defeated the Egyptian king Ptolemy Philometor at a battle east of the Nile Delta. Ptolemy lost the battle because he was betrayed by counselors who sat at his own dinner table (v. 26).

While returning to his land with great riches, his heart shall be moved against the holy covenant; so he shall do damage and return to his own land. At the appointed time he shall return and go toward the south; but it shall not be like the former or the latter. For ships from Cyprus shall come against him; therefore he shall be grieved, and return in rage against the holy covenant, and do damage. So he shall return and show regard for those who forsake the holy covenant (vv. 28–30).

Antiochus advanced in a second military campaign against Egypt, but was stopped by Roman ships sailing from Cyprus. In his fury, he turned toward Palestine, breaking his peace treaty with the children of Israel. He wooed and flattered Jews who were willing to "forsake the holy covenant."

"And forces shall be mustered by him, and they shall defile the sanctuary fortress; then they shall take away the daily sacrifices, and place there the abomination of desolation" (v. 31).

Armed with information from spies, Antiochus came against Jerusalem in 171 B.C. In a violent rage of frustration, he murdered more than forty thousand Jews and sold an equal number into slavery. He took away the daily sacrifice from the temple (Zerubbabel's temple, which had been erected by the returned exiles on the Temple Mount), offered the blood of a pig upon the altar, and set up an image of Jupiter to be worshiped in the holy place.

The Origin of Hanukkah

Ever wonder where the Jewish holiday of Hanukkah originated? You'll find the answer in Daniel's prophetic timeline and in the history of Antiochus and his blasphemy upon the Temple Mount.

Antiochus began his anti-Jewish campaign on September 6, 171

B.C., and continued until December 25, 165, when Judas Maccabeus restored true worship in the temple. This accounts for the 2,300 days of Daniel 8:14.[8] Chanukah, or Hanukkah, the eight-day festival that the children of Israel celebrate on the twenty-fifth day of the Hebrew month of Kislev, commemorates the victory of Judas Maccabeus and his followers over the forces of Antiochus Epiphanes. According to Talmudic legend, when the Hasmoneans recaptured and cleansed the temple, they were able to find only a single cruse of oil with the high priest's seal, sufficient for only one day's lighting of the menorah. But a miracle occurred, and the menorah burned for eight days.[9]

> Those who do wickedly against the covenant he shall corrupt with flattery; but the people who know their God shall be strong, and carry out great exploits. And those of the people who understand shall instruct many; yet for many days they shall fall by sword and flame, by captivity and plundering. Now when they fall, they shall be aided with a little help; but many shall join with them by intrigue. And some of those of understanding shall fall, to refine them, purify them, and make them white, until the time of the end; because it is still for the appointed time. (Dan. 11:32–35)

In this portion of Daniel's prophecy we can see that the years ahead were to be a time of great suffering. Gentile nations would continue to batter the nation of Israel—Syria from the north, Egypt from the south, Rome from the west. Many people would fall away from the faith and try to immerse themselves in the predominant culture. Others would remain faithful to the God of Abraham, Isaac, and Jacob. Those people, like the Maccabees, would be strong and "carry out great exploits." Some would fall and get up, being purged, refined, and strengthened as the end of time approaches.

Antiochus Epiphanes	The Antichrist
(Dan. 11:21–35)	(Dan. 11:36–39; 8:23–26)
A vile person	The man of sin
Works through intrigue	Works through intrigue
Is a warrior	Honors the god of "fortresses" or military might
Defiles the temple	Will defile the temple
Known as a peacemaker	Will destroy with peace
Was destroyed and defeated	Will be utterly defeated

Prophecy of the Willful King

Then the angel took Daniel over a prophetic gap of time. He moved from foretelling the future about Antiochus Epiphanes to speaking about a man who is very much like that pagan Syrian. The angel began to speak of the Antichrist, and Daniel dutifully recorded the description:

Then the king shall do according to his own will: he shall exalt and magnify himself above every god, shall speak blasphemies against the God of gods, and shall prosper till the wrath has been accomplished; for what has been determined shall be done. He shall regard neither the God of his fathers nor the desire of women, nor regard any god; for he shall exalt himself above them all. But in their place he shall honor a god of fortresses; and a god which his fathers did not know he shall honor with gold and silver, with precious stones and pleasant things. Thus he shall act against the strongest fortresses with a foreign god, which he shall acknowledge, and advance its glory; and he shall cause them to rule over many, and divide the land for gain. (Dan. 11:36–39)

No doubt Daniel realized that he had heard about this willful prince before. He had seen the Antichrist in his vision of the four beasts (Dan. 7), heard the man speaking pompous words, and watched until the beast was slain, "its body destroyed and given to the burning flame" (Dan. 7:11).

Daniel had also learned about the Antichrist in his vision of the ram and goat. Here the angel told Daniel:

> A king shall arise,
> Having fierce features,
> Who understands sinister schemes.
> His power shall be mighty, but not by his own power;
> He shall destroy fearfully,
> And shall prosper and thrive;
> He shall destroy the mighty, and also the holy people.
> Through his cunning
> He shall cause deceit to prosper under his rule;
> And he shall exalt himself in his heart.
> He shall destroy many in their prosperity.
> He shall even rise against the Prince of princes;
> But he shall be broken without human means.
> And the vision of the evenings and mornings
> Which was told is true;
> Therefore seal up the vision,
> For it refers to many days in the future. (Dan. 8:23–26)

Just like Antiochus Epiphanes, the Antichrist will make his debut upon the stage of world history with hypnotic charm and charisma. In Revelation 13:1, John described him: "Then I stood on the sand of the sea. And I saw a beast rising up out of the sea, having seven heads and ten horns, and on his horns ten crowns, and on his heads a blasphemous name."

This man, the Antichrist who lives in the eschatology of all three major world religions, will make Antiochus Epiphanes look like a choir boy. He will walk over the ancient streets of Jerusalem and gloat because he is treading triumphantly over the streets of the City of God.

Nine
Satan's Messiah

Just as we do not question the sincerity of the sentiments of others toward their holy sites in Jerusalem, we expect that others will not question the Jewish people's deep, awesome attachment to Jerusalem and its holy sites—from which we will never again be parted.

—*Shlomo Ben-Ami, Israeli foreign minister* [1]

It is not up to Israel to decide who will be sovereign over the Old City's shrines. It is a Muslim, Christian, and Arab decision.

—*Yasser Arafat, responding* [2]

As the battle over Jerusalem continues, one man will step in to find a peaceful solution—the Beast. Notice that in Daniel's vision of the Antichrist, the Beast rises from the sea—the sea, in prophetic symbolism, represents the gentile world. He will come from the European Union or a country or confederation that was once part of the Roman Empire, which stretched from Ireland to Egypt and included Turkey, Iran, and Iraq. In Daniel's vision of the four beasts, the fourth beast had ten horns that represented ten kingdoms (Dan. 8:19–25). The "little horn" sprouted from among the other ten, which we know are ten divisions of the old Roman Empire.

I find it interesting that he will come from the European Union and be a man of "fortresses," or military might. Until the year 2000, the European Union had no military, but now they are not only organizing an army, but also considering a peacekeeping action . . . in Jerusalem.

In his rise to power, the Antichrist will weave his hypnotic spell first over one nation in the ten-kingdom federation, then over all ten. He will conquer three of the ten nations, hence the seven heads and ten crowns of John's vision, then assume primacy over all of them. He may well be doing this during the time right before the Rapture or during the time of the Gog-Magog war. The Bible tells us that after his position is secure in the ten-nation federation, he will turn his ravenous eyes toward the apple of God's eye—Israel.

While Israel is cleaning up after the terrible destruction of the war with Russia and its Arab allies, it is quite likely that this man will sense an opportunity to catapult himself onto the world's stage. He will already have amalgamated his power in Europe, but here, in Israel, is his chance to become a world peacemaker.

The Antichrist will be a man who has "paid his dues" in the military and the political arenas, and many will willingly follow him. He will rule over those in his federation with absolute authority and will do as he pleases (Dan. 11:36).

We also know the Antichrist will enter the world stage with a reputation of being a powerful man of peace. Perhaps he will be a Nobel Peace Prize winner. He will defeat and merge three kingdoms. Daniel 8:25 says that by peace he "shall destroy many." He will step in and guarantee peace for Israel and the Middle East, which won't be difficult after Russia's Pan-Islamic military juggernaut is destroyed. After all, those who have eyes to see have just realized that God Himself defends Israel (Ps. 125:1–2).

But you can dangle the truth right before some people, and they won't believe it. Even after Israel's miraculous deliverance, millions of people will prefer to believe that mankind can solve the problems. They'll credit Israel's deliverance to a fluke, a force of nature, or technology. And when this international peacemaker steps in to offer a seven-year treaty guaranteeing the peace of Israel, he will be applauded, lauded, and hailed as the Messiah—a false messiah, the world's new Caesar.

First John 2:18 boldly declares, "Little children, it is the last hour; and as you have heard that the Antichrist is coming, even now many antichrists have come, by which we know that it is the last hour." The Antichrist—capital *A*—is coming. Though many people through the years have been against Christ, there is coming a man who is the devil incarnate, the son of Satan, evil personified.

The Antichrist's three-point plan for world domination consists of a one-world economic system in which no one can buy or sell without a mark sanctioned by the Antichrist's administration, a one-world government, and a one-world religion that will eventually focus its worship on the Antichrist himself.

The One-World Economy

As our present economy shudders and sways above a crumbling foundation of global instability, the Antichrist will step in and end all our problems. What could make more sense than a global monetary system? When Brazil devalues its currency, investors in America lose millions, so why not establish a currency that will bring parity to all nations?

The European Union has implemented a European monetary system. *Time* magazine notes, "One month after the latest monetary crisis, Cabinet officers, legislators, and bankers on both sides of the Atlantic are intensely debating a lengthening list of ideas" for developing "a global financial system." Bank of America has advertised the slogan, "The whole world welcomes world money."

The Antichrist's economy will be a cashless society in which every financial transaction can be electronically monitored. John, writing in the book of Revelation, described the situation: "He causes all, both small and great, rich and poor, free and slave, to receive a mark on their right hand or on their foreheads, and that no one may buy or sell except one who has the mark or the name of the beast, or the number of his name" (Rev. 13:16–17).

A cashless society may be presented as a foolproof way to end theft or to control drug lords, or as the ultimate shopping convenience. If you want to go to the grocery store, you can simply pass your hand—in which a microchip has been inserted under the skin—beneath a computer scanner. The amount of your purchase will instantly be deducted from your bank account.

This scenario doesn't sound nearly as far-fetched as it did in my father's day. My bank offers a debit card; today I don't need money to go to the grocery store. Everything is scanned these days, from library cards to thumbprints, and it doesn't require a great leap of imagination to see how this cashless, computerized system of buying and selling will be placed into operation. A day is coming when you will not even be able to buy a pack of gum without the proper approval, without having a chip in your hand or forehead.

The computer revolution has placed this phenomenal accomplishment well within our grasp. We have become accustomed to being managed by our "numbers." We cannot deduct our children on our income tax forms unless they have a Social Security number. We give our phone numbers to a representative from a catalog company, and the salesclerk can find our address, sales history, and past purchases in an instant.

American politicians are now talking about implementing a national identity card, ostensibly to control illegal aliens. Our government is putting on a full-court press that will ultimately give it the power to control cash transactions.

I believe the main reason the Antichrist will cause everyone to receive what is known as the "mark of the beast" is to crush all who worship the God of Abraham, Isaac, and Jacob. If he cannot personally have the joy of controlling or killing them, he will have the satisfaction of knowing they will starve to death. Without his mark, no one will be able to buy a loaf of bread or a drop of milk. Believers may not be able to buy homes or make rent payments. They may not be able to hold jobs.

The One-World Government

Never in history has one government completely ruled the world, but the false man of peace will "devour the whole earth" (Dan. 7:23). He will rule over the people by their own consent and with absolute and total authority (Dan. 11:36). His personality will be marked by great intelligence, persuasiveness, subtlety, and craft. His mouth will speak "pompous words" (Dan. 7:8), and he will be a "master of intrigue" (Dan. 8:23 NIV). He will be the world's most prominent, powerful, and popular personality.

The world—which no longer will have the true church sprinkled throughout its nations—will not hesitate to give this man its full attention. The Antichrist will be free to set up his one-world government, but there's nothing new about his new world order! Satan has been scheming to institute one ever since Nimrod proposed to build a mighty tower on the plains of Shinar. The purpose of what we know as the Tower of Babel was to defy God's authority on earth—to cast God out and institute the government of man.

God commanded men to "be fruitful and multiply, and fill the earth" (Gen. 9:1); however, the people of that day had a different idea: "Now the whole earth had one language and one speech. And it came to pass, as they journeyed from the east, that they found a plain in the land of Shinar, and they dwelt there . . . And they said, 'Come, let us build ourselves a city, and a tower whose top is in the heavens; let us make a name for ourselves, lest we be scattered abroad over the face of the whole earth'" (Gen. 11:1–2, 4). God endured the builders' brashness for a limited time, then He scattered them across the earth.

After World War I, "the war to end all wars," President Woodrow Wilson crafted the League of Nations to uphold peace through a one-world government. Adolf Hitler told the German people he would bring a "new order" to Europe. He did, dragging Europe into the bowels of a living hell and turning the streets crimson with rivers of human blood.

The Communists of the former Soviet Union pledged to institute a new world order and erected an atheistic empire that collapsed like a house of cards. Now the United Nations wants to establish a new world order!

What does it mean? Brock Chisolm, former director of the United Nations World Health Organization, said, "To achieve world government, it is necessary to remove from the minds of men their individualism, loyalty to their families, national patriotism, and religion."

Think about it. After the Rapture, after the Gog-Magog war of Ezekiel 38–39 when every nation experiences terrible earthquakes, after nuclear war falls even upon nations not directly involved in the conflict, what hopes and ideals will remain to support mankind? True religion will be reduced to a dying ember—it will flame again, but not for a while. National patriotism will be trampled in the weariness of devastation. Loyalty to families may still exist, but even today it is waning. Our families are so fractured that family loyalty seems a thing of the past. And individualism? What's the point?

I believe simple apathy may be the prime force that will draw men to the Antichrist. As men and nations struggle to pick up the pieces after the Rapture and the terrifying Gog-Magog war, they will look to one who promises peace, economic prosperity, and simple government. Why not hand him the reins of control?

The Antichrist's One-World Religion

What is the Antichrist's chief desire? He is a false christ. Satan knows the prophecy that one day every knee will bow before Jesus Christ, but so great is his hatred toward God that he's determined to lash out at God by keeping as many people from salvation as possible. Satan thinks he can defeat the Lord God! During the Antichrist's limited time on earth, he wants to be worshiped. But he will proceed carefully, solidifying his positions in religion and politics, maintaining his false front as a global peacemaker.

Nowhere will he be more careful and diplomatic than in Jerusalem. The Jewish temple will be rebuilt in the Holy City either shortly before or during the Antichrist's rise to power. During the first three and one-half years of the time of Tribulation, the Antichrist will allow the Jewish people to resume making daily sacrifices in the temple. They will rejoice, and many of them may believe him to be their Messiah.

In A.D. 1200, Moses Maimonides, a Jewish rabbi who wrote part of the Talmud, prophesied about the temple of the last days: "In the future, the Messianic king will arise and renew the Davidic dynasty, restoring it to its initial sovereignty. He will rebuild the Beis Ha Mikdash [the temple] and gather in the dispersed remnant of Israel."[3]

It could very well be that Maimonides was prophesying about Jesus and the millennial temple, but thousands of Jews may read this prophecy and link it with the Antichrist who has promised peace and allowed them to resume daily temple sacrifices.

As we've already discussed, the Temple Institute in Jerusalem has created the implements necessary for temple worship to be reinstated exactly as in the days of Moses. Every detail in every instrument and every fabric for the priests' clothing has been replicated as they prepare to again make sacrifices in the temple.

After the war of Gog-Magog, the hearts of the children of Israel will turn toward the God of Abraham, Isaac, and Jacob. In a surge of reawakening religious interest, they will rebuild the temple. In a public show of support, the Antichrist will praise these endeavors.

The Second Seal: The Rider on the Red Horse

Shortly after the opening of the first seal, John the Revelator saw Jesus break the second seal: "Another horse, fiery red, went out. And it was granted to the one who sat on it to take peace from the earth, and that people should kill one another; and there was given to him a great sword" (Rev. 6:4).

Under the red horseman, anarchy will reign as societies break down, the haves rioting against the have-nots. The Antichrist's "peace" will be false and short-lived, for the second seal will propel the world toward increasing violence. I believe the rider on the red horse will instigate actual warfare between countries as well as violence between man and his neighbors. Remember the condition of the earth—there are no Christians, and much of the world may be recovering from damage inflicted by nuclear fallout from the Gog-Magog war. As the rider of the red horse takes peace from the earth, people will kill one another on battlefields, in subways, on highways, in cities, in country fields. Such concepts as common decency and human kindness will fade to vague memories from another age. Nation will rise against nation; man will rise against his friend; children will rise against their parents. As cities turn into armed camps and nations hurl weapons at one another, the world will fall under a cloud of hopelessness and despair.

Remember the apocalyptic visions of a future world in movies such as *Mad Max* and *Blade Runner*? Welcome to the world under the red horseman.

The Third Seal: The Rider on the Black Horse

John looked again and saw "a black horse, and its rider was holding a pair of scales in his hand. And a voice from among the four living beings said, 'A loaf of wheat bread or three loaves of barley for a day's pay. And don't waste the olive oil and wine'" (Rev. 6:5–6 NLT).

Fact: in 1995, for the third year in a row, the world produced less food than it ate, and its "carry-over" stocks of emergency grain supplies sank to a record low. Lester Brown, president of the Worldwatch Institute, says we may now be witnessing a shift in the world's food economy "from a long-accustomed period of overall abundance to one of scarcity."[4]

Make no mistake, famine is on its way. The color of the black horse symbolizes the deep mourning that will fall upon the people of the earth as the third seal is broken. As a result of war and God's mighty hand, the world will be stricken with a famine unlike anything in its past.

Listen to the prophet Jeremiah describe death by famine:

Now their appearance is blacker than soot;
They go unrecognized in the streets;
Their skin clings to their bones,
It has become as dry as wood.
Those slain by the sword are better off
Than those who die of hunger;
For these pine away,
Stricken for lack of the fruits of the field. (Lam. 4:8–9)

While the Antichrist keeps himself aloof from the trouble, while violence and war wreak havoc in every nation, men, women, and children will begin to die of starvation. You'll notice that the rider of the black horse is told not to touch the wine and the olive oil.

The wine and oil symbolize luxuries enjoyed by wealthy people. The rich will be able to obtain food and luxuries during this time, but middle-class and poor people will not.

The Fourth Seal: The Rider on the Pale Horse

As John the Revelator watched, Jesus opened the fourth seal. A living creature beckoned John to "come and see."

"I looked," John wrote, "and behold, a pale horse. And the name of him who sat on it was Death, and Hades followed with him. And power was given to them over a fourth of the earth, to kill with sword, with hunger, with death [pestilence], and by the beasts of the earth" (Rev. 6:8).

Notice that Death and Hades rode together. J. Vernon McGee explained the pairing: "While Death takes the body, Hades is the place where the spirit of a lost man goes."[5]

Incredible! One-fourth of the earth's population will die as the rider on the pale horse goes forth. As anarchy, war, and famine continue, two new factors will be added to the scenario: pestilence and wild animal attacks. One agent could account for both—biological warfare. For the same reason a rabid raccoon will attack almost anything in its path, a biological or chemical attack could affect animals so that they lose their natural fear of man and attack without provocation.

Dr. Frank Holtman, head of the University of Tennessee's Bacteriological Department, said, "While the greater part of a city's population could be destroyed by an atomic bomb, the bacteria method might easily wipe out the entire population within a week."[6]

The prophet Ezekiel foretold the path of the pale rider: "For thus says the Lord GOD: 'How much more it shall be when I send My four severe judgments on Jerusalem—the sword and famine and wild beasts and pestilence—to cut off man and beast from it?'" (Ezek. 14:21).

Notice that the order of the first four seals exactly follows Jesus' prediction about the beginning of the Tribulation: "For nation will rise against nation and kingdom against kingdom [the red horse]. And there will be famines [the black horse], pestilences [the pale horse], and earthquakes in various places. All these are the beginning of sorrows" (Matt. 24:7–8).

The Fifth Seal: Prayers of the Martyrs

When Jesus opened the fifth seal, John saw under the altar:

> the souls of those who had been slain for the word of God and for the testimony which they held. And they cried with a loud voice, saying, "How long, O Lord, holy and true, until You judge and avenge our blood on those who dwell on the earth?" Then a white robe was given to each of them; and it was said to them that they should rest a little while longer, until both the number of their fellow servants and their brethren, who would be killed as they were, was completed. (Rev. 6:9–11)

The martyrs under the altar are those who will be beheaded by the Antichrist in the first three and one-half years of the Tribulation. They will be martyred in Daniel's seventieth week, between the Rapture and the fifth seal, for the same reason John was on the isle of Patmos (Rev. 1:9–10). Notice that they are conscious and fully aware, not in "soul sleep."

The Sixth Seal: Nature Revolts

Jesus broke the sixth seal, and John recorded:

> Behold, there was a great earthquake; and the sun became black as sackcloth of hair, and the moon became like blood. And the stars of

heaven fell to the earth, as a fig tree drops its late figs when it is shaken by a mighty wind. Then the sky receded as a scroll when it is rolled up, and every mountain and island was moved out of its place. And the kings of the earth, the great men, the rich men, the commanders, the mighty men, every slave and every free man, hid themselves in the caves and in the rocks of the mountains, and said to the mountains and rocks, "Fall on us and hide us from the face of Him who sits on the throne and from the wrath of the Lamb! For the great day of His wrath has come, and who is able to stand?" (Rev. 6:12–17)

John described what seems remarkably like a meteor shower colliding with the earth. Scientists tell us that a huge meteor would result in an explosion much like a nuclear bomb, accompanied by enormous tidal waves, hurricanes moving at six hundred miles per hour, the speed of sound, and months of darkness, caused by thick clouds of dust.[7] Astronomers predict that the earth's next close brush with a meteor will be in 2126 when the comet Swift-Tuttle comes near, but I believe God could bring a comet any time He chooses to accomplish His purposes.

The Seventh Seal: Silence in Heaven

Just before the seventh seal was broken, John heard that 144,000 children of Israel, 12,000 from each tribe, were sealed. Terrible judgment was about to fall on the earth, and if they were not sealed and divinely protected, they would not escape.

These are the children of Israel who will spread the gospel throughout the entire world during the Tribulation. Notice that in Matthew 24, when Jesus described the Tribulation, He mentioned the martyrs (v. 9), false prophets (v. 11), and this great evangelistic team: "And this gospel of the kingdom will be preached in all the world as a witness to all the nations, and then the end will come" (v. 14).

Next John saw a great multitude of Gentiles who came out of

the Tribulation. They were clothed in white robes, and John was told that they came "out of the great tribulation, and washed their robes and made them white in the blood of the Lamb" (Rev. 7:14).

They are those who will be executed by the Antichrist during the Tribulation for "the word of their testimony, and they did not love their lives to the death" (Rev. 12:11). People will come to Christ during the Tribulation. They will hear the gospel preached by angels flying through the heavens, saying, "Fear God and give glory to Him, for the hour of His judgment has come; and worship Him who made heaven and earth" (Rev. 14:7). They will refuse to take the mark of the Antichrist, and they will be killed.

Perhaps the Antichrist will charge them with treason. Perhaps he will condemn them for following what he calls "a dead religion for dead people." In any case, these martyrs will die for their faith, and their souls will wait in heaven until the Lord's purpose is complete.

Next, Jesus, the Judge of the earth, stepped forward and broke the seventh seal. A solemn, tense hush fell over the assembly, and the silence lasted for "about half an hour" (Rev. 8:1).

It was not a hesitation or moment of indecision. It was the lull before the storm. The host of heaven saw what God was preparing to do, and they stood in absolute awe, total silence, of the coming divine annihilation of men on earth. The Great Tribulation, when the full fury of the Lamb is unleashed, is coming next.

The Antichrist Reveals His Character

Let's look back and see what Daniel had to say about these latter days and the evil man who will influence them:

> Then the king shall do according to his own will: he shall exalt and magnify himself above every god, shall speak blasphemies against the God of gods, and shall prosper till the wrath has been

189

accomplished; for what has been determined shall be done. He shall regard neither the God of his fathers nor the desire of women, nor regard any god; for he shall exalt himself above them all. (Dan. 11:36–37)

The Antichrist shall do "according to his own will," or as he pleases. If he has counselors, they are mere window dressing, for in the end he will do only what he wants to do. Compare his example to that of Jesus, the One he imitates. Jesus said, "I can of Myself do nothing. As I hear, I judge; and My judgment is righteous, because I do not seek My own will but the will of the Father who sent Me" (John 5:30). In the Garden of Gethsemane, Jesus prayed, "O My Father, if it is possible, let this cup pass from Me; nevertheless, not as I will, but as You will" (Matt. 26:39).

The Antichrist will not only be willful, but Daniel told us he will not regard the "desire of women." This phrase could mean several things. First, and most obvious, it could mean that he will care nothing for the company of women—he will not possess normal desires for love, sex, and marriage. He may be a homosexual, or given that Daniel was writing in a pagan culture that exalted everything from gods of war to gods of childbirth, it may mean that the Antichrist will not honor the gods of men or those traditionally favored by women.

In examining the context of these verses, some prophecy scholars interpret this phrase to mean that the Antichrist will not regard the desire of Hebrew women to be the mother of the Messiah. The Messiah had not yet come at the time of Daniel's writing, and nearly every Hebrew woman yearned to be the mother of the One who would bring salvation to Israel. Daniel might have been saying, "He shall honor neither the true God, nor the coming Messiah, nor any god at all."

Though the Antichrist will come to the forefront of world events under a banner of peace and tolerance, he will quickly reveal his true colors. He will begin to persecute those who do not accept the mark that would allow them to buy and sell in the world markets, and he will portray those who refuse to swear allegiance to him as anarchists and dangerous subversives. His campaign of terror will escalate as he begins to criticize Bible-based worship in all its forms. He will promote a one-world religion and New Age concepts tolerant of all except Christians and Jews. The Antichrist will stop the daily sacrifice in the temple at Jerusalem, and he will demand that *he* be worshiped.

The Antichrist Cult on the Temple Mount

Jerusalem is a monument to the faithfulness of God. The psalmist wrote,

> Those who trust in the LORD
> Are like Mount Zion,
> Which cannot be moved, but abides forever.
> As the mountains surround Jerusalem,
> So the LORD surrounds His people
> From this time forth and forever. (Ps. 125:1–2)

Jerusalem is a living testimonial to all believers. We are sheltered in the arms of God, just as Israel is cradled by the mountains and defended by God Himself.

Knowing all this, the Antichrist will decide to center his religious cult in Jerusalem, in the very heart of the temple itself. He knows full well that his actions are an affront to holy God and His chosen people, the Jews.

Jesus confirmed that Satan's messiah would demand worldwide worship in Jerusalem. He said,

> "Therefore when you see the 'abomination of desolation,' spoken of
> by Daniel the prophet, standing in the holy place" (whoever reads,

let him understand), "then let those who are in Judea flee to the mountains." (Matt. 24:15–16)

The Antichrist's Cohort—the False Prophet

The Antichrist will not be alone in his diabolical deeds. He will have an assistant who is as thoroughly committed to evil as he is.

Remember this principle—Satan loves to mimic God's truth. He will continue doing so until the end of the age, and he will be particularly active during the last days.

The Antichrist will be part of a perverted satanic trinity that functions in much the same way as the Father, Son, and Holy Spirit. Satan, the "first person" of this triune partnership, will supply power to the Antichrist, who will be aided by the devilish False Prophet.

And he [the False Prophet] deceives those who dwell on the earth by those signs which he was granted to do in the sight of the beast, telling those who dwell on the earth to make an image to the beast who was wounded by the sword and lived. He was granted power to give breath to the image of the beast, that the image of the beast should both speak and cause as many as would not worship the image of the beast to be killed. (Rev. 13:14–15)

The image of the Antichrist will be made to speak like a man. When it does, most people will bow and worship on the spot. Anyone who has ever been to Disney World and its Hall of Presidents will tell you that the creation of a lifelike talking statue is no big deal. Either this statue possesses powers beyond what we're accustomed to, or the lesson here is the same lesson Daniel and his three friends learned in Nebuchadnezzar's court. If you'll recall that story, Nebuchadnezzar had his craftsmen create a golden image of himself, ninety feet tall and nine feet wide. Then he commanded the people to fall down and worship it whenever they heard the musical cue (Dan. 3). Shadrach, Meshach, and Abed-Nego refused to bow and soon found themselves enjoying the roaring welcome of a fiery furnace. But God delivered them from the flames, sending His own Son to keep the young men company. Nebuchadnezzar was rightfully astonished, and he praised the Hebrews by saying, "Blessed be the God of Shadrach, Meshach, and Abed-Nego, who sent His Angel and delivered His servants who trusted in Him . . . [because they would] not serve nor worship any god except their own God!" (Dan. 3:28).

In the same way, the False Prophet will erect an image or statue of the Antichrist, and everyone will be commanded to worship it. And just as He did generations ago, God will deliver those who refuse to bow.

To fully understand the Antichrist's agenda, we must grasp Satan's overall strategy. His goal is to "be like the Most High" (Isa. 14:14). He wants, in fact, to *dethrone* the Most High. Prior to the dawn of time, Satan, the most perfect angelic being ever created, convinced one-third of the angels to join him in his reckless attempt to overthrow God as the ruler of all. Though he was decisively defeated in a supernatural war, Satan has continued in open opposition to God, seeking every possible opportunity to lash out and attempt to destroy, deceive, or discredit what is important to Him.

The very name *antichrist* reveals Satan's agenda. The Greek prefix *anti-* has two meanings. The first is the most obvious: "against." The second is far more interesting, for *anti-* also means "in place of." Both definitions apply here. Satan and his unholy conspirators are against God and seeking to take His place.

Since Satan and his demons know what the Word of God says about their ultimate doom, why do they persist in this futile endeavor? Part of the answer undoubtedly lies in their evil, spiteful characters. Perhaps they truly believe they can alter their destiny and dethrone God Almighty. After all, Satan's defining sin is pride.

I believe one of Satan's purposes in the Tribulation is to imitate the worldwide rule of God in the golden era of peace. During the time of Great Tribulation, Satan may feel he has the best shot he has ever had at usurping God's place. But though Satan seeks to impose a world government, the Antichrist will spend this half of the Tribulation fighting off one challenge after another. He will never fully succeed in claiming the world as his own.

Let's compare the two world rulers—Satan in the Tribulation, and Jesus in the Millennium:

The Antichrist will reign through seven years of war, violence, and chaos, but Jesus will rule a world of peace and prosperity.

The Antichrist offers eternal damnation for those foolish enough to worship him, while Jesus offers eternal salvation to those who trust Him.

The False Prophet testifies of the Antichrist and enforces allegiance to him through threats, deception, and ruthless aggression, while the Holy Spirit testifies of Jesus and provides comfort, joy, and strength to those who trust the Savior.

When Satan seeks to impose a world religion, a "great multitude no one can count" rejects him and recognizes Jesus as the Messiah.

While the Antichrist offers temporal salvation (the ability to buy and sell) to those who follow him, Jesus offers eternal salvation to those who trust Him.

The Wounding

At some point in the Great Tribulation, the Antichrist will appear to be fatally wounded, perhaps by an assassination attempt, but he will not die. John said, "I saw one of his heads as if it had been mortally wounded, and his deadly wound was healed. And all the world marveled and followed the beast" (Rev. 13:3).

The prophet Zechariah called the Antichrist a "worthless shepherd" and told us that he will be wounded in the right eye and have a blind eye:

Woe to the worthless shepherd,
Who leaves the flock!
A sword shall be against his arm
And against his right eye;
His arm shall completely wither,
And his right eye shall be totally blinded. (Zech. 11:17)

It's entirely possible that an attack on the Antichrist will leave him with a withered arm and a blind eye. His wound will be so severe that any other man would die, but the Antichrist will not. He will emulate the death and resurrection of Jesus Christ. Just as he entered the stage of world prophecy riding a white horse to imitate Christ, he will also appear to die and miraculously rise again.

The Number of a Man

In Daniel, the Antichrist is the "little horn" of chapter 7, the "king of fierce features" of chapter 8, the "prince who is to come" of chapter 9, and the "willful king" of chapter 11. John the Revelator gave us another way to identify him: "Here is wisdom. Let him who has understanding calculate the number of the beast, for it is the number of a man: His number is 666" (Rev. 13:18).

"The number of a man," according to Bible scholars, is *six*. Under Old Testament law, man's labor was limited to six days, for God commanded man to rest on the seventh day. The seventh day is God's day, and throughout the Scripture, seven is the number of divine completeness. Six falls short of seven, just as anything done by created beings falls short of the Creator's perfection.

The Antichrist's number, 666, could represent the satanic trinity: Satan, the Antichrist, and the False Prophet. For just as six falls short of seven, Satan falls short of being God the Father, the Antichrist falls short of being God the Son, and the False Prophet falls short of being God the Holy Spirit.

Another explanation for the Antichrist's number lies in the ancient Jewish practice of gematria. As the apostle John wrote Revelation, he certainly knew that his readers were familiar with this practice, which involves substituting letters for numbers. The letters of the alphabet designated certain numbers in the same way that Roman numerals represent numbers. It would be a simple matter for members of the early church to convert a number into a name or a name into a number.

In Revelation 13:18, John made it possible for the world to identify the Antichrist by the number 666. This cryptic puzzle is not intended to point a finger at some unknown person. It is, however, intended to confirm someone already suspected of being the Antichrist.

This information is of no practical value to the church because we will be watching from the balconies of heaven by the time this lawless ruler is revealed. But for those of you reading this book after the church has been taken away, you should be able to confirm which personality arising out of a European federation is the devil incarnate, the son of Satan.

During the late 1930s and early 1940s, a flurry of pamphlets identified Adolf Hitler as the Antichrist. Others declared that Mussolini was the Antichrist because of his close relationship to Rome.

In his book *Is the Antichrist Alive and Well?*, Ed Hindson lists several world leaders who have been suspected of being the Antichrist. The list includes Kaiser Wilhelm, Joseph Stalin, Nikita Khrushchev, John F. Kennedy, Mikhail Gorbachev, Ronald Wilson Reagan (nominated because he had six letters in each of his three names), Saddam Hussein, and Bill Clinton, with Hillary as the False Prophet.[8] But no one can possibly know who the Antichrist is because he will not make his appearance upon the world stage until the church has been removed.

This so-called man of peace, this false messiah, is probably alive

Christ	The Antichrist
Christ came from heaven (John 6:38).	The Antichrist will come from hell (Rev. 11:7).
Christ came in His Father's name (John 5:43).	The Antichrist will come in his own name (John 5:43).
Christ humbled Himself (Phil. 2:8).	The Antichrist will exalt himself (2 Thess. 2:4).
Christ was despised and afflicted (Isa. 53:3).	The Antichrist will be admired and lauded (Rev. 13:3–4).
Christ came to do His Father's will (John 6:38).	The Antichrist will come to do his own will (Dan. 11:36).
Christ came to save (Luke 19:10).	The Antichrist will come to destroy (Dan. 8:24).
Christ is the Good Shepherd (John 10).	The Antichrist will be the evil shepherd (Zech. 11:16–17).
Christ is the truth (John 14:6).	The Antichrist will be "the lie" (2 Thess. 2:11).
Christ is the "mystery of godliness," God manifested in the flesh (1 Tim. 3:16).	The Antichrist will be the "mystery of lawlessness," Satan manifested in the flesh (2 Thess. 2:7–9), the living son of Satan.

now and may even know his predestined demonic assignment. Though we do not know who he *is*, we certainly know what he will *do*.

The Antichrist Reveals His Agenda

The Antichrist will care only about exalting himself. He will set up his image in the city of Jerusalem and demand that the nations of the world worship him—or face death by decapitation (Rev. 20:4). Daniel made it clear that the temple offerings stop three and one-half years (1,290 days) before the end of the Tribulation. Why? Just like his forerunner, Antiochus Epiphanes, the Antichrist will introduce idolatrous worship inside the holy temple and set himself up as God:

> He will make a treaty with the people for a period of one set of seven [seven years], but after half this time, he will put an end to the sacrifices and offerings. Then as a climax to all his terrible deeds, he will set up a sacrilegious object that causes desecration, until the end that has been decreed is poured out on this defiler. (Dan. 9:27 NLT)

Paul also understood what would happen during the time of Great Tribulation:

> He [the Antichrist] will exalt himself and defy every god there is and tear down every object of adoration and worship. He will position himself in the temple of God, claiming that he himself is God . . . And you know what is holding him back, for he can be revealed only when his time comes. (2 Thess. 2:4, 6 NLT)

The Antichrist will speak so artfully, with such graceful deception, that those who heard the gospel and rejected it before the Rapture will be caught up in his lies. Paul told us,

The coming of the lawless one is according to the working of Satan, with all power, signs, and lying wonders, and with all unrighteous deception among those who perish, because they did not receive the love of the truth, that they might be saved. And for this reason God will send them strong delusion, that they should believe the lie, that they all may be condemned who did not believe the truth but had pleasure in unrighteousness. (2 Thess. 2:9–12)

The son of Satan will be a counterfeit of the Son of God. But we learn even more about the personality and plan of the Antichrist by understanding how completely opposite he is from Jesus. (See chart on p. 207.)

The Two Witnesses

The Antichrist will be impeded, however. Along with a multitude of people who refuse to submit to his program, God will send two witnesses who will be thorns in his side. Many Bible scholars believe that the two witnesses who will appear on the earth during the Tribulation are Elijah and Enoch or Elijah and Moses (Rev. 11:1–15). I do not believe we can be dogmatic about who they are, for John didn't identify them, but there is a biblical basis for believing they could be Elijah and Moses.

The prophet Malachi wrote about the last days: "Behold, I will send you Elijah the prophet before the coming of the great and dreadful day of the LORD" (4:5). Over the years, tradition has added the practice of "looking for Elijah" to the Jews' observance of the Passover Feast. On the seder table you will also find a special cup set for Elijah. Because the prophet is supposed to return as a forerunner of the Messiah, a cup is poured for him in the hope that he will appear, thus speeding the Messiah's appearance. Jesus Himself referred to this prophecy when He said, "Elijah is coming first and will restore all things" (Matt. 17:11).

Moses is a possible candidate for one of the two witnesses for several reasons. First, the miracles the witnesses perform are similar to those Moses enacted during the Exodus. Second, some have suggested that Satan's effort to claim Moses' body (Jude 1:9) may have been motivated in part by his desire to prevent Moses' appearance at the Transfiguration and as one of these two witnesses. Moses is also given the nod by some scholars because he appeared with Elijah at the Transfiguration (Matt. 17:3).[9]

Whoever they are, these two witnesses will be filled with the Holy Spirit. They will preach the gospel and perform great miracles for three and one-half years. They will have the power to perform miracles, call down fire from heaven, and proclaim drought on the earth. They will be supernaturally protected until their mission is complete, then the Antichrist will kill them, leaving their bodies exposed for the world to see.

Scripture tells us that their dead bodies will literally lie in a street of Jerusalem for three and a half days. The entire world, via television, will see their bodies and rejoice. No one will suggest that they be given a proper burial. Human decency and kindness are not to be found in Satan's kingdom, and they certainly won't be found in the Antichrist's Jerusalem. The bodies of the two witnesses will lie in the gutter like dead animals while "those who dwell on the earth will rejoice over them, make merry, and send gifts to one another, because these two prophets tormented those who dwell on the earth" (Rev. 11:10).

Perhaps the witnesses will die during Christmas, so the gift sending and receiving is part of those festivities. With no Christians to reinforce the *real* meaning of Christmas, the holiday will become totally pagan. I can just see a husband and wife toasting each other before a tinsel-draped fireplace, waiting for Santa and watching CNN's display of two dead bodies in the street. "Christmas came early for us this year," the newscaster says in a voice-over. "We finally got rid of those two cursed prophets! Glory to our leader, and happy holidays to all!"

But after three and a half days, God will raise His prophets from the dead and take them to heaven. Before the unblinking eye of television cameras, they will stand to their feet, brush the dust and dried spittle from their rough garments, and lift their faces to heaven. The sky will thunder with a loud voice saying, "Come up here!" and up they'll go, courtesy of a heavenly cloud.

In that same hour there will be a great earthquake, and a tenth of Jerusalem will fall. Seven thousand people will be killed, but the trembling survivors will recognize the power of God.

The Seventh Seal Leads to Seven Trumpets

When He opened the seventh seal, there was silence in heaven for about half an hour. And I saw the seven angels who stand before God, and to them were given seven trumpets . . . So the seven angels who had the seven trumpets prepared themselves to sound. (Rev. 8:1–2, 6)

The seventh seal inaugurates the seven trumpet judgments of Revelation 8:7–9:21, which are reminders of the ten plagues God poured out on Egypt (Ex. 7–11). The first four judgments will affect the natural world; the last three will affect the unredeemed people of the earth. Everyone except the 144,000 Jewish evangelists will be subject to the plagues of the trumpet judgments. The horror heralded by the first six trumpets is beyond comprehension, but the seventh trumpet announces the glory of the kingdom of Christ, which is to come.

In the Old Testament we learn that God commanded that trumpets be used for calling the congregation together, either to go to war or to sound an alarm. In Numbers 10:9, we read, "When you go to war in your land against the enemy who oppresses you, then you shall sound an alarm with the trumpets, and you will be remembered before the LORD your God, and you will be saved from your enemies."

J. Vernon McGee said, "As the trumpets of Israel were used at the battle of Jericho, so the walls of this world's opposition to God will crumble and fall during the Great Tribulation."[10] Amen!

The Trumpet Judgments

At the beginning of the Great Tribulation, the angels of heaven will blow the trumpets against the earth ruled by the Antichrist. They will be sounding an alarm and a warning, for God will be about to pour out the full fury of His wrath.

"The first angel sounded: And hail and fire followed, mingled with blood, and they were thrown to the earth. And a third of the trees were burned up, and all green grass was burned up" (Rev. 8:7).

This first judgment will be against the earth itself. Burning hail will destroy one-third of all plant life—trees, shrubs, grass, forests, gardens, parks. God used water, a flood, in His first judgment against the earth; in this judgment He will use fire. Plants were the first life-forms to be created; they will be the first to be destroyed.[11]

"Then the second angel sounded: And something like a great mountain burning with fire was thrown into the sea, and a third of the sea became blood. And a third of the living creatures in the sea died, and a third of the ships were destroyed" (vv. 8–9).

Another natural disaster will strike as God moves His mighty hand. A massive meteor will strike the earth, causing tidal waves and vast pollution that will contaminate our oceans.

I don't know if you've seen a red tide before, but when it strikes beaches, hundreds of thousands of dead fish wash up on the shore, polluting the water for miles. This judgment will be far worse than a case of red tide; it will be the supernatural act of a wrathful God. One-third of all living creatures in the sea—dolphins and sharks, jellyfish and squid, microscopic plankton and great whales—will die, as well as any unfortunate sailors out on the ocean.

"Then the third angel sounded: And a great star fell from heaven, burning like a torch, and it fell on a third of the rivers and on the springs of water. The name of the star is Wormwood. A third of the waters became wormwood, and many men died from the water, because it was made bitter" (vv. 10–11).

The second trumpet will affect the salt water of the oceans. The third trumpet will affect *fresh* water, without which human life cannot exist. Chronic water shortages already affect 40 percent of the world's population, and when the angel poisons the waters, the situation will become dire. "Water wars" between countries over shared lakes and rivers could break out, with the Holy Land and northeast Africa being the most dramatically affected areas. According to Washington's Worldwatch Institute, many of the skirmishes between Israeli settlers and Arabs have been exacerbated by the conflict over water rights.[12]

When I last talked with General Ariel Sharon in Israel, he told me the Six-Day War of 1967 began over a water issue. Israeli intelligence discovered that Syria had bulldozers trying to reroute the three rivers that feed the Sea of Galilee. If the water could be rerouted, the Sea of Galilee, Israel's only source of fresh water, would dry up. Result? No water for crops, livestock, or human consumption. Such a situation would produce economic disaster, famine, and death. Israel went to war instantly!

If water is such an urgent concern now, can you imagine how horrible the situation will be when Wormwood pollutes one-third of the world's fresh water?

"Then the fourth angel sounded: And a third of the sun was struck, a third of the moon, and a third of the stars, so that a third of them were darkened. A third of the day did not shine, and likewise the night" (Rev. 8:12).

Like the heavy darkness that fell upon Egypt when Pharaoh made the lives of the Jewish people harsh with bitter bondage, darkness will cover the earth when the fourth angel sounds his trumpet. In

Matthew 24:29, Jesus predicted that the heavens would declare the Tribulation: "Immediately after the tribulation of those days the sun will be darkened, and the moon will not give its light; the stars will fall from heaven, and the powers of the heavens will be shaken."

Whether from supernatural provision or the result of the fire, the hail, and the meteor, God will allow a veil of thick fog to dim the light of sun, moon, and stars. He will not totally blot out sunshine and starshine, for He specifically promised,

> While the earth remains,
> Seedtime and harvest,
> Cold and heat,
> Winter and summer,
> And day and night
> Shall not cease. (Gen. 8:22)

God will keep His covenant with man. The earth will still know day and night, but it will be darkened under a black cloud that brings humanity deep depression and unspeakable emotional torment.

"And I looked, and I heard an angel flying through the midst of heaven, saying with a loud voice, 'Woe, woe, woe to the inhabitants of the earth, because of the remaining blasts of the trumpet of the three angels who are about to sound!'" (Rev. 8:13).

The angel warned that the judgments brought by the next three trumpets will be far worse than the others. The first four were judgments upon creation; the next three terrors will be judgments on mankind.

Three Trumpets of Terror

Then the fifth angel sounded: And I saw a star fallen from heaven to the earth. To him was given the key to the bottomless pit. And he opened the bottomless pit, and smoke arose out of the pit like the smoke of a great furnace. So the sun and the air were darkened because of the smoke of the pit. Then out of the smoke locusts came upon the earth. (Rev. 9:1–3)

These unnatural, demonic locusts will be released from the very pit of hell to torment men. The "star fallen from heaven" is Satan himself, and he is given the authority to release these locusts upon the earth. Normal locusts eat plants, but these creatures will not. They will sting men who are not sealed with the seal of God. Their terribly painful sting will make men want to die, but they will not. For five months these locusts, led by their demonic king Abaddon, will torment men upon the earth (vv. 4–11).

John described the locusts as being like horses prepared for battle, their faces like the faces of men, their teeth like lions' teeth, and the sound of their wings like the sound of chariots with many horses running into battle (vv. 7–10). The scene will be one of unspeakable and unstoppable terror! The intelligent, spiritual beings will be capable of commands and following the demonic leadership of Abaddon. Some Bible teachers believe that these are helicopters, but they are not.

Then the sixth angel sounded: And I heard a voice from the four horns of the golden altar which is before God, saying to the sixth angel who had the trumpet, "Release the four angels who are bound at the great river Euphrates." So the four angels, who had been prepared for the hour and day and month and year, were released to kill a third of mankind. (Rev. 9:13–15)

The four angels who were bound at the Euphrates are evil angels, or they would not have been bound. But they will be loosed to kill one-third of mankind, and they will immediately commence their evil assault. With one-quarter of humanity already dead from hunger, pestilence, sword, and wild beasts (Rev. 6:8), these angels will lead a demonic army 200 million strong. John saw the hellish horsemen with "breastplates of fiery red, hyacinth blue, and sulfur yellow; and the heads of the horses were like the heads of lions; and out of their mouths came fire, smoke, and brimstone" (Rev. 9:17).

I do not know if these are physical horses or symbols of a future weapon, but I do find the color combination intriguing. Last year I picked up a *Newsweek* magazine and read an article on the European Union's new Euro dollar. In the picture, two men were dressed in colorful uniforms, and behind them a large circle, spangled with stars, displayed the emblem of the new currency.[13] The colors of their uniforms and the display? Hyacinth blue and yellow. Coincidence? I don't know. Perhaps the Antichrist will add his signature color, red, to the mix, and the horsemen of Revelation 9 will wear the official colors of his new world government.

More than one-half of the world's population will die in the Tribulation, yet the remainder will persist in idolatry, immorality, and rebellion against God (Rev. 9:20–21).

This demonic army will issue from the vicinity of the Euphrates River. J. Vernon McGee pointed out that this area has great spiritual significance:

> The Garden of Eden was somewhere in this section. The sin of man began here. The first murder was committed here. The first war was fought here. Here was where the Flood began and spread over the earth. Here is where the Tower of Babel was erected. To this area were brought the Israelites of the Babylonian captivity. Babylon was the fountainhead of idolatry. And here is the final surge of sin on the earth during the Great Tribulation.[14]

The Angel and the Little Book

An interlude will fall between the sixth and seventh trumpet judgments. In Revelation 10:1–11, John prophesied the completion of the mystery of God concerning the nation of Israel. God's kingdom on earth will be established, but at a high cost to those who reject Him.

At that point in his vision, an angel gave John a "little book" and cried with a loud voice. He was answered by seven thunders, but John was not allowed to write the words he heard. This part of his revelation is the only part that remains sealed.

The angel planted one foot on the land and one on the sea—claiming God's dominion over both—and swore by God the Creator that the seventh trumpet was about to sound, and the "mystery of God" would be finished. Then John was commanded to take the book from the angel's hand and eat it. "It will make your stomach bitter," he was told, "but it will be as sweet as honey in your mouth."

So John ate. To that point, he had seen the destruction of Gentiles, but from that point on, he would see judgment upon his own people. At the beginning of Revelation 11, an angel told John to measure the temple of God, the altar, and the worshipers. He added that the outer court had been given to the Gentiles, who "will tread the holy city underfoot for forty-two months" (Rev. 11:2).

The forty-two months correspond to the three and one-half years the Antichrist will control the temple (Dan 12:11).

The Seventh Trumpet

At the blowing of the seventh trumpet, loud voices in heaven cried out, "The kingdoms of this world have become the kingdoms of our Lord and of His Christ, and He shall reign forever and ever!" (Rev. 11:15). As the end of the Great Tribulation approaches, the world's suffering will be very nearly finished, and Jesus Christ will be ready to claim His kingdom.

The twenty-four elders on their thrones fell on their faces and worshiped God, saying,

We give You thanks, O Lord God Almighty,
The One who is and who was and who is to come,
Because You have taken Your great power and reigned.
The nations were angry, and Your wrath has come,
And the time of the dead, that they should be judged,
And that You should reward Your servants the prophets and the saints,
And those who fear Your name, small and great,
And should destroy those who destroy the earth. (Rev. 11:17–18)

The Three Angelic Evangelists

The three angels (Rev. 14:5–13) are heavenly beings who will be sent to preach the message of God's righteous judgment on all the nations of the earth. They will invite people to fear and glorify God before final judgment; they will announce the ultimate downfall of wicked Babylon, and they will warn against worshiping the Antichrist.

"How tragic," writes Harold Willmington, "that Christ, at Calvary, drank this cup of wrath for the very sinners now forced to drink it again."[15]

The Great Harlot

There is a vast difference between ignoring Scripture and interpreting Scripture. To ignore the prophetic teaching of Revelation 17 would be cowardly and irresponsible. But anyone who interprets Revelation 17 runs the risk of being labeled bigoted, extremist, and politically incorrect.

In the New Testament, we find a very clear presentation of an apostate church that professed Christ without *possessing* Him. In 1 Timothy 4:1, Paul wrote, "Now the Spirit expressly says that in latter times some will depart from the faith, giving heed to deceiving spirits and doctrines of demons." And in 2 Peter 2:1–2, the apostle Peter told us: "But there were also false prophets among the people, even as there will be false teachers among you, who will secretly bring in destructive heresies, even denying the Lord who bought them, and bring on themselves swift destruction. And many will follow their destructive ways, because of whom the way of truth will be blasphemed."

After the rapture of the true church, or believers in Christ, a church will still exist on the earth, but it will be an *apostate* church. Revelation 17:1 labels the heretic church of the last days as "the great harlot who sits on many waters." A harlot is an individual who has been unfaithful in her wedding vows. Here John portrayed an apostate church that professed to be loyal to Christ but in fact cleaved to idols and a false religious system. This is spiritual adultery.

The apostate church will wield worldwide influence. God Himself told John the interpretation of the phrase "many waters" as "peoples, multitudes, nations, and tongues" (v. 15). This is a worldwide false religious system.

In verse 2, we discover that this "great harlot" seduced "the kings of the earth," not just the general population. The kings of the earth "were made drunk with the wine of her fornication." They had been stupefied and mesmerized by the global religious system.

John further wrote, "So he carried me away in the Spirit into the wilderness. And I saw a woman [the great harlot] sitting on a scarlet beast which was full of names of blasphemy, having seven heads and ten horns" (Rev. 17:3). If you go back to Revelation 13:1, you will read, "Then I stood on the sand of the sea [the world]. And I saw a beast rising up out of the sea, having seven heads and ten horns." What we see in Revelation 17:3 and 13:1 is the same, so the beast the great harlot sits upon refers to the revived Roman Empire under the control of the Antichrist. John described a world where the apostate church and the Antichrist will join forces to rule the earth.

Beautiful but Deadly

In Revelation 17:4, John described the apparel of the great harlot: "The woman was arrayed in purple and scarlet, and adorned with gold and precious stones and pearls." She had the outward appearance of royalty; she was wearing gold and an array of jewels, symbolizing her unlimited wealth. In her hand was "a golden cup full of abominations and the filthiness of her fornication." To all outward appearances, the great harlot was beautiful, but the contents of her cup were poison to the nations of the world.

John identified the great harlot by saying,

On her forehead a name was written: MYSTERY, BABYLON THE GREAT, THE MOTHER OF HARLOTS AND OF THE ABOMINATIONS OF THE EARTH. (Rev. 17:5)

The word *mystery* in the New Testament refers not to something mysterious, but to some truth not previously made known by God to men. The mystery God is revealing is that in the last days there will be a worldwide apostate church that will reject Christ, dishonor God, and join forces with the Antichrist.

To identify Babylon, we must go to Genesis 10:8 and read about Nimrod, the arch-apostate of the postdiluvian world. Nimrod, who lived four generations after the Flood, is called "the mighty hunter before the LORD. And the beginning of his kingdom was Babel" (vv. 9–10). The word *Bab-el* means the "gate of God."

Nimrod's generation built the Tower of Babel for the purpose of casting God and His influence out of the earth. They proposed to build a great tower that would reach into heaven so they could have the benefits *of* God without submitting *to* God. In response to their presumptuous action, God confounded their language and scattered them over the earth.

This is the critical point—the first organized idolatrous religious system in the history of the world was introduced at Babel. That's why John called Babylon "the mother of harlots" (Rev. 17:5). Babylon was the birthplace of spiritual adultery. So the spiritual adultery of the end times is called by the name Babylon, the mother of harlots.

What will be the end of this great harlot? Look carefully at Revelation 17:16–17:

> The ten horns which you saw on the beast [the European confederation which will produce the Antichrist], these will hate the harlot, make her desolate and naked, eat her flesh and burn her with fire. For God has put it into their hearts to fulfill His purpose, to be of one mind, and to give their kingdom to the beast, until the words of God are fulfilled.

John was saying that in the middle of the Tribulation, members of the European confederation that arises from the old Roman Empire will realize they are mere puppets of the great harlot. The Antichrist, who rules over the confederation, will be content for a time to share his power, then he will turn on her and destroy her with a vengeance. By eliminating the false church, the Antichrist will be clearing the way for his own cult and his own worship.

The Sea of Glass and the Seven Vials

The last set of judgments described in Revelation comes with the seven vial, or bowl, judgments (Rev. 16:1–21). A vial is a bowl, and these seven bowls of fierce judgment will be poured out in rapid succession at the end of the Great Tribulation. Just as the seventh seal introduced the seven trumpet judgments, the seventh trumpet judgment introduces the seven bowl judgments, especially their final outcome. The bowl judgments are similar in kind to the trumpet judgments. But whereas the judgments of the trumpets are partial in their effects, the judgments poured from the bowls are complete and final. The seventh and last bowl presages the great Battle of Armageddon and foretells the final ruin of the Antichrist.

In Revelation 15:1–8, John the Revelator saw another seven angels preparing to pour out the seven last plagues. He described something "like a sea of glass mingled with fire" and told us that those who were victorious over the Beast were standing on the sea of glass, singing the song of Moses and the song of the Lamb. While John listened to their hymns of praise, the temple of the tabernacle in heaven opened and out stepped the seven angels, clothed in pure white linen, having their chests girded with golden bands.

Without any delay, the angels were commanded to pour out the bowls of God's wrath upon the earth. Terrible plagues followed one another in quick succession.

The first angel poured out "foul and loathsome" sores upon those who had the mark of the Beast (Rev. 16:1–2).

The second angel poured his bowl on the sea, and it became like the thick, coagulated blood of a dead man. Every living creature in the sea died (v. 3).

The third angel poured his bowl on the rivers and springs of fresh water, and they, too, became like blood. The angel of the waters made a telling comment:

> You are righteous, O Lord . . .
> For they have shed the blood of saints and prophets,
> And You have given them blood to drink.
> For it is their just due. (vv. 5–6)

The fourth angel poured his bowl on the sun, which began to burn hot enough to "scorch men with fire." Men cursed God, but they did not repent or give Him glory (vv. 8–9).

The fifth angel poured his bowl on the throne of the Beast, and his kingdom filled with dense darkness. His followers chewed their tongues in pain from the sores, the heat, and their thirst, but they did not repent (vv. 10–11).

The sixth angel poured out his bowl on the "great river Euphrates," and its waters dried up so the "kings of the east" could march across the dry riverbed and join God's other enemies for battle. At that time, three demons went forth to entice the kings of the world to gather at Armageddon. "You want a fight?" Satan was saying to God. "We're going to give You one" (vv. 12–16).

The seventh angel poured his bowl into the air, and a voice from heaven proclaimed, "It is done!" (v. 17). A mighty earthquake unlike any other shook the earth. Every city was destroyed; every mountain laid low. Every island vanished into the sea as seventy-five-pound hailstones (one talent weight) fell from the sky (vv. 18–21).

Yet men still continued to curse and blaspheme God.

The Reaping Angels

The reaping angels (Rev. 14:14–20) are angels who go forth at God's command to bring the wrath of God upon the unbelieving world. In this sneak preview of Armageddon, John saw that Christ will return to earth and, joined by these two reaping angels, will begin to harvest the earth with sharp sickles, resulting in a river of human blood two hundred miles long and as high as a horse's bridle.

The Old Testament prophets often spoke of the latter days in terms of harvest. Joel wrote,

> Put in the sickle, for the harvest is ripe.
> Come, go down;
> For the winepress is full,
> The vats overflow—
> For their wickedness is great. (3:13)

Isaiah 63, the passage that inspired "The Battle Hymn of the Republic," the glorious old song sung throughout the Civil War, shares Joel's vision of a vat of ripe grapes, ready to be trampled underfoot:

> Who is . . .
> This One who is glorious in His apparel,
> Traveling in the greatness of His strength? . . .
> Why is Your apparel red,
> And Your garments like one who treads in the winepress?
> "I have trodden the winepress alone,
> And from the peoples no one was with Me.
> For I have trodden them in My anger,
> And trampled them in My fury;
> Their blood is sprinkled upon My garments,
> And I have stained all My robes.
> For the day of vengeance is in My heart,
> And the year of My redeemed has come." (vv. 1–4)

This is no weak-wristed, smiling Jesus come to pay the earth a condolence call. This is a furious Christ, ready to confront the gathered armies of the world on a plain called Armageddon.

The first time He came to earth, He was the Lamb of God, led in silence to the slaughter. The next time He comes, He will be the Lion of the tribe of Judah, who will trample His enemies until their blood stains His garments, and He shall rule an age of peace with a rod of iron.

Jerusalem will receive its King.

Ten

The Final Peace Accord

General William Sherman defined war as hell, but the definition of a modern peace is far worse and unprintable. War is a terrible thing, but wars will continue until the caliber of our statesmen equals the caliber of our guns.

I have a foolproof plan for world peace—let all nations agree not to begin another war until the last one is completely paid for! Quite seriously, friend, let me assure you: peace will never come to Israel nor to the world until the world has a conference with the Prince of Peace.

War is the whip God uses to chastise rebellious nations, and the sword with which He delivers the oppressed. As you read the pages of the Old Testament, you can see how often Israel went to war. The prophet Jeremiah told the people of Israel that God would take them to war for a purpose:

> You are My battle-ax and weapons of war:
> For with you I will break the nation in pieces;
> With you I will destroy kingdoms. (Jer. 51:20)

God set Israel free from Egypt by crushing the Egyptian army beneath a wall of water. Next, the slashing swords of Joshua's men smashed Amalek. The spears of Israel cleared out the godless Canaanites. God used the blades of Israel as a surgeon uses his scalpel to cut out a cancer.

Jesus said, "You will hear of wars and rumors of wars. See that you are not troubled; for all these things must come to pass, but the end is not yet" (Matt. 24:6). In other words, war will be a way of life on earth until the end of time. Why? Because Satan is the god of this world, and his objective is to rob and kill and destroy. Men and nations under his control are driven like the swine of Galilee into the abyss of war.

But a day is coming, my friend, when we shall no longer worry about war. Jesus Christ will descend to the Mount of Olives, and with His army of saints He will destroy the Antichrist and all those who would oppress and oppose His chosen people. Then He will set up His kingdom, and the final peace accord, the *lasting* peace accord, will be instituted on earth.

What Lies Ahead for Israel?

God's megaphones came in human form. He chose righteous men to preach His message and proclaim prophecy. Zechariah was such a man. Born of priestly lineage, Zechariah lived during one of the most significant periods of upheaval in the saga of Israel. Struggling exiles returning from Babylon rebuilt the blackened ruins of Jerusalem and the temple. Zechariah knew God was getting ready to do a great thing. However, in writing to encourage the weary laborers, he also left us with vital clues to understand God's everlasting plan.

Zekar-yah, the prophet's name in Hebrew, means "God remembers." In fact, Zechariah's theme is that Israel will be blessed precisely because God remembers the covenants and agreements He made with the patriarchs. No one was better equipped to explore the mind of God than this walking symbol of the faithful memory of almighty God Himself.

The prophet bequeathed to us a simple statement that remains the most important guiding principle by which any nation or individual can live. Speaking to the Jewish people flowing back into their ancient homeland, Zechariah wrote, "For thus says the LORD of hosts: 'He sent Me after glory, to the nations which plunder you; for he who touches you touches the apple of His eye'" (2:8). If the prophet had written nothing but this one line, his contribution would be worthy of a special place in Scripture's hall of fame.

Through His prophets, God made sure the chosen people knew what was coming while the rest of the world was left wondering. Zechariah, for instance, wasn't surprised when he got the message about the future. Another prophet had already described what lay ahead for Israel. Isaiah foresaw the coming fall and conquest of the Hebrews by Babylonian hordes, and Isaiah gave Zechariah his first inkling of an astonishing divine surprise awaiting Jerusalem and the Jews.

As we talk about Israel and end times, one painful conundrum arises: How can Christians rejoice to think of the Lord's coming, knowing that it will bring not only joy, but also a time of great tribulation to Israel?

In his book *The End of Days: Fundamentalism and the Struggle for the Temple Mount*, Gershom Gorenberg often visits the painful problem. He quotes Chuck Missler, a Christian prophecy teacher, who told an evangelical crowd in Jerusalem that the coming Antichrist would betray Israel during the Tribulation:

> He'll issue in a time of trouble for Israel the likes of which have never occurred at that time, nor ever would happen again. And those words echo in our ears as we think of Auschwitz, Dachau, the horrors of Europe in the thirties and forties, and realize that what Jesus is saying is it's going to be worse next time around . . . So if we watch the Temple being positioned, on the one hand we're excited because God's plans are unfolding as He said they would. On the other hand, if you have friends, if you have a heart for Israel, you can't help but feel pain for them because they have no idea what's coming.

Gorenberg further says, "On the Christian side are those who want to 'bless' Israel, and provide it with what they believe is the fuse for Armageddon." He observes that the "Endtime drama" script "is somewhat rougher on Jews than on born-again Christians. In fact, the Christians will safely exit to the wings, while on stage, the Jews will find themselves at the center of the apocalypse."[1]

The truth of Bible prophecy is this: Israel and Jerusalem are about to enter a dark hour of suffering in which God personally comes to their defense (Ezek. 38–39). This hour of darkness will be followed by the Messiah and the golden age of peace, lasting one thousand years.

The apostle Paul wrote, "I consider that the sufferings of this present time are not worthy to be compared with the glory which shall be revealed in us" (Rom. 8:18).

Do you see? Heartbreak and sorrow and trial last only a short while, and this present earthly lifetime is only the blink of an eye in the span of God's eternity. The joy and the glory to come are worth the pain of today and what might come tomorrow.

Most thinking Christians are not indifferent to the suffering that will come during the Tribulation—that is one reason we are engaged in spreading the news of the gospel of Jesus Christ. And not only the Jews will suffer in the Tribulation; the entire *world* will suffer the effects of the judgments of God. The Antichrist will put the nations of the globe under his thumb, and everyone who does not take his mark and swear allegiance to his regime will be persecuted.

God will be faithful to His covenant people. The 144,000 Jews who are sealed as witnesses immediately after the Rapture will be granted divine protection so that they may be preserved during the time of Tribulation. God's judgment and wrath will be evident, yes, but so will His mercy. Once the church has been removed, God will act to bring the nation of Israel to faith in Him. The Holy Spirit, while not indwelling believers as He did in the church age, will move to convict and enlighten. The Jews will see miraculous signs of God's work—the destruction of Gog and Magog chief among them. The 144,000 will minister, and the two witnesses will walk the streets of Jerusalem and preach the need for repentance and salvation.

Yes, God will pour out His wrath upon the world, but the nation of Israel will be granted mercy in the form of signs, witnesses, and the ministry of the omnipresent Holy Spirit. If you've heard that the Holy Spirit will be inoperative during the Tribulation, think again! Jesus told Nicodemus that a man must be born of the Spirit in order to be saved (John 3:5–6), and He had that conversation with Nicodemus prior to the Spirit's descent at pentecost.

Let's not forget the benefits of suffering. The apostle Paul wrote, "We also glory in tribulations, knowing that tribulation produces perseverance; and perseverance, character; and character, hope" (Rom. 5:3–4).

Believers in God, including the Old Testament prophets, the New Testament saints, and contemporary Christians, have been persecuted throughout history. Millions of people have lost homes, health, and life itself for our Savior's sake, and persecution will not end with the Rapture.

But those who lose their lives in the Tribulation period will be rewarded. Read the explanation in Scripture:

> I saw thrones, and they sat on them, and judgment was committed to them. Then I saw the souls of those who had been beheaded for their witness to Jesus and for the word of God, who had not worshiped the beast or his image, and had not received his mark on their foreheads or on their hands. And they lived and reigned with Christ for a thousand years. (Rev. 20:4)

Jesus said that when we are persecuted, we should "rejoice and be exceedingly glad, for great is your reward in heaven, for so they persecuted the prophets who were before you" (Matt. 5:12).

What is this life, compared to the glory that awaits us in heaven? It is but the blink of an eye in the time of eternity.

God Blesses Those Who Bless Israel

In the Tribulation period, as now, God will extend His blessing to those who encourage, support, and bless Israel.

In Genesis, the Bible tells us that Jacob agreed to work seven years for Laban in order to earn the right to marry Laban's daughter Rachel. Aided by darkness and a heavy wedding veil, Laban deceived Jacob and gave his daughter Leah in marriage instead. Jacob was forced to work another seven years for Rachel's hand.

Over the course of those fourteen years, Laban changed Jacob's wages ten times and began to look with disfavor on him. Fearful of his future prospects, Jacob fled with Leah and Rachel, their children, and all their possessions. When Laban heard that Jacob had fled, he followed. When he finally caught up with his son-in-law, he asked why Jacob had left his camp. Jacob answered, "You have changed my wages ten times, each time to my hurt, and you deceived me into marrying your homely daughter."

Laban, Jacob's gentile employer, answered, "Please stay . . . for I have learned by experience that *the LORD has blessed me for your sake*" (Gen. 30:27, emphasis added). Laban knew from firsthand experience that God blessed Gentiles through the Jewish people.

Three times in Acts 10 the Bible declares that Cornelius, a Roman centurion who lived in Caesarea and gave alms to the Jewish people, was a man of "good reputation among all the nation of the Jews" (v. 22). Cornelius was a righteous man who benefited from the principle of "I will bless those who bless you." How did God bless him?

Soon after Christ's ascension to heaven, God gave the apostle Peter a vision of a prayer shawl descending from heaven held by the four corners. All manner of four-footed beasts and wild beasts and creeping things and fowls of the air crawled inside the prayer shawl. This vision broke down the religious barrier forbidding Jews from associating with Gentiles in spiritual matters.

Understanding the message of the vision, Peter went to the house of gentile Cornelius, preached the gospel, and rejoiced when those in Cornelius's household were saved: "While Peter was still speaking these words, the Holy Spirit fell upon all those who heard the word. And those of the circumcision [the Jews] who believed were astonished, as many as came with Peter, because the gift of the Holy Spirit had been poured out on the Gentiles" (Acts 10:44–45).

What made this possible? A Roman centurion—a Gentile— blessed the Jewish people, and God opened the windows of heaven and poured upon him and his house blessing he could not contain.

The principle of blessing the Jews is as applicable today as it was in Old and New Testament times. It will also be applicable in days to come, including the Tribulation and millennial kingdom.

Israel Will Know Great Joy

The Millennium will be a time of great rejoicing for God's people. Jesus Christ, the Lord of glory, will regather, regenerate, and restore faithful Israel. He will call the remnant hiding in Petra and welcome them back into Jerusalem.

Isaiah prophesied,

> For the LORD will comfort Zion,
> He will comfort all her waste places;
> He will make her wilderness like Eden,
> And her desert like the garden of the LORD;
> Joy and gladness will be found in it,
> Thanksgiving and the voice of melody . . .
> For you shall go out with joy,
> And be led out with peace;

The mountains and the hills
Shall break forth into singing before you,
And all the trees of the field shall clap their hands. (Isa. 51:3; 55:12)

We who have returned in the armies of heaven will follow our King as He revisits His promised land. The barren, devastated lands around Jerusalem will miraculously burst forth with new life as the Messiah passes by, and we will breathe in the scents of sweet jasmine, the rose of Sharon, and lily of the valley. The faithful Jews who have anticipated His coming will follow us, rejoicing in the arrival of their long-awaited Messiah. What a victory parade that will be!

Daniel 12:11–12 indicates there will be a period of seventy-five days between Christ's second coming and the institution of the millennial reign. Dr. S. Franklin Logsdon explains it this way:

We in the United States have a national analogy. The President is [ideally!] elected in the early part of November, but he is not inaugurated until January 20th. There is an interim of seventy-plus days. During this time, he concerns himself with the appointment of Cabinet members, foreign envoys and others who will comprise his government. In the period of 75 days between the termination of the Great Tribulation and the Coronation, the King of glory likewise will attend to certain matters.[2]

But before Christ establishes His millennial kingdom, a judgment must occur.

The Judgment of the Nations

After the defeat of the Antichrist, Jesus will sit down on His throne and begin to execute judgment. This is not the Great White Throne Judgment, at which every unbeliever will be judged for his deeds, but a judgment to judge the gentile nations of earth for the manner in which they treated the Jewish people and Israel (Gen. 12:1–3). Let's see how Jesus described it:

> When the Son of Man comes in His glory, and all the holy angels with Him, then He will sit on the throne of His glory. All the nations will be gathered before Him, and He will separate them one from another, as a shepherd divides his sheep from the goats. And He will set the sheep on His right hand, but the goats on the left. Then the King will say to those on His right hand, "Come, you blessed of My Father, inherit the kingdom prepared for you from the foundation of the world: for I was hungry and you gave Me food; I was thirsty and you gave Me drink; I was a stranger and you took Me in; I was naked and you clothed Me; I was sick and you visited Me; I was in prison and you came to Me." Then the righteous will answer Him, saying, "Lord, when did we see You hungry and feed You, or thirsty and give You drink? . . ." And the King will answer and say to them, "Assuredly, I say to you, inasmuch as you did it to one of the least of these My brethren, you did it to Me." Then He will also say to those on the left hand, "Depart from Me, you cursed, into the everlasting fire prepared for the devil and his angels: for I was hungry and you gave Me no food; I was thirsty and you gave Me no drink . . ." Then they also will answer Him, saying, "Lord, when did we see You hungry or thirsty or a stranger or naked or sick or in prison, and did not minister to You?" Then He will answer them, saying, "Assuredly, I say to you, inasmuch as you did not do it to one of the least of these, you did not do it to Me." And these will go away into everlasting punishment, but the righteous into eternal life. (Matt. 25:31–37, 40–42, 44–46)

This judgment is for Gentiles, who will be judged according to how they treated Jesus' "brethren," or the Jews, from the time of Genesis 12 to the judgment of the nations. God will judge Egypt and the Pharaoh that knew not Joseph for making the lives of the Jewish people bitter with harsh bondage. God will judge the Babylonians and the Persians. He will judge the Roman Church that decreed the Jews were "sons of the devil," that they could not own land, that they could not vote or hold public office, that they could not practice their professions, that they must wear distinctive clothing marking them as Jews, that they could not live with Christians, and that it was good form to kill the "Christ killers" during Holy Week.

During the Holy Inquisition, the bones of dead Jews were dug up and put on trial in Spain. When the dead Jews could not prove they were not heretics, their fortunes were confiscated by the Roman Catholic Church.

The British Empire will be called to the judgment bar for its White Paper Policies during World War II and before. As Hitler was killing 25,000 people a day, multitudes of Jews tried to escape. Yet the British White Paper Policy allowed only 5,000 Jews a year to immigrate to Israel. Israel, under control of the British, returned helpless Jews to Hitler's death camps. The British captured Jews sneaking into Israel in leaky ships. The British closed the gates of mercy on Jews trying to escape. Almighty God will remember their actions on this judgment day.

The PLO will answer for its terrorist activities, for bombs placed on public buses where children were killed. The group will answer for every kidnapping, every murder, every threat made against God's people.

The Gentiles who live during the Tribulation will answer for their treatment of the Jewish people. You will recall that during the Tribulation, God will seal a believing remnant of Israel, 144,000 strong, to witness during the entire seven-year period. In Matthew 24:14, Jesus told us that this remnant will preach the "gospel of the kingdom . . . in all the world as a witness to all the nations, and then the end will come." These believing Jews will be successful in their endeavors, for in Revelation 7:9–17, we see that a great multitude will be redeemed during the dark days of the Tribulation.

From a casual reading of Matthew's passage, you might think these Gentiles are being judged by their works—if they gave food and water to the ministering Jews, they will be allowed to obtain eternal life. This idea, however, contradicts the entire body of Scripture, for nowhere does God allow man to be saved through his own efforts. We are saved through faith in Jesus Christ, and our salvation *results* in good works. The acts of kindness and compassion detailed in Jesus' words are not the criteria upon which these people are judged, but *evidence* of the transformation of their hearts.

God will look at each individual who has come out of Tribulation terror and ask, "How did you treat the witness who came to visit you? Did you give him food and water and listen to his message? Or did you call the authorities and attempt to have him cast into prison?" I believe society will be so dark and dismal and paranoid that kindness and compassion will be found only in those whose hearts have been regenerated by the Spirit of God.

After this judgment, the "goats" will follow the Antichrist and the False Prophet into the lake of fire and brimstone. As they followed him in life, they will follow him in eternity. The "sheep" who know the Good Shepherd, Jesus, will follow Him to a glorious marriage feast.

Israel in the Kingdom of Peace

Though the subject is not often preached from Sunday pulpits, the Bible has much to say about the Millennium. It is known in Scripture as "the world to come" (Heb. 2:5), "the kingdom of heaven" (Matt. 5:10), "the kingdom of God" (Mark 1:14), "the last day" (John 6:40), and "the regeneration" (Matt. 19:28). Jesus told His disciples, "Assuredly I say to you, that in the regeneration, when the Son of Man sits on the throne of His glory, you who have followed Me will also sit on twelve thrones, judging the twelve tribes of Israel" (Matt. 19:28).

The golden era of peace was foreshadowed in the Old Testament by the Sabbath, a time of rest. A rest was to be observed after six work days, six work weeks, six work months, and six work years. In God's eternal plan, the earth will rest after six thousand years as well, as He ushers in the millennial kingdom of the Messiah.

The Millennium will be a time of rest for the people of God. Hebrews 4:8–9 tells us "for if [Jesus] had given them rest, then He would not afterward have spoken of another day. There remains therefore a rest for the people of God."

The prophet Isaiah echoed the thought:

> And in that day there shall be a Root of Jesse,
> Who shall stand as a banner to the people;
> For the Gentiles shall seek Him,
> And His resting place shall be glorious. (11:10)

During the golden era of peace, the geography of Israel will be changed. For the first time in history Israel will possess all the land promised to Abraham in Genesis 15:18–21. God promised Abraham that Israel would become a mighty nation, which has already come to pass, and that his seed would someday own the promised land forever (Gen. 12:7; 13:14–17).

Israel rightfully owns all the land God gave to Abraham by blood covenant, "from the river of Egypt to the great river, the River Euphrates," and "from the wilderness and Lebanon . . . even to the Western Sea" (Gen. 15:18; Deut. 11:24). Ezekiel 48:1 establishes the northern boundary of Israel as the city of Hamath; the southern boundary is established in Ezekiel 48:28 as the city of Kadesh. In modern terms, Israel rightfully owns all of present-day Israel, all of Lebanon, half of Syria, two-thirds of Jordan, all of Iraq, and the northern portion of Saudi Arabia. When Messiah comes, the seed of Abraham will be given that land down to the last square inch.

Not only will Israel's geography be enlarged, but it will be changed. The desert will become a fertile plain, and a miraculous river will flow east to west from the Mount of Olives into both the Mediterranean Sea and the Dead Sea. But it will be "dead" no longer!

Hear how Ezekiel described it:

When I returned, there, along the bank of the river, were very many trees on one side and the other. Then he said to me: "This water flows toward the eastern region, goes down into the valley, and enters the [Dead] sea. When it reaches the sea, its waters are healed. And it shall be that every living thing that moves, wherever the rivers go, will live. There will be a very great multitude of fish, because these waters go there; for they will be healed, and everything will live wherever the river goes. It shall be that fishermen will stand by it from En Gedi to En Eglaim; there will be places for spreading their nets. Their fish will be of the same kinds as the fish of the Great Sea, exceedingly many. (Ezek. 47:7–10)

Ezekiel described fishermen catching all the fish at En Gedi (a city on the Dead Sea) that can be caught in the Mediterranean Sea. Indeed, the Dead Sea shall live, as will everything during the millennial kingdom when the Giver of Life sits upon the throne of His father, King David.

Ezekiel also said there will be trees on each side of this river, flowing out of the Temple Mount, and John the Revelator further revealed that these trees will bear twelve kinds of fruit, one for each month of the year. The leaves of these trees are for the healing of the nations (Rev. 22:2). Isaiah told us that we will enjoy unparalleled health: "In that day the deaf shall hear the words of the book, and the eyes of the blind shall see out of obscurity and out of darkness" (29:18).

Zechariah also described the millennial kingdom of Israel:

And in that day it shall be
That living waters shall flow from Jerusalem,
Half of them toward the eastern sea
And half of them toward the western sea;
In both summer and winter it shall occur . . .
All the land shall be turned into a plain from Geba to Rimmon
south of Jerusalem. Jerusalem shall be raised up and inhabited in
her place from Benjamin's Gate to the place of the First Gate and
the Corner Gate, and from the Tower of Hananel to the king's
winepresses.
The people shall dwell in it;
And no longer shall there be utter destruction,
But Jerusalem shall be safely inhabited . . .
And it shall come to pass that everyone who is left of all the nations
which came against Jerusalem shall go up from year to year to worship the King, the LORD of hosts, and to keep the Feast of
Tabernacles. (14:8, 10–11, 16)

Jerusalem, the apple of God's eye, will become the joy of the
world, for Jesus will reign from the Temple Mount. The city will
become the international worship center, and people from all over
the world will make pilgrimages to worship in the temple. Kings,
queens, princes, and presidents shall come to the Holy City so "that
at the name of Jesus every knee should bow, of those in heaven . . .
and that every tongue should confess that Jesus Christ is Lord, to the
glory of God the Father" (Phil. 2:10–11).

Of the millennial kingdom the prophet Isaiah wrote,

> Awake, awake!
> Put on your strength, O Zion;
> Put on your beautiful garments,
> O Jerusalem, the holy city!
> For the uncircumcised and the unclean
> Shall no longer come to you. (52:1)

The prophet Micah also wrote of the millennial kingdom, and the poetry of his verse has inspired many a public building (including the United Nations headquarters) to be inscribed with a portion of his words. But Micah wasn't writing about the United Nations, London, or New York; the prophet was writing about God's millennial capital, Jerusalem:

> Now it shall come to pass in the latter days
> That the mountain of the LORD's house
> Shall be established on the top of the mountains,
> And shall be exalted above the hills;
> And peoples shall flow to it.
> Many nations shall come and say,
> "Come, and let us go up to the mountain of the LORD,
> To the house of the God of Jacob;
> He will teach us His ways,
> And we shall walk in His paths."
> For out of Zion the law shall go forth,
> And the word of the LORD from Jerusalem.
> He shall judge between many peoples,
> And rebuke strong nations afar off;
> They shall beat their swords into plowshares,
> And their spears into pruning hooks;
> Nation shall not lift up sword against nation,
> Neither shall they learn war anymore. (4:1–3)

The Holy City, now six miles in circumference, will occupy an elevated site and will be named *Jehovah Shammah*, meaning "the Lord is there" (Ezek. 48:35), and *Jehovah Tsidkenu*, meaning "the Lord our righteousness" (Jer. 33:16).

Can you imagine one thousand years of perfect peace? The earth will cease from strife, and the lion shall lie down by the lamb without even showing his claws! Satan will be bound in the bottomless pit, and earthly problems will fade away.

Jesus Christ Will Rule Jerusalem

God promised Abraham, "I will make you exceedingly fruitful; and I will make nations of you, and kings shall come from you" (Gen. 17:6). God was revealing how He planned to eventually rule over all the earth through a king of His appointment.

At the close of the first book of Moses, Jacob the patriarch called his twelve sons around his bed to give them a final blessing and to speak a prophetic word over each of them. His word over Judah was especially provocative:

> Judah, you are he whom your brothers shall praise;
> Your hand shall be on the neck of your enemies;
> Your father's children shall bow down before you . . .
> The scepter shall not depart from Judah,
> Nor a lawgiver from between his feet,
> Until Shiloh comes. (Gen. 49:8, 10)

The word *Shiloh* may be rendered "He whose right it is to rule." Jacob thus prophesied that a man who had the right to be king would come out of Judah's lineage.

In 2 Samuel 7:16, God made this promise to King David: "Your house and your kingdom shall be established forever before you. Your throne shall be established forever." There are three important words in this verse: *house, kingdom,* and *throne.* "Your house" designates the descendants of David who would sit on his throne. "Your kingdom" represents the kingdom of Israel. "Your throne" is David's royal authority, the right to rule as God's representative. Twice in this one verse God assured David that his dynasty, kingdom, and throne would last *forever.*

The gospel of Matthew opens with God breaking a silence of more than four hundred years. God proclaimed Jesus' royal lineage to Israel by saying, "The book of the genealogy of Jesus Christ, the Son of David, the Son of Abraham."

If Jesus Christ is the Son of Abraham, He is the One through whom all the families of the earth should be blessed (Gen. 12:3). If Jesus Christ is the Son of David, He is the One who has the right to rule. He is Shiloh!

The angel of the Lord appeared to the Virgin Mary and said,

> Do not be afraid, Mary, for you have found favor with God. And behold, you will conceive in your womb and bring forth a Son, and shall call His name JESUS. He will be great, and will be called the Son of the Highest; and the Lord God will give Him the throne of His father David. And He will reign over the house of Jacob forever, and of His kingdom there will be no end. (Luke 1:30–33)

Jesus Christ was born, lived as an observant Jew, and was crucified by the Roman government on a Roman cross. When He ascended to heaven, God the Father said to Him, "Sit at My right hand, till I make Your enemies Your footstool" (Matt. 22:44).

Jesus Christ will rule the Millennium because He alone is worthy. He will rule by heritage, by holy decree, and by divine appointment. Blessing and honor and glory and power be to Him who will sit on the throne of His father, David!

Israel Is Not Forgotten

We would be remiss if we thought the golden era of peace was nothing but a time of celebration and rest for Christians. In the Millennium, Israel and the Jewish people will enjoy a glorious, triumphant era.

We have already seen that Israel will receive great measures of mercy during the Tribulation period. When will the children of Israel welcome their Messiah? Look at Romans 11:25: "For I do not desire, brethren," Paul wrote, "that you should be ignorant of this mystery, lest you should be wise in your own opinion, that blindness in part has happened to Israel until the fullness of the Gentiles has come in." The word translated "fullness" is the Greek word *pleroma*. The word refers not to a numerical capacity, but to a sense of *completeness*.

"The completion of the mission to the Gentiles will result in, or lead to, Israel's 'fullness' or 'completion' (Rom. 11:12), her 'acceptance' (Rom. 11:15)," write scholars Walter C. Kaiser Jr., Peter H. Davids, F. F. Bruce, and Manfred T. Brauch in *Hard Sayings of the Bible*.

> Paul proclaims this future realization of God's intention as "a mystery" (Rom. 11:25) . . . The most instructive parallel to this text—which envisions the grafting of both Gentile and Jew into the same olive tree—is Ephesians 3:3–6, where Paul says that the content of the "mystery of Christ" is the inclusion of the Gentiles as fellow heirs of the promise with Jews in the new community of Christ's body.[3]

Bible scholars agree that Paul's statement that "all Israel will be saved" means Israel "as a whole," not every single individual. Just as the phrase "the fullness of the Gentiles" (Rom. 11:25) does not mean every single Gentile will accept Jesus as Messiah, even so, not every single child of Israel will place his faith in Christ. But when the "fullness of the Gentiles" has come and the church age is completed, then God will remove the Jews' blindness (Rom. 11:10) to the identity of Messiah, and "all Israel will be saved" (Rom. 11:26).

"What is also clear from the whole thrust of the discussion in Romans 9–11," write the authors of *Hard Sayings of the Bible*, "is that God's purposes for the salvation of Israel will be realized in no other way and by no other means than through the preaching of the gospel and the response of faith."[4] Israel, unsaved at the beginning of the Tribulation, will receive a multitude of witnesses and signs, so that individuals will experience salvation throughout the seven-year period and the nation will be saved at Jesus' return:

And so all Israel will be saved, as it is written:
"The Deliverer will come out of Zion,
And He will turn away ungodliness from Jacob;
For this is My covenant with them,
When I take away their sins." (Rom. 11:26–27)

The King and His Vice-Regent

Dr. Harold Willmington points out that though Jesus Christ will be supreme Ruler during the golden era of peace, some prophetic passages strongly suggest that He will be aided by a second in command: David, the man after God's own heart![5]

Let's look at the Scripture:

> But they shall serve the LORD their God,
> And David their king,
> Whom I will raise up for them. (Jer. 30:9)

Jeremiah wrote four hundred years after David's death, so he could not have been referring to David's earthly reign.

> I will establish one shepherd over them, and he shall feed them—My servant David. He shall feed them and be their shepherd. And I, the LORD, will be their God, and My servant David a prince among them. (Ezek. 34:23–24; see also 37:24–25)

> Afterward the children of Israel shall return and seek the LORD their God and David their king. They shall fear the LORD and His goodness in the latter days. (Hos. 3:5)

But King David won't be the only ruler. He will be assisted by the following:

233

- The church (1 Cor. 6:3)

- The apostles (Matt. 19:28)

- Nobles (Jer. 30:21)

- Princes (Isa. 32:1; Ezek. 45:8–9)

- Judges (Zech. 3:7; Isa. 1:26)

- Tribulation martyrs (Rev. 20:4)

- Lesser authorities (Zech. 3:7)[6]

If there is a lesson here for us, the waiting church, it is that those who are faithful now will be given greater responsibility in heaven. "Well done, good and faithful servant," Christ told the man who multiplied the talents he had been given, "you have been faithful over a few things, I will make you ruler over many things. Enter into the joy of your lord" (Matt. 25:23).

The Final Test of Peace

Millions of babies will be born during this thousand-year period of peace, and they will be babies just like you and I once were, prone to sin and bent toward trouble. Though the Christian parents who enter the Millennium will teach their children right from wrong, some of these children will exercise their free will to choose wrong.

Some of them, Zechariah told us, will "not come up to Jerusalem to worship the King, the LORD of hosts," so on them "there will be no rain" (14:17). Christ will have to rule with "a rod of iron" (Rev. 19:15).

Dr. René Pache explains the situation:

As beautiful as the Golden Era of Peace is, it will not be heaven . . . Sin will still be possible during the thousand years. Certain families and nations will refuse to go up to Jerusalem to worship the Lord.

Such deeds will be all the more inexcusable because the tempter will be absent and because the revelations of the Lord will be greater.[7]

Sin will still have a foothold in creation, and it must be eradicated. And at the end of the thousand-year reign of Christ, the final conflict between God and Satan will take place.

Unfortunately, just as men failed in previous ages, mankind will fail during this period too. Though many will obey Christ, others will rebel against God and His righteousness. At the end of the golden era of peace, Satan will be loosed from his prison, and thousands of people from all the nations of the earth will believe his lies and follow him. They will gather around Jerusalem, Christ's capital city, and wage a great war.

> Now when the thousand years have expired, Satan will be released from his prison and will go out to deceive the nations which are in the four corners of the earth, Gog and Magog, to gather them together to battle, whose number is as the sand of the sea. They went up on the breadth of the earth and surrounded the camp of the saints and the beloved city. (Rev. 20:7–9)

What will make these people follow Satan? Who can understand what drives men to sin? For those who are living in earthly bodies, even as we are now, the law of sin is like the law of gravity. No matter how much we want to rise above it, it draws us down. Only through the power of Christ can we rise above sin at all.

The Millennium will be a time similar to the Garden of Eden. In a perfect environment created by God, Adam and Eve chose to sin. Under ideal circumstances—an abundant earth, no sickness, and no war—the human heart will prove that it remains unchanged unless regenerated by the power of Christ. When Satan is loosed on the earth, many will turn their backs on the God who has sustained them and follow the evil one.

Notice that Revelation mentions Gog and Magog in this passage describing the final conflict, but this is not the same Gog-Magog war described in Ezekiel 38–39. J. Vernon McGee believed that "the rebellion of the godless forces from the north will have made such an impression on mankind that after one thousand years, the last rebellion of man bears the same label—Gog and Magog."[8] Just as we have called two conflicts World War I and World War II, the people may call this last battle Gog-Magog II.

These people will mount an army and advance against Jerusalem, where Jesus rules and reigns from the Temple Mount. There they will learn that rebellion always ends in destruction. To purge creation of the evil effects of sin finally and forever, God will destroy the earth with great heat and fire. Peter told us,

> The heavens will pass away with a great noise, and the elements will melt with fervent heat; both the earth and the works that are in it will be burned up . . . Nevertheless we, according to His promise, look for new heavens and a new earth in which righteousness dwells. (2 Peter 3:10, 13)

John wrote,

> And fire came down from God out of heaven and devoured them. The devil, who deceived them, was cast into the lake of fire and brimstone where the beast and the false prophet are. And they will be tormented day and night forever and ever. (Rev. 20:9–10)

Our enemy—the one who has tormented, tempted, and tested Christians for generations—will be permanently put away. He will enter hell for the first time—during the golden era of peace, he was chained in the bottomless pit, and today he roams the earth, seeking those he may lead into deception. But at the end of the Millennium, praise God, Satan the destroyer will receive God's permanent justice.

As judgment for sin, fire will come down from out of heaven and devour the millennial earth. The rebels who chose to side with Satan will be destroyed. God will bring an end to rebellion as all rebels, human and immortal, will face judgment and be confined to eternal hell and torment. And then God will create a new heaven and a new earth that will last for all eternity.

> "For as the new heavens and the new earth
> Which I will make shall remain before Me," says the LORD,
> "So shall your descendants and your name remain.
> And it shall come to pass
> That from one New Moon to another,
> And from one Sabbath to another,
> All flesh shall come to worship before Me," says the LORD.
> "And they shall go forth and look
> Upon the corpses of the men
> Who have transgressed against Me.
> For their worm does not die,
> And their fire is not quenched.
> They shall be an abhorrence to all flesh." (Isa. 66:22–24)

Stand by Jerusalem

The future of the Holy City is the centerpiece of God's blueprint for history. Make no mistake, God will reorder, restore, redouble, redistribute, reclaim, remove, renovate, recycle, recommit, and redeem until Jerusalem has become the crowning gem of all the cities on earth!

The Jews are God's covenant people and will remain so to the end of time. By divine agreement, Jerusalem was ordained to be Jehovah's everlasting city. The heavenly Father never intended the Holy City to be a divided municipality. Any individual, group, race, or country attempting to end Jewish control and carve up

Jerusalem streets is in direct opposition to the known will of God.

Consequently, Christians must stand with Israel in maintaining a unified status. Never has this stance been more important than in the present hour of continuing attack.

From out of the death camps of Europe and crematoriums of Auschwitz echoes the cry, "Never again!" The young nation of Israel was birthed around this conviction of fire and blood. It is now Christianity's turn to insist on the same mandate. With all our might we must resist any effort to partition the Holy City. Let our resolve be felt in the halls of Congress, through the corridors of the United Nations, and to every enemy of Israel. Never again will Jerusalem be divided!

Prophecy in the Second Psalm

I'd like to close with a teaching from Psalm 2, one of the many written by David, the warrior king after God's own heart. This is a prophetic and messianic psalm, and it holds keys to understanding the future of Jerusalem.

There are four speakers in this psalm:

- David speaks in verses 1–3.

- God the Father speaks in verses 4–6.

- God the Son speaks in verses 7–9.

- God the Holy Spirit speaks in verses 10–12.

Look at the first three verses:

> Why do the nations rage,
> And the people plot a vain thing?
> The kings of the earth set themselves,
> And the rulers take counsel together,

Against the LORD and against His Anointed, saying,
"Let us break Their bonds in pieces
And cast away Their cords from us."

The *nations* are the gentile, or non-Jewish, nations. *Rage* implies a violent hatred toward God, and the world *plot* refers to a battle in the mind. The godly use their minds to meditate upon God. The godless use their minds to consider how to get rid of God. Never has this been more evident than in today's world. This rebellion against God is premeditated. It is a plan conceived and carried out.

A certain youth pastor in Florida helps in a student-run prayer meeting before school. One day he noticed two adults in the room. They didn't say anything as the students watched a Christian music video and then took prayer requests. These two adults, a man and a woman, just sat with stony expressions.

The next week he learned that they were wiccans—witches! They had come to the meeting to observe the students and promptly went home to develop a plan for shutting down the volunteer, before-school prayer meeting. They went to the school principal and demanded that they be allowed to offer a meeting for witches!

Premeditated planning with godlessness as the goal. We are surrounded by people who despise the gospel!

Notice, too, that the psalmist wrote, "the kings of the earth set themselves, and the rulers take counsel together." The rulers gather by appointment. They come together in formal meetings and debate how they can do away with God.

In the coming months, friend, watch the United Nations closely. You may soon see a UN resolution that would deny Israel the right to its own sacred and capital city.

Why do the nations rage and people imagine a vain thing? Why do the kings of the earth and the rulers take counsel against the

Lord? This rebellion against God is not imposed on the masses—it is a popular, grassroots movement.

Do you doubt that godlessness has already taken hold in America? Look around! Look at the rock concerts, where thousands of young people flash satanic gestures, dress in black, and sing songs of violence and cruelty. Consider our mainline denominations, most of which deny that the Bible is the infallible, inerrant Word of God. Consider our Supreme Court, which took public prayer out of schools. Consider our schools. Consider our television programs, which revel in immorality and decadence.

Consider your life: Have you attempted to get rid of God? When you don't pray, you're living without God. When you ignore the reading of His Word, you're living apart from His guidance. When you willfully sin, you're thumbing your nose at His holy standards for your life. When you cherish and protect your hidden sin, you're attempting to get rid of God.

Notice that those who rage against God are against Him and His anointed, or Jesus Christ. They say, "Let us break Their bonds in pieces and cast away Their cords from us."

Men want to get rid of God's "cords and bonds," or the restraints the Bible places on society. We don't want God's morality; we want to create our own. We create new names for old sins and turn God's *covenant* love into a *convenient* love. We call abortion "choice." We call homosexual perversion "an alternate lifestyle." We call lying "fudging the truth." We call immorality "private behavior." We call fornication "free love." We call euthanasia "a good death" and infanticide "an alternative to a poor quality of life."

May heaven have mercy on us for our rebellion against God's authority! We've become adept at saving our ire for sin as *we* define it, not as God has defined it. Liberal theologians mock salvation by blood as "slaughterhouse religion," when the Bible clearly says that without the shedding of blood there is no remission for sin (Matt. 26:28; Heb. 9:22). What can wash away my sin? Nothing but the blood of Jesus!

Let's consider God's reaction to those who would rage against His standards and sacrifice:

He who sits in the heavens shall laugh;
The LORD shall hold them in derision.
Then He shall speak to them in His wrath,
And distress them in His deep displeasure:
"Yet I have set My King
On My holy hill of Zion." (Ps. 2:4–6)

God laughs! That's His answer to puny, ignorant people who have sworn to throw Him out of the affairs of men!

If you can remove God, then you can lasso the stars from the heaven, pull down the blazing sun at noon, and command the wind and waves. Jesus commanded the wind and waves, and He controls the sun and stars.

Man, for all his talents, is still man. God is God—eternal, almighty, and infallible. He is all-knowing, all-powerful, and holy. He is sitting in the highest heaven, adored by angels and worshiped by men. There is no one like Him!

When the last peal of God's chilling laughter dies away, it will be replaced by a tide of fearful, holy wrath. God will speak to man from a well of deep displeasure and determination. He says, "Yet"—after all this—"I have set My King on My holy hill"—the Temple Mount—"of Zion."

Notice that though God speaks of things to come, He uses the past tense. As far as He's concerned, Jesus' appearance on the Temple Mount is a done deal!

Now God's glorious Son speaks:

I will declare the decree:
The LORD has said to Me,
"You are My Son,

Today I have begotten You.
Ask of Me, and I will give You
The nations for Your inheritance,
And the ends of the earth for Your possession.
You shall break them with a rod of iron;
You shall dash them to pieces like a potter's vessel." (Ps. 2:7–9)

If there is any doubt that the "Son" is Jesus, all doubts are erased by Scripture. John the Revelator referred to this psalm in Revelation 12:5 when he wrote of a woman, representing Israel, who "bore a male Child who was to rule all nations with a rod of iron. And her Child was caught up to God and His throne."

Notice Jesus' *Sonship*. If all the atheists, humanists, Communists, New Agers, and satanists exerted all their power at one given moment, they would not have the power to change this fact: Jesus is God's Son! Despite the inscriptions on the walls of the Dome of the Rock that read "God is One and has never fathered a child," Jesus is God's Son!

Notice Jesus' *sovereignty*. God has promised to give Him anything He asks. In the temptation of Christ, Satan said, "Ask me for the kingdoms of the earth and I will give them to You," but Jesus refuted him with the Word of God.

What are you lacking today, and who are you asking to meet your needs? If you ask God for guidance, deliverance, healing, peace, salvation, and forgiveness, He will answer. The Bible says, "You do not have because you do not ask" (James 4:2).

Finally, notice Jesus' *severity*. In one moment the Antichrist will be strutting into Jerusalem—the next, he and his armies will be dashed with a rod of iron, completely annihilated. Like a piece of pottery in the hands of a craftsman, the Antichrist will be shattered into pieces!

When Jesus reigns in the Millennium, He will come as the Son of Abraham, He will possess the land of Israel in God's name, and He will assume the throne of David. He will be manifested as the

Son of man, and as such will execute judgment at the inception of the kingdom and throughout the period of one thousand years. He will be a King of righteousness and King over all the earth. He will be manifested as God the Son, so all can say "the tabernacle of God is with men" (Rev. 21:3). He will be Redeemer, Judge, Rewarder of the saints, Teacher, King, Prophet, Lawgiver, and Shepherd.[9]

In the kingdom of peace we will see the full manifestation of the glory of Jesus Christ. We will see the glory of *dominion* over the physical earth, to replace the dominion Adam lost when he sinned. We will see the glory of God in *government,* to replace every flawed government the world has ever known. We will see the glory of God in the *judiciary,* in which Christ, as the spokesman for God, will announce God's will and judge through the age. We will see the glory of God in the *temple,* in which Christ will reign.[10]

Let's consider the words of God's Holy Spirit:

> Now therefore, be wise, O kings;
> Be instructed, you judges of the earth.
> Serve the LORD with fear,
> And rejoice with trembling.
> Kiss the Son, lest He be angry,
> And you perish in the way,
> When His wrath is kindled but a little.
> Blessed are all those who put their trust in Him. (Ps. 2:10–12)

Ah, this is no simpering Spirit! Kings and judges are commanded to serve the Lord with fear, or awed respect. The fear of the Lord is the beginning of wisdom.

The apostle John walked and talked with Jesus for more than three years during His earthly ministry. Jesus counted John as one of His closest friends. But when John saw Jesus in the vision given to him in the Revelation, he "fell at His feet as dead" (Rev. 1:17).

I have a problem with Christians who "see the Lord" every

Thursday night and demand that God perform for them. I have a problem with people who come to church late week after week, as though worshiping God were as casual a thing as going to the movies. I have a problem with people who stand chatting in the aisle while the choir is singing the call to worship.

Look at verse 12: "Kiss the Son, lest He be angry." Remember that God the Son is holy and powerful and deserving of awed respect.

Love and anger go together; in fact, anger is love's clearest voice. When you shout at a child to come away from the street or to pull his hand away from a hot stove, you're shouting to get his attention. When that child deliberately disobeys and runs toward the street anyway, your anger flares, and you run after him because of love.

The Spirit ends with this promise: "Blessed are all those who put their trust in Him." Hear me, friend! The world has not seen the last of Jesus. He is coming again with power and great glory! Jerusalem will see Him, the Antichrist will tremble before His power, and Israel will recognize its Messiah and King.

Today this same Jesus offers you peace and salvation. Embrace Him today. Kiss Him. For tomorrow will come wrath and judgment.

I can think of no better way to end this book than with the promise spoken by the prophet Isaiah:

> I have set watchmen on your walls, O Jerusalem;
> They shall never hold their peace day or night.
> You who make mention of the LORD, do not keep silent,
> And give Him no rest till He establishes
> And till He makes Jerusalem a praise in the earth. (62:6–7)

Glory and hallelujah! Even so, come Lord Jesus!

Notes

Chapter One

1. John L. Lyons, "Jerusalem: Besieged by the Sacred," *The World & I*, 1 March 1997, 60.

2. "Mistrust Encases Jerusalem: Idea of Ancient City Touches Emotions," *Dallas Morning News*, 30 July 2000, 40A.

3. Gershom Gorenberg, *The End of Days* (New York: Free Press, 2000), 6.

4. Michael Hirsh, "The Lost Peace Plan," *Newsweek*, 25 September 2000.

5. Daniel Klaidman, "Walking Off a Cliff," *Newsweek*, 27 November 2000, 53.

6. Lally Weymouth, "Ariel Sharon: Don't Blame Me," *Moscow Times*, 10 October 2000.

7. Briefing, "Chronology of Events Leading to the Temple Mount Riots," American Jewish Committee, New York, 6 October 2000.

8. Ibid.

9. "Growing Concern Over Probability of Temple Mount Unrest," *IsraelWire*, 28 September 2000.

10. "Chronology of Events Leading to the Temple Mount Riots."

11. Ibid.

12. Ibid.

13. Ibid.

14. Ibid.

15. Ibid.

16. "Talking Points on Anti-Israeli Violence," Anti-Defamation League, International Affairs Division, 10 October 2000.

17. William A. Orme Jr., "Clashes Kill 12, Hurt 500 Palestinians: Protesters' Battles with Israelis Among Bloodiest in Four Years," *Dallas Morning News*, 1 October 2000, 1A.

18. Mark Lavie, "Israel: Boy Likely Shot by Palestinians," *Tampa Tribune*, 28 November 2000, A5.

19. Orme, "Clashes Kill 12," 1A.

20. Ibid.

21. Staff, "Politics: U.N. to Hold Emergency Special Session on Palestine," InterPress Service English News Wire, 18 October 2000.

22. Judy Lash Balint, "First Person: The Pain—and Grace—of Lynching Victim's Family," Jewish Telegraphic Agency, Inc.

23. Steven Komarow, "*Cole* Probers Get Bomb Threat," *USA Today*, 27 October 2000, 20A.

24. Voice of America, "Cohen Warns Israeli-Palestinian Conflict Could Spread," *Israel Faxx*, 20 November 2000.

25. Sheikh Dr. Ahmad Abu Halabayah, member of Palestinian Authority, Religious Consultative Council, Palestinian television broadcast.

26. "Renewed Violence Disrupts Once-Peaceful Haifa: Signs Show Leaders' Efforts to Restore Coexistence Starting to Work," *Dallas Morning News*, 24 November 2000, 62.

27. Dan Ephron, "'This Isn't Intifada. This Is War': Arafat, Peres Reach Agreement on Cease-fire," *Washington Times*, 2 November 2000.

28. Thomas L. Friedman, "Arafat's War," *New York Times*, 13 October 2000.

29. Ibid.

30. Lee Hockstader, "Arab Uprising Spreads to Israel; Israeli Defends Visit to Contested Site," *Washington Post*, 2 October 2000.

31. Ibid.

32. Robert Fisk, "Bloodbath at the Dome of the Rock," *Independent*, 30 September 2000.

33. "Talking Points on Anti-Israel Violence," Anti-Defamation League, International Affairs Division, 10 October 2000.

34. Sandro Contenta, "Israelis Aim to Kill Us: Palestinians," *Toronto Star*, 5 October 2000.

35. Noah Adams and Linda Wertheimer, "Analysis: Cease-fire Between Israelis and Palestinians Fails to Stem Violence Raging Throughout Palestinian Territories," *All Things Considered*, National Public Radio, 3 October 2000.

36. Weymouth, "Ariel Sharon."

37. Christopher Dickey, "War on Two Fronts," *Newsweek*, 11 December 2000, 51.

38. Barbara Slavin, "Experts Fear No One Can End Latest Unrest in Mideast Quickly," *USA Today*, 14 November 2000, 22A.

Chapter Two

1. Lyons, "Jerusalem: Besieged by the Sacred," 60.

2. Gorenberg, *The End of Days,* 61.

3. Daniel Klaidman and Jeffrey Bartholet, "The Real Jerusalem," *Newsweek,* 24 July 2000, 18 ff.

4. A .B. Yehoshua quoted in Special Dispatch no. 83, <http://memri.org/sd/SP8300.html>.

5. Joan Peters, *From Time Immemorial* (New York: Harper and Row, 1984), 391–412.

6. Yehoshua, Special Dispatch no. 83.

7. Gorenberg, *The End of Days,* 112.

8. Midrash Tanchuma, *Qedoshim,* <http://www.templemount.org/>.

9. Gorenberg, *The End of Days,* 14–15.

10. Randall Price, "Time for a Temple?" <http://www.foigm.org/IMG/timetemp.htm>.

11. Ibid.

12. Ibid.

13. Ibid.

14. Jeremy Shere, "Holy Cow," *Jerusalem Post,* 23 May 1997.

15. Gorenberg, *The End of Days,* 17.

16. Shere, "Holy Cow."

17. Herb Keinon, "They've Got the Temple in Their Sights," *Jerusalem Post,* 6 March 1998.

18. Gorenberg, *The End of Days,* 150–51.

19. Ibid., 43.

20. Ibid., 44.

21. Ibid., 190.

22. "The Story of Sufyani," <http://alislam1.org/mahdi/Chapt10.htm.>

23. Gorenberg, *The End of Days*, 194.

24. Ibid., 44.

25. Gershom Gorenberg, "Jerusalem Dispatch," *New Republic*, 20 November 2000.

26. Marvin J. Rosenthal, "Jerusalem's Tunnel and the Temple Mount: Rioting, Bloodshed, and World Condemnation," <http://www.zionshope.org/html/tunnel.html>.

27. "Tunnels Under the Al-Aqsa Mosque," <http://www.stir.ac.uk/Departments/Arts/ReligiousStudies/afa/jerusalem/News.htm>.

28. Andrea Levin, "Media Mute on the Temple Mount Desecrations," *On Camera*, 14 July 2000.

29. "Jew Arrested for Closing Eyes on Temple Mount," <http://www.templemount.org/recent.html>.

30. Gershon Salomon, "The Voice of the Temple Mount," Spring 1999, <http://www.templemountfaithful.org/s5759.htm>.

31. Price, "Time for a Temple?"

32. Ibid.

33. Grant Jeffrey, *Final Warning* (Toronto, Ontario: Frontier Research, 1995), 147.

34. Gorenberg, *The End of Days*, 65.

Chapter Three

1. Lyons, "Jerusalem: Besieged by the Sacred."

2. Ibid.

3. Ramon Bennett, *Philistine: The Great Deception* (Jerusalem: Arm of Salvation, 1995), 25.

4. Gorenberg, *The End of Days*, 82.

5. Ibid., 83.

6. Nick Goldberg, "Setting the Stage for Conflict: A History of Palestine Under British Rule Shows How Little Has Changed in the Battle Between Arabs and Jews," *Newsday*, 18 November 2000.

7. Bennett, *Philistine: The Great Deception*, 46–47.

8. Ibid., 48.

9. Ibid., 44.

10. Ibid., 55.

11. Moris Farhi, *The Last of Days* (New York: Kensington Publishing Corporation, 1983), 201.

12. Ibrahim Sarbal, leader of the Islamic Jihad movement in Palestine—Al-Aqsa Brigades. Quote is provided by the Anti-Defamation League of B'nai B'rith.

13. Bennett, *Philistine: The Great Deception*, 42, emphasis in original.

14. Quote provided by the Anti-Defamation League of B'nai B'rith.

15. Joseph Farah, "Myths of the Middle East," WorldNetDaily.com.

16. Ibid.

17. Ibid.

18. Ibid.

19. Bennett, *Philistine: The Great Deception*, 45.

20. Dr. Manfred R. Lehmann, "Recent Developments in the News Regarding the Temple Mount," 6 October 2000, <http://www.templemount.org/recent.html>.

21. Gorenberg, *The End of Days*, 70.

22. Ben Barber, "History Echoed in Crisis," *Washington Times*, 15 October 2000, C1.

23. Dan Ephron, "Palestinians' 'Day of Rage' Kills Nine and Wounds Dozens," *Washington Times*, 7 October 2000.

24. Ibid.

25. Ibid.

26. <http://www.abcnews.go.com/reference/bios/ arafat.html>.

27. John Laffin, *The PLO Connections* (Great Britain: Corgi Books, 1982), 19.

28. Ibid., 18.

29. Ibid., 18–19.

30. Ibid.

31. Ibid.

32. Ibid., 19.

33. <http://www.abcnews.go.com/reference/bios/arafat.html>.

34. Douglas J. Feith, "Wye and the Road to War," *Commentary* (The American Jewish Committee), 1 January 1999, 43.

35. Martin Regg Cohn, "Decades-old Palestinian Charter Thorn in Mideast Peace Process," *Toronto Star*, 23 November 1998.

36. Cal Thomas, "Gingrich Insightful, Not Inciting," *Kansas City Star*, 29 May 1998.

37. Ibid.

38. Ibid.

39. "The Status of Jerusalem," 14 March 1999, report from the Consulate General of Israel.

40. Dr. David R. Reagan, "Yasser Arafat: Man of Peace or an International Thug?" <http://www.lamblion.com/Web08-02.htm>.

41. Ibid.

42. Ibid.

43. Ibid.

44. Ibid.

45. Hani Al-Hassan quoted by Charles Krauthammer, "Arafat's Strategy," *Washington Post*, 20 October 2000.

46. Golda Meir quoted by Cal Thomas in "Piecemeal Destruction of Israel," *Washington Times*, 11 October 2000.

47. Krauthammer, "Arafat's Strategy."

48. Ibid.

49. Louis Rene Beres, professor of international law, "Oh Ye Who Are Jews . . . Long for Death," 6 November 2000, <http://www.gamla.org.il/english/article/2000/nov/ber2.htm>.

50. Ibid.

51. Ibid.

52. Jonathan Torop, "Arafat and the Uses of Terror," *Commentary*, 1 May 1997, 30.

53. Ibid.

54. Ibid.

55. Ibid.

56. Thomas, "Piecemeal Destruction of Israel."

57. Torop, "Arafat and the Uses of Terror."

58. Arafat's quote from press bulletin issued from the Israel Government Press Office, 2 December 1998.

59. Torop, "Arafat and the Uses of Terror."

60. Ibid.

61. Beres, "Oh Ye Who Are Jews."

62. Torop, "Arafat and the Uses of Terror."

63. Arafat's quotes from press bulletin issued from the Israel Government Press Office, 2 December 1998.

64. Nadav Shragai, "Refusal to Recognize Israel Widespread on Palestinian TV," *Ha'aretz News*, 3 September 1998.

65. Uzi Benziman, "Arafat Wants to Kill Israelis," *Ha'aretz*, 27 November 2000.

66. Heidi Kingstone, "Interview: Binyamin Netanyahu," *New Statesman*, 10 October 1997, 10.

67. Ibid.

68. Binyamin Netanyahu, speech, "A Night to Honor Israel," San Antonio, Texas, 17 November 2000.

69. Chris Hedges, "The Deathly Glamour of Martyrdom," *New York Times*, 29 October 2000.

70. Michael Finkel, "Playing War," *New York Times Magazine*, 24 December 2000, 50.

71. Ibid.

72. Golda Meir quoted by Sarah Braham, "Reminder to Yasser Arafat: That Nobel Prize You Received Was for Peace," Crisis in the Middle East, Jerusalem Center for Public Affairs.

73. Ibid.

Chapter Four

1. Kingstone, "Interview: Binyamin Netanyahu."

2. Torop, "Arafat and the Uses of Terror."

3. Carol Clark, "The Israeli Elections: More Choices, Weaker Voices," <http://www.cnn.com/SPECIALS/1999/ israeli.elections/stories/overview/>.

4. George Will, "Israel Faces Greatest Risk of Its History: Nation's Multiplying Problems Include Western Media," *Calgary Sun*, 14 October 2000.

5. Ibid.

6. Ibid.

7. Norman Atkins, *Jerusalem* (Singapore: APA Publications, 1999), 59.

8. Klaidman and Bartholet, "The Real Jerusalem," 18.

9. Atkins, *Jerusalem*, 61.

10. Klaidman and Bartholet, "The Real Jerusalem."

11. Yoram Hazony, *The Jewish State: The Struggle for Israel's Soul* (New York: Basic Books, 2000), back cover copy.

12. Atkins, *Jerusalem*, 63.

13. Ibid., 65.

14. Grant R. Jeffrey, *Armageddon* (Toronto: Frontier Research Publications, 1997), 140.

15. Leo B. Roberts, "Traveling in the Highlands of Ethiopia," *National Geographic*, September 1935, 297.

16. Atkins, *Jerusalem*, 67.

17. Ibid., 68.

18. Ibid., 69.

19. Gorenberg, *The End of Days*, 163.

20. Michael S. Arnold, "Palestinians for Jesus?" *Jerusalem Post*, 8 March 2000.

21. Ibid.

22. Ibid.

23. Ibid.

24. Ibid.

25. Atkins, *Jerusalem*, 71.

26. Ibid.

27. Ibid.

28. "Renewed Violence Disrupts Once-Peaceful Haifa,"
    62.

29. Ibid.

30. Noah Adams, "Analysis: Israeli Jews Debate What
    Went Wrong to Reignite Violence Between Them and
    Arab Israelis," *All Things Considered*, National Public
    Radio, 22 November 2000.

31. "Renewed Violence Disrupts Once-Peaceful Haifa,"
    62.

32. Atkins, *Jerusalem*, 73.

33. Ibid.

34. Ibid., 74.

35. Alan Unterman, *Dictionary of Jewish Lore and Legend*
    (London: Thames and Hudson, 1991), 203.

Chapter Five

1. Daniel Schorr, "No Time to Stall on Foreign Policy,"
   Christian Science Monitor, 1 December 2000, 11.

2. R. W. Apple Jr., "Lingering Doubts of Legitimacy, for
   Whoever Wins," *New York Times*, 19 November 2000,
   1A.

3. Jonathan Weisman, "Economic Storm Could Await
   Next President," *USA Today*, 6 December 2000, 5A.

4. Liane Hansen, "Analysis: Russia Makes Major Foreign Policy Decisions Regarding Middle East and Iran as U.S. Has Remained Paralyzed by Election Chaos," *Weekend Edition—Sunday,* National Public Radio, 26 November 2000.

5. Weisman, "Economic Storm Could Await Next President," 5A.

6. Ibid.

7. Senate Record Vote Analysis, Resolution 277, "Israeli Loan Guarantees," 1 April 1992.

8. Clyde R. Mark, "85066: Israel: U.S. Foreign Assistance," Foreign Affairs and National Defense Division, 31 October 1996.

9. Ibid.

10. *Al-Ayyam* (Palestinian Authority), 9 August 2000.

11. *Al-Quds al-Arabi* (London), 9 August 2000.

12. *Al-Wafd* (Egypt), 9 August 2000.

13. Deborah Sontag, "Barak Steps Down, Forcing an Election by Early February," *New York Times,* 10 December 2000, 1A.

Chapter Six

1. Klaidman and Bartholet, "The Real Jerusalem."

2. Gorenberg, *The End of Days,* 3.

3. Shelese Emmons, "Russian Jewish Immigration and Its Effect on the State of Israel," paper submitted to Indiana University School of Law, Bloomington, Indiana.

4. Gorenberg, *The End of Days,* 29.

5. "Tell the Truth, Mr. Boies," *Washington Times,* 1 December 2000.

6. Unterman, *Dictionary of Jewish Lore and Legend,* 72.

7. <http://www.infoplease.com/ipa/A0197837.html>.

8. Jesus Film Project Web page,
   <http://www.jesusfilm.org/updates/statistics.html>.

9. Special Dispatch no. 59, Egypt, 19 November 1999,
   Middle East Media and Research Institute.

10. Ibid.

11. "Germ Warfare," *Primetime Live,* 29 July 1998, tran-
    script.

12. Marc Peyser, "Gay All the Way," *Newsweek,* 27
    November 2000, 78.

13. Caryn James, "In a Gay World Without the Usual
    Guides," *New York Times,* 3 December 2000, AR27.

14. Peyser, "Gay All the Way," 78.

Chapter Seven

1. Matthew Fisher, "America Fiddles While Israel Burns,"
   Ottawa Sun, 24 November 2000, 13.

2. Holger Jensen, "Despite New Cease-fire Bids, Oslo
   Peace Process Is Dead," *Denver Rocky Mountain News,* 2
   November 2000, 36A.

3. John Maggs, "Economy: Over a Barrel," *National
   Journal,* 4 November 2000.

4. Ibid.

5. Ibid.

6. "Political, Economic, Social, Cultural, and Religious
   Trends in the Middle East and the Gulf and Their
   Impact on Energy Supply, Security, and Pricing,"
   Center for International Political Economy, April 1997.

7. Maggs, "Economy: Over a Barrel."

8. Ibid.

9. Ibid.

10. "We May Be Heading for Hard Economic Landing," *Toronto Star,* 19 November 2000.

11. Ibid.

12. Ibid.

13. Staff, "Taxes: With Debt Still Looming, Large Tax Cut Is Reckless," *Atlanta Constitution,* 5 September 2000, A10.

14. "Concord Coalition."

15. Jeanne Hardy, "The Crash That 'Didn't Happen.' Yet," *Countryside & Small Stock Journal,* 1 March 1994, 62.

16. Ibid.

17. Eric Black, "A Glimmer Behind the Deficit Glaze," *Minneapolis Star Tribune,* 8 February 1998, 21A.

18. James C. Lawson, "The U.S. Debt Debacle," *The World & I,* 1 January 1996, 96.

19. Ibid.

20. Alexander Tyler quoted by Ron Blue, *Master Your Money* (Nashville, TN: Thomas Nelson Publishers, 1986), 15.

21. William F. Lauber, "America's Failed War on Poverty," *The World & I,* 1 September 1995, 28.

22. Ibid.

23. Ibid.

Chapter Eight

1. Thomas, "Piecemeal Destruction of Israel," A17.

2. Ibid.

3. "Our Say . . . Position on Jerusalem," *Star* (Jordan), 3 August 2000.

4. "Russia Backs European Plan for New Force," *New York Times*, 26 November 2000, A22.

5. Ibid.

6. John Wesley White, *Thinking the Unthinkable* (Lake Mary, FL: Creation House, 1992), 150.

7. J. Vernon McGee, *Ezekiel* (Nashville, TN: Thomas Nelson Publishers, 1991), 187.

8. *Encarta® 99 Desk Encyclopedia.* Copyright © 1998 Microsoft Corporation. All rights reserved.

9. Press bulletin from the Israel Government Press Office, 2 December 1998.

10. Ibid.

11. "Russia," *Microsoft® Encarta® Encyclopedia 2000.* © 1993–1999 Microsoft Corporation. All rights reserved.

12. Uri Dan and Dennis Eisenberg, "Kremlin's Lust for Oil," *Jerusalem Post*, 19 September 1996, 6.

13. Ibid.

14. Stephen Blank, "Russia's Return to the Middle East," *The World & I*, 1 November 1996.

15. Ibid.

16. Ibid.

17. Scott Peterson, "Israel Uses 'Deliberate Ambiguity' in Nuclear Policy," *Washington Times*, 12 August 1998, A13.

18. Stan Goodenough, "A Narrowing of Choices," *Jerusalem Post*, 12 April 1995.

19. Ibid.

20. "Researcher Says Russians Have Nuclear Doomsday Device," *All Things Considered*, National Public Radio, 8 October 1993, transcript.

21. Howard Marlowe, "Coastal Dwellers Not to Blame," *USA Today*, 27 July 2000, 16A.

22. Tim Zimmermann, "Just When You Thought You Were Safe . . . ," *U.S. News & World Report*, 10 November 1997, 38–40.

23. White, *Thinking the Unthinkable*, 145.

24. Tim LaHaye, *The Beginning of the End* (Wheaton, IL: Tyndale, 1988), 65.

25. Peter C. Craigie, *Ezekiel* (Philadelphia, PA: Westminster Press, 1983), 273.

Chapter Nine

1. Matthew Fisher, "Middle East Disturbs the World," *Edmonton Sun*, 24 November 2000, 11.

2. Ephron, "'This Isn't Intifada. This Is War,'" A1.

3. "European Union Countries Pledge to Form 60,000-Member Military," *Tampa Tribune*, 21 November 2000.

4. Deborah Kovach Caldwell, "Apocalypse Soon? As New Millennium Rapidly Approaches, Interest in End of World Is at All-time High," *Dallas Morning News*, 24 October 1998, 1A.

5. J. Dwight Pentecost, *Things to Come* (Grand Rapids, MI: Zondervan, 1964), 46.

6. R. B. Girdlestone quoted in Pentecost's *Things to Come*, 47.

7. Harold Willmington, *Basic Stages in the Book of Ages* (Lynchburg, VA: Thomas Road Bible Institute, 1975), 373.

8. Harold Willmington, *Willmington's Bible Handbook* (Wheaton, IL: Tyndale, 1997), 437.

9. Peter S. Knobel, ed., *Gates of the Seasons* (New York: Central Conference of American Rabbis, 1983), 90.

Chapter Ten

1. "Israel Insists on Claims to Jerusalem," *Xinhua* (China), 18 September 2000.

2. Ibid.

3. Jeffrey L. Sheler and Mike Tharp, "Dark Prophecies," *U.S. News & World Report*, 15 December 1997, 62.

4. David Nicholson-Lord, "What's Going to Get You First?" *Independent on Sunday*, 5 January 1997, 4–5, 7.

5. J. Vernon McGee, *Revelation, Chapters 6–13* (Nashville, TN: Thomas Nelson Publishers, 1991), 45.

6. Frank Holtman quoted by McGee, *Revelation, Chapters 6–13*, 48.

7. Nicholson-Lord, "What's Going to Get You First?" 4–5, 7.

8. Ed Hindson, *Is the Antichrist Alive and Well?* (Eugene, OR: Harvest House, 1998), 19–21.

9. Willmington, *Bible Handbook*, 801.

10. McGee, *Revelation, Chapters 6–13*, 86.

11. Ibid., 90.

12. Nicholson-Lord, "What's Going to Get You First?" 4–5, 7.

13. For photo, see "The Euro: No Worries in Washington," *Newsweek*, 19 January 1999, 41.

14. McGee, *Revelation, Chapters 6–13*, 106.

15. Harold Willmington, *Willmington's Guide to the Bible* (Wheaton, IL: Tyndale, 1997), 803.

Chapter Eleven

1. Gorenberg, *The End of Days*, 27.

2. S. Franklin Logsdon, *Profiles of Prophecy* (Grand Rapids, MI: Zondervan, 1964), 81.

3. Walter C. Kaiser Jr., Peter H. Davids, F. F. Bruce, and Manfred T. Brauch, *Hard Sayings of the Bible* (Downers Grove, IL: InterVarsity Press, 1996), 569–70.

4. Ibid., 570.

5. Harold Willmington, *The King Is Coming* (Wheaton, IL: Tyndale, 1988), 250.

6. Adapted from Willmington, *The King Is Coming*, 250.

7. René Pache, *The Return of Jesus Christ* (Chicago, IL: Moody Press, 1955), 428.

8. J. Vernon McGee, *Revelation, Chapters 14–22* (Nashville, TN: Thomas Nelson Publishers, 1991), 152.

9. J. Dwight Pentecost, *Things to Come* (Grand Rapids, MI: Zondervan, 1958), 480.

10. Ibid., 480–81.

About the Author

Dr. John Hagee, author of the bestsellers *From Daniel to Doomsday, His Glory Revealed, Beginning of the End, Day of Deception,* and *Final Dawn Over Jerusalem,* is the founder and senior pastor of the 17,000-member Cornerstone Church in San Antonio, Texas. He is also the president of Global Evangelism Television, which broadcasts Pastor Hagee's daily and weekly television and radio programs throughout the United States and around the world. John and his wife, Diana, have five children: Tish, Christopher, Christina, Matthew, and Sandy.

Other Titles by John Hagee

In his first novel, John Hagee tells a powerful story of a Christian family caught in the persecutions of Rome. With an array of intriguing characters set against a sweeping historical background, *Devil's Island* paints an emotionally vivid picture of believers struggling to live out their faith in an era of oppression.

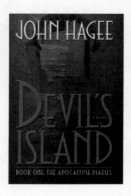

07852-6787-5 • Hardcover • $19.99
07852-6401-9 • Paperback • $14.99

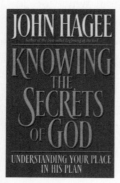

Through the ages past, God has longed for fellowship with man. Like an eager suitor, He is still pursuing the hearts of men and women today. Citing examples from eras past, present, and yet to come, Dr. Hagee skillfully uses Scripture to illustrate the compelling and provocative pictures God wants modern man to see and understand.

07852-6589-9 • Tradepaper • $14.99

John Hagee says, "The world as we know it will end, neither with a bang nor a whimper, but in stages clearly set forth in God's Word." Taking cue from a cultural icon, the ticking clock, Hagee presents a prophetic "Doomsday Clock" and counts down the minutes— through prophetic events—which must occur before that fateful moment when every unredeemed individual must face God on Judgment Day. Citing examples from national and international media and using Scripture to confirm his insights, he presents a compelling argument to prove that time is indeed running out.

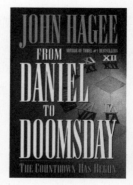

07852-6966-5 • Hardcover • $19.99
07852-6818-9 • Tradepaper • $14.99